CONTEMPORARY FATHERING

Theory, policy and practice

Brid Featherstone

This edition published in Great Britain in 2009 by

The Policy Press
University of Bristol
Fourth Floor
Beacon House
Queen's Road
Bristol BS8 1QU
UK

Tel +44 (0)117 331 4054
Fax +44 (0)117 331 4093
e-mail tpp-info@bristol.ac.uk
www.policypress.org.uk

North American office:
The Policy Press
c/o International Specialized Books Services
920 NE 58th Avenue, Suite 300
Portland, OR 97213-3786, USA
Tel +1 503 287 3093
Fax +1 503 280 8832
e-mail info@isbs.com

British Library Cataloguing in Publication Data
A catalogue record for this book is available from the British Library.

Library of Congress Cataloging-in-Publication Data
A catalog record for this book has been requested.

ISBN 978 1 86134 987 3 paperback
ISBN 978 1 86134 988 0 hardcover

The right of Brid Featherstone to be identified as author of this work has been asserted by her in accordance with the 1988 Copyright, Designs and Patents Act.

The statements and opinions contained within this publication are solely those of the author and not of the University of Bristol or The Policy Press. The University of Bristol and The Policy Press disclaim responsibility for any injury to persons or property resulting from any material published in this publication.

The Policy Press works to counter discrimination on grounds of gender, race, disability, age and sexuality.

Cover design by Robin Hawes
Front cover: image kindly supplied by Paul Green
Printed and bound in Great Britain by T.J. International Ltd, Padstow

This book is dedicated to my dear father and mother,
John and Julia, in loving memory.

Contents

Acknowledgements

I have been very fortunate to receive so much support with the writing of this book. Ian Burkitt, Richard Collier, Malcolm Cowburn, Andrea Doucet, Jacqui Gabb, Wendy Hollway, Nancy Kelly and Sandy Ruxton were kind enough to read and comment on drafts and I benefited greatly from their expertise and generosity. As always, Ruth Lister was a great source of expertise and support. Claire Fraser undertook a valuable literature search for Chapter Seven. Cathy Ashley and other colleagues on the Fathers Matter project and Martin Manby provided me with important opportunities to do some of the research informing the book. Frank McLoughlin and Margot Puddepha were sources of great inspiration and support. Many fathers and workers in a range of projects offered their very valuable insights on policy and practice. My colleagues at the universities of Huddersfield and Bradford took an active interest in the work and provided great environments in which to work. I have been very lucky, indeed, in drawing on the support of so many. It is, of course, important to note that responsibility for the limitations of, and any mistakes in, the text is mine alone.

ONE

Introduction

There has been increasing interest in fathers, fathering and fatherhood from a diverse range of constituencies in the last decades in the UK.[1] Research has blossomed, successive governments have legislated and, particularly since 1997, child welfare services have been faced with new demands to engage fathers or develop father-inclusive services.

This book emerges from work by the author, as a researcher and educator since 1999, on the issues posed by this agenda for child welfare practitioners in a variety of contexts (Sure Start, the voluntary sector and social work/social care). It is hoped that, by locating fathers, fatherhood and fathering within a historical and social landscape, the book can open up issues seldom addressed in practice settings. Furthermore, while it emerges from a particular research and education background, its concern to offer practitioners the opportunity to explore theoretical, research and policy debates should ensure that it is of interest to those studying and researching fathers and families today.

This introduction offers some preliminary observations on the practice and policy context and sketches out the key elements of the feminist perspective informing the book. However, first, it is important to signpost features of the contemporary landscape in which men father (these are dealt with at length in Chapter Two). Morgan (2002) suggests the addition of the word 'fathering' to the terms 'fathers' and 'fatherhood' in recognition of the current plurality of practices. Technological developments alongside divorce and the increased visibility of gay parenting offer a range of differing fathering narratives. There have been a series of demographic changes in a range of countries over the last decades: declining fertility rates, ageing populations, falling marriage rates and an increase in cohabitation, which open up differing and fluid possibilities (O'Brien, 2004). The opportunities and constraints open to men who father continue to vary according to class, sexuality, ethnicity, disability, age and their intersections. Moreover, biographical experiences of being fathered and fathering are crucial aspects of diversity to consider.

Individual life stories can encompass considerable complexity and fluidity (Lee, 2008). As O'Brien (2005: 19-20) notes:

[I]t would not be uncommon for a contemporary divorced father to have caring and economic responsibilities to a non-resident biological child living with his ex-wife, a biological child living with him and his new partner, as well as a co-resident, non-biological child from his second partner's first marriage. Probably more than at any time in history fathers, both biological and social, confront a range of decisions about how to conduct their kin and non-kin relationships.

Locating service provision issues within contemporary political developments

There are three key areas in relation to political developments highlighted here to signpost some of the themes of the book. First it is important to locate the current focus on engaging fathers within a specific political moment. New Labour, elected to power in 1997, promoted something of a shift in constructions of fathers. The demands of the various fathers' organisations and the interrelation between politics and research also constitute key sites of political contestation.

Within New Labour's desire to redraw the welfare state an emphasis on investing in children has been very important (see Fawcett et al, 2004; Featherstone, 2004; Lister, 2006; Parton, 2006). As explored in Chapter Eight, considerable attention has been devoted to ensuring that children's outcomes are improved and that parents meet their responsibilities towards their children. To this end, a range of supportive and controlling measures have been put in place to facilitate engagement in paid work for both men and women, and the meeting of an expanded range of responsibilities in relation to children's behaviour, school attainments and so on.

In general, in relation to fathers, despite some welcome moves in relation to paternity and parental leave and flexible working, the approach has been considered disappointing by many interested in a gender equality project when contrasted with the kinds of support evident in other countries (see Chapter Eight). Certainly, it would appear that, although there have been important moves to support both mothers and fathers to work and care, the policies, in the main, support fathers as providers of cash rather than of care. This has occurred despite the increasing consensus among policy makers that fathers have a vital contribution to make to children's development, beyond the provision of cash (Collier and Sheldon, 2008). Moreover, some of the initiatives in relation to flexible working seem precarious and may be threatened by economic developments as government ministers search for ways to help businesses survive the economic downturn (Grice, 2008).

There is an unprecedented focus on the role of services (such as children's centres) in developing father-inclusive practices. While welcome for a range of reasons as outlined in this book, this is not explicitly located within a gender equality project and exemplifies a general tendency towards exhortation rather than the entrenching of concrete entitlements. Given that many services are staffed by poorly paid women workers, it could be construed as inviting them to bear the brunt of a project that actually requires change at a range of levels in society (see Chapter Ten).

Moreover, the barriers to fathers' involvement with services are often located exclusively in the failings of the service and female service providers (see, for example, HM Treasury/DfES, 2007). This service deficit model can reinforce a sense of fathers as victims. This impedes engagement with men's agency, which may take a variety of forms including active resistance:

> The government believes that much more can be done to release the potential improvements in outcomes for children through better engagement between fathers and services for children and families. This requires a culture change – from maternity services to early years, and from health visitors to schools – changing the way that they work to ensure that services reach and support fathers as well as mothers. (HM Treasury/DfES, 2007: 34-5)

This statement captures key themes in the current policy and practice climate. Here, some of the difficulties and opportunities it highlights in relation to current developments are explored. Who is considered the father may not be straightforward and this is not acknowledged adequately. As discussed in Chapter Eight, there is a strengthening of the rights and responsibilities attached to birth fathers, which obscures the complexities of fathering practices in families today and may be out of line with the wishes of those 'doing family' in specific arrangements (see Lee, 2008). What about stepfathers, a mother's long-term partner, the 'father' in a gay male relationship? Thus, practitioners may be faced with difficult issues that they may not feel equipped to tackle. For example, what about situations where there is a birth father and stepfather in dispute? Moreover, what about services where a considerable number of the children do not have a father present or involved in their lives?

(See Roskill et al, 2008 for an analysis of some of the complexities of the families who come to the attention of social care services.)

In many of the documents directed at practitioners, there is a failure to adequately locate fathering within relationships with women, partners and wider kin. This obscures the complexities of many practice situations. For example, research outlined in Chapter Nine with mothers involved with social care services suggests that many would welcome service engagement with fathers, and feel that it would support them and their children (see Roskill et al, 2008). However, others may not in a context where children appear to be a site of gendered power battles for some mothers and fathers (see Chapters Six and Seven).

Generally, there is a failure to recognise the important roles played by women in facilitating men's fathering and the costs and privileges accruing. Policies and practices are not located within an understanding of the complexities of the gendered dynamics of mothering and fathering and, in particular, of maternal gatekeeping (see Doucet, 2006a; and Chapters Five, Six, Nine and Ten in this book).

Moreover, the possible risks to women of father engagement appear to be poorly understood in a policy context where there is little join up between fostering such engagement and tackling domestic violence. For example, the Children's Plan notes the need for public services to engage with both mother and father except where there is a clear risk to the child to do so (DCSF, 2007). Interestingly, the risks highlighted relate only to the child, which is of concern given the evidence of sexual violence towards women (see, for example, Chapter Two). As explored in a number of chapters throughout this book, the risks for women/mothers increasingly appear negated by the framing of domestic violence as a child welfare/protection issue. There is little acknowledgement of the possibility that, in cases of domestic violence, father involvement with children may be pursued as part of a project to undermine mothers (Featherstone and Peckover, 2007).

Overall, the emphasis placed by New Labour on the importance of child outcomes carries important possibilities for improving children's welfare but the gendered implications have often been ignored. Lister (2006), for example, has pointed out how, under New Labour, a focus on abolishing children's poverty has occluded discussions of their mothers' poor pay and gendered inequalities in the workplace. This, of course, has comparable implications for poor men/fathers although current demographic trends would suggest a disproportionate impact on women.

There is literature on how a language of child welfare can construct women as obstructive/bad mothers if they do not facilitate contact post-divorce (see, for example, Wallbank, 2007). It is important that the promotion of father involvement in children's services does not reproduce this with a disproportionate impact on particular groups of women (those who are poor and subject to state surveillance). Such women may be constructed as not acting in children's best interests if they do not facilitate father involvement with their children. However, they may also be seen as not protecting their children if violent fathers are involved with their children.

It has become apparent that services can be premised on such narrow constructions of child development and the imperatives for parents to meet children's needs that wider questions, in relation to the material and emotional landscapes occupied by men and women in terms of mothering and fathering, are screened out. While there is a long and worrying tradition of this in relation to women, there are dangers of it now being extended to men. There is a concern that the kind of support that is offered to fathers reinforces and exacerbates gender inequalities in childcare – for example, offering leisure activities to fathers while offering parenting skills training to mothers or supporting fathers to pronounce on what children need, but abdicating responsibility for the work required to meet those needs. Indeed, it is possible to see the current political project in relation to fathers as promoting a form of fathering that is premised on fathers developing emotional connections with their children rather than actively sharing in their care.

Fathers need to be located within not only households and domestic triangles but also the state and the market (Morgan, 2002: 274). What are the rights, duties and obligations associated with fathers in differing welfare regimes? As we will see in Chapter Eight, these vary. As Morgan notes, the historic dominance of notions of the father as economic provider underscores the importance of the relationship with the market. Such relationships need to be understood at local as well as global levels as a consultation with a group of South Asian fathers reinforced (Fraser and Featherstone, 2007). The majority worked either in catering or as taxi drivers and a key factor for them was that services did not take account of shift patterns. They were often financially supporting parents and family in Pakistan as well as families in the UK. As O'Brien (2005: 21) notes, most discussions of work–life balance invoke the image of a couple alone negotiating the competing roles of carer and financial provider. The reality for many South Asians living in Britain may be very different, with complex, sometimes multi-site, households being common. Moreover, this is not just an issue for such fathers. Increasing interest in global chains of care obliges recognition of the dispersal of some fathers' caring practices across time and space.

Services need to be rooted in an understanding of the realities of local labour markets as well as wider global trends. It is important, too, to exercise caution about a climate where particular groups of men can use privileges deriving from class and ethnicity to enjoy parenting while buying themselves out of much of the work involved (often through the employment of economically disadvantaged men and women) and use the free time and mobility to acquire status and recognition. Henwood and Procter (2003: 340) note Lazar's argument that the image of:

> [T]he new man who is devoted and nurturing at home, successful outside it, and with a similarly successful female partner, should be interpreted not as the antithesis of conservative masculinity, but as a hybridized form of masculinity enjoying the best of both worlds at little significant cost and much convenience, eg, by projecting aggression, domination and misogyny onto other subordinated groups of men.

The public fatherhood espoused by some high-profile politicians fits within the approach of the men identified by Lazar and has not led to wider discussions about differing models of masculinity or serious discussion of cash/care issues. Moreover, such men may promote their credentials as good 'involved' fathers in ways that seek to marginalise and demonise other groups of fathers, while rendering invisible the constraints within which fathering practices can operate.

Discussion resulting from the tragic deaths of young boys (primarily from Black and minority ethnic backgrounds) through gun/knife crime often falls back on assumptions about fathers as the cause of or solution to quite complex social problems. Furthermore, when such calls may be considered politically sensitive, equally problematic one-dimensional tropes such as Black male role models are invoked (see Harker, 2007a, 2007b). For example, an independent report commissioned by the government to raise the attainment of young Black boys called for more successful male role models (Reach, 2007). It drew on social learning and functionalist theories about role modelling, which have been criticised by academic research as inadequate in engaging with the complexities of how we connect or identify with differing ways of being men, women, mothers and fathers (see Chapters Five and Six).

Research carried out with a small number of young men who are themselves fathers, from Black and minority ethnic backgrounds, suggests their investment in models of masculinity that are highly committed to strong relations with children, but deeply distrustful of the mothers of their children, within a context of feeling marginalised by what they perceive as a feminised state and state services (see Featherstone and White, 2006; and Chapters Seven, Nine and Ten in this book).

Politics and fathers' organisations

The current policy context is the subject of demands from a variety of fathers' organisations that are, in the main, concerned with birth fathers. The majority, and those most well known and long-standing, focus on private law (relating to contact issues post-divorce/separation) and child support. One organisation (the Fatherhood Institute) is concerned with issues such as employment practices and has a particular focus on services such as children's services. Despite public and academic characterisation of fathers' groups as concerned with fathers' rights, they increasingly couch their demands in terms of children's rights, welfare or outcomes. This is not to say that 'fathers' rights' talk is not mobilised, but it is often hidden or fused with talk of children's rights or welfare. Many say they want equality between men and women. However, the equality arguments used by fathers' organisations are usually focused on legal status rather than equality in everyday parenting, and there is little emphasis on tackling the gendered inequalities – for example, in pay – outlined in Chapter Two (see Flood, 2004).

The concern by some activists to argue for equality in relation to their legal status as fathers appears to be rooted in their desire to stress that fathers and mothers are absolutely interchangeable and to screen out, for example, any discussion of bodily differences between men and women (see Hollway, 2006; and Chapter Four). For example, in 2007, the UK government opened up a consultation on whether joint birth registration should be legally binding. In their response to the consultation some fathers' activists stressed that mothers and fathers be treated 'identically' (see DCSF/DWP, 2008).[2] However, this stress on identical treatment appears out of line with how many mothers and fathers perceive their roles in children's lives (see Doucet, 2006a; Dermott, 2008; and Chapter Six).

It is important to note that, while biological differences are sometimes screened out as irrelevant, they can also be mobilised to stress the differences between mothers and fathers and hence the unique role fathers play with children (see Chapter Six). Activists seem also to seek to use the law to shore up what is considered the societal downgrading of the importance of the father–child link (see Chapter Two).

The key organisations pitch their demands either explicitly or, by omission, within the language associated with identity politics and are focused mainly on the needs or rights, or both, of birth fathers. There can be a deliberate attempt to separate fathers into the safe birth father and the dangerous step- or social father, as is explored in Chapter Seven.

Men and masculinities scholars are often very suspicious of calls by fathers' organisations, although Flood (2004) argues that it is important to engage with the pain and vulnerability motivating some of these men's actions. Many are going through profoundly destabilising experiences of loss in the context of divorce and relationship breakdown. Fatherhood activists and scholars, in turn, often ignore or actively reject the crucial insights contained in the men and masculinities literature, as discussed in Chapters Six and Seven. There can be a mirroring process at work, with fathers' organisations stressing their problems/troubles and victim status as fathers, and men and masculinities scholars stressing their problematic, troublesome and victimiser status. This book will argue that it is important to be able to engage with both/and rather than either/or (see Featherstone et al, 2007, for a discussion of this approach more generally in relation to working with men).

Overall, it is important to recognise complexity and diversity within and between groups. Collier and Sheldon (2006) note that activists are steeped in the discourse of the good father – good fathers fight to stay involved with their children. But wanting more nurturing relationships with children may also coexist with a desire to turn the clock back in relation to gender equality. Indeed, the two may be linked (see Chapter Seven). The Fatherhood Institute does make the case for supporting both parents to be earners and carers through better social policies, which is an important element of a gender equality project and explicitly distances itself from other fathers' organisations (see Chapters Seven and Eight).

However, it is rare to find the case being made by such organisations that encouraging active fatherhood might contribute to a restructuring of masculinity in a progressive way and support women, or indeed that it might harm women by contributing to a restructuring of masculinity, which might strengthen men's power over women (see Segal, 1999, for an elaboration of this point).

Despite their visibility it is important to remember that fathers' groups do not speak for all, or indeed many, fathers, although they are important in that they can have some influence on policy makers (see Chapter Seven). We are dealing with a complex and diverse picture and, while often visible and vocal, fathers' organisations are a small part of this picture and need to be located within broader inquiries into men's hopes, fears, opportunities and constraints today.

Research and politics

In terms of the interrelationship between research and politics, it has long been understood that research around family issues and change has been discussed as if in a 'war zone' (Featherstone, 2001a). This is especially so in relation to research on fathers. Daniels (1998: 1), in her wide-ranging edited collection, bringing together key protagonists in the US, argues that those involved in the debates could not even agree on the most fundamental terms such as the prevalence of children living without fathers, what is a father, do children need fathers, and is 'there a relation between fatherlessness and rising rates of crime and destitution, or does father talk serve as mere subterfuge for more fundamental discussions of poverty and inequality?'. Stacey (1999) has documented the increased blurring of lines in the US between the academy and influential think tanks locked in bitter combat about what is happening in families with the role of fathers the lightning rod for tensions.

In the UK scholarly divisions are not as intense, although the uses and abuses of research are evident from activists. For example, one website accessed for Chapter Seven outlined a host of statistics about the adverse effects on children of being 'without fathers', which did not seem to fit with any academic scholarship encountered by the author. Flood (2004) notes a range of problematic features about the way research is used in a number of countries: bogus statistics, the confusion of correlation and causation, the reduction of multiple social variables to bivariate associations, the highly selective use of research evidence, and the treatment of small differences as if they were absolute.

Much of the research drawn on by policy makers in the UK comes from psychology and is concerned with the impact of father involvement on outcomes for children (see Featherstone, 2006; and Chapter Five). This is linked to the preoccupations of the current policy context as outlined previously. Outcome-focused research has long been a contested feature of the debates about the impact of divorce on children (see Smart and Neale, 1999, and Chapter Five, for a discussion of the theoretical and methodological issues here). In recent years, there appears to have been an extension from this specific legal and policy area to broader family and children's services with similarly problematic conceptual and methodological practices being repeated. As explored in Chapter Five, leading fatherhood researchers make quite careful and nuanced statements about the relationship between father involvement and outcomes for children. Such statements and research are very helpful in indicating the complexities of family systems and the need to engage with the child's emotional ecology. Lewis and Lamb (2007: 13-14) stress the importance of understanding that all family relationships are highly interrelated and the dangers of seeing any one parent as making some magical contribution. However it is apparent that such nuances are sometimes lost when incorporated into government policy, where research on father involvement is inappropriately used to justify particular policy measures (see discussion in Chapter Five).

This book highlights research from a range of disciplines and is particularly concerned to highlight that which engages with fathers, mothers and children about their hopes and fears today, and is not just focused on outcomes.

To conclude this section, it is important to note that, despite the dangers, the current policy and practice landscape offers important opportunities. The opening up of a language around mothers and fathers, rather than parents, is key to encouraging changes in practice. Using terms such as mothers and fathers can encourage discussions about change, continuity and cultures, and can lead to the problematising of assumptions of fathers as threats or irrelevant (see Featherstone, 2004; Scourfield, 2006). It can open up a language around fathers as resources for children and can lead to their engagement in the care of their children offering themselves, mothers and children much needed opportunities. It can challenge their neglect by services and support those who are vulnerable in getting their needs addressed. Crucially, the absence of a focus on men by practitioners and services has led either to mother-blaming and/or an expectation that child welfare and protection is women's business and the current climate opens up possibilities to challenge this (Scourfield, 2003, 2006).

It is hoped that this book will contribute to services that encourage men and women to work together to challenge a government-sponsored language in relation to child outcomes, and to fight for social policies that support their needs as individual men and women in order to earn, care and simply 'to be' (see Lister, 2006; and Chapter Eight of this book). This requires ongoing dialogue about the tensions and difficulties of trying to develop policies and practices that engage with men's, women's and children's hopes and fears, and challenging the current policy climate where the improvement of children's welfare or outcomes is intoned as *the* consideration that trumps all else.

Locating this book: theoretically (and politically) speaking

Currently, leading researchers in the area of fathering express concern about the lack of theory in much of the research, allowing political assumptions/prejudices to be hidden behind assertions of empirical 'facts' (Lewis and Lamb, 2007). It may, however, be a trifle optimistic to think that, in this very anxiety-ridden area, theory will trump politics.

An aim of this book is to trace the lineage of many taken-for-granted ideas about fathers and to identify the ways in which they function to open up and close down possibilities in relation to gender and gender relations. A large part of this exploration is structured through concentrating on three disciplines: psychoanalysis, psychology and sociology. This is partly because the anticipated audience of social work and social care practitioners will usually have been trained in psychology and sociology.

The importance of the 'psy complex' in western thought is also of relevance here. As is well known, Foucault (1979) identified the rise of the psy professions (such as psychoanalysis, psychiatry and psychology) as crucial in the process of developing fundamental 'truths' about the self. 'It has become impossible to conceive of personhood, to experience one's own or another's personhood, or to govern oneself or others without "psy"' (Rose, 1991: 139).

There are, however, very important limitations and difficulties with structuring chapters in this way, as there is a considerable amount of research that is interdisciplinary, particularly from feminists and scholars in the men and masculinities field. In relation to the latter, for example, while these are located in the chapter exploring sociology, this can be misleading, although it reflects a crucial aspect of much of that work, which is its concern to locate individual practices by men within wider social-structural processes.

Moreover, it needs to be noted here that the author's approach is interdisciplinary and can be summarised briefly as follows. Gender is not an essence or an inner truth, and it is not simply learned. It is achieved and performed (Hicks, 2008). When politicians and practitioners tell us that boys need fathers or male role models, they are producing rather than articulating a 'truth' and, in the process, privileging certain ways of ordering the world. For example, functionalist sociology, discussed further in Chapter Six, promotes a certain model of the family with discrete roles for men and women and the necessity and desirability of socialising individuals into these roles. While Hicks (2008) notes this is particularly evident in sociology, it also has a considerable history in psychology and, indeed, many versions of psychology and psychoanalysis produce their own regimes of truth in relation to gender and gender relations (see Chapters Four and Five).

As Burkitt (2008: 134-5) notes:

> There is a powerful argument, backed by historical studies, that the contemporary Western belief that sex is a fundamental truth of our identities is a cultural invention of recent date (from around the 18th century onwards) and is also geographically specific. Evidence also exists that the bipolar model of sex as divided into male and female, seen as mutually exclusive categories, is equally recent and local, and like the idea of sex as truth, is dependent on the growth of the biomedical sciences ... the bipolar model of sex cannot be separated from the growing cultural distinction of what today we would call gay men and lesbians ... with the creation of the medical terms 'homosexuality' and heterosexuality.

A key point is that our gender is continually referencing and improvising a socially scripted performance, parts that were written before we were born, rather than constituted by a nature we were born with. Furthermore, we live our gender in interaction with others.

Language does not merely reflect a world of pre-existing women and men. It produces men and women, mothers and fathers and, as is shown in Chapters Seven, Nine and Ten, this is very important in understanding claims for recognition, rights and so on. Social work and social care practices construct families, gender and gender relations in everyday encounters. Studies of 'talk' are important in exploring such processes (see Taylor and White, 2000; Scourfield, 2003; Featherstone and White, 2006).

Writings from within the field of men and masculinities make crucial links often obscured in the individualist focus of the work from some psychologists on fathers, as we will see in Chapter Six. While mindful of Dermott's (2008) warning about conflating fatherhood and masculinity, it is important not to disassociate them either. In previous work exploring the issues involved in working with men we identified the following summary from Connell et al (2005), which can be applied most usefully to thinking about men as fathers also:

> ... men and masculinities are socially constructed, produced and reproduced, variable and changing across time and space, within societies and through life courses and biographies, men have a relationship, albeit differentially, with gendered power. Both material and discursive aspects need to be analysed in the context of how gender and other social divisions intersect in their construction. (Featherstone et al, 2007: 20)

Furthermore, although psychoanalytic perspectives have historically played contradictory roles, in that some have strongly affirmed rigid and fixed norms about gender roles, others have offered important insights into the conflict-ridden and contradictory nature of gender constructions and relations (see Chapter Four).

It is important to signpost here that there have been, and continue to be, differences between feminists about what should be aimed for, policy-wise, which are connected to differing understandings of gender and gender relations. These debates reoccur throughout the book, and the policy implications are a specific focus of Chapter Eight:

> Theoretically and politically, the feminist position that guides my work on fathers calls for the inclusion of men where it does not work to undermine women's own caregiving interests ... my feminist position on fathering is one that works towards challenging gendered asymmetries around care and employment, encouraging and embracing active fathering, while always remembering and valuing the long historical tradition of women's work, identities and power in caregiving. (Doucet, 2006a: 30)

Keeping women/mothers in the frame is crucial in the current policy climate where, as indicated previously, the dominant constructions can efface the contributions they make to supporting men's fathering as well as their contributions to their children.

Doucet (2006a) is highly influential in relation to the perspective informing this book and, indeed, her research with fathers in Canada (explored in Chapter Six) is an exemplary account of the theoretical, political and methodological challenges and opportunities for feminist work in this area.

As she notes, a key set of debates cohere around equality and difference feminism. Equality feminism is a strand of feminism underpinned by liberal feminism, which minimises or denies differences between women and men because they represent obstacles to socioeconomic equality. There is a strong emphasis on facilitating women's participation in paid work on an equal footing. Difference feminism covers a broad and very contested spectrum of approaches but a key theme is the celebration of work associated with women as well as challenging the value accorded it by society. In recent years, many feminists have aligned with the ethic of care that values women's work as caregivers and extends the implications to men and wider social policies and structures (see, for example, Williams, 2004).

There is a consensus among scholars that, in certain theoretical and historical contexts, the concepts of gender equality and gender differences are highly interdependent. Doucet (2006a) argues that, in order to move out of the equality–difference gridlock, the following is of use. She shifts her analytic lens from equality to differences and disadvantages, and the difference that difference makes. This is very important when applied to everyday life. Difference does not always lead to disadvantage and difference does not always mean unequal. Doucet suggests that gender difference can coexist with equality and she further suggests the elaboration of a notion of gender symmetry rather than equality. However, as explored in Chapter Eight, the notion of equality as developed by feminists such as Lewis and Campbell (2007) moves us a long way from a liberal notion of equality that was premised on ignoring the private and can be useful.

An interesting issue raised by Doucet (2006a) concerns 'the epistemology of reception', which obliges the consideration of how knowledge is received, evaluated and acted upon, and under what circumstances. She reflects on this in a context where fathers' rights activists seized on her work to support claims she disagreed with politically. More generally, working in the area of fathering can be difficult for feminists on a range of levels. Judith Stacey (1998) has argued that it would be a mistake not to engage even when debates are on terrain that many feminists strongly object to. She argues that, although many discussions of fatherlessness in the US are profoundly problematic, even a displaced discussion on the crises of contemporary masculinities is better than none at all. 'For this reason I think it would be a mistake if feminists and other progressives were to abdicate the arena of the politics of fatherlessness entirely' (Stacey, 1998: 76-7). Certainly, bringing talk about fathers into practice and education arenas has opened up discussions about gender relations in a climate where such discussions are not usually held (see Featherstone, 2004). More positively, the research by Doucet (2006a) with primary caregiver fathers renders visible their worlds and destabilises, in exciting ways, our assumptions when male voices speak in a language of care. It offers joyful and much needed opportunities to hear about men's abilities and desires in relation to care. Sadly, public and private discourses are too often saturated with counter-examples.

Flax (1992) provides an important cautionary note about engaging with feminist theory, which the author considers highly pertinent, particularly in the context of her anticipated audience. Articulating why she promoted an engagement between feminism, psychoanalysis and postmodernism, Flax said:

> Postmodernism calls into question the belief (or hope) that there is some form of *innocent* knowledge to be had. This hope recurs throughout the history of Western philosophy (including much of feminist theory). While many feminists have been critical of the content of such dreams, many have also been unable to abandon them…. By innocent knowledge I mean the discovery of some sort of truth which can tell us how to act in the world in ways that benefit or are for the (at least ultimate) good of all. Those whose actions are grounded in or informed by such truth will also have *their* innocence guaranteed. They can only do good not harm to others. (Flax, 1992: 447, emphasis added)

For example, it is important at this juncture to note a danger of the feminist perspective espoused in this book. In the desire to counter the subsuming of women's needs to those of men, are children's own voices and perspectives ignored? More generally, feminist perspectives, as outlined in a range of places in this book, alert us to the wider picture of institutionalised discrimination and systemic gendered inequalities in pay, care taking and patterns of violence, from which many men benefit. However, a weakness can be, certainly in some versions, that the focus on the wider picture can render us less than sympathetic to individual men's pains and the harms they suffer. This can be compounded by the exclusive use of rational sociological theories. For example, the author remains unconvinced by explanations positing monocausal explanations for men's campaigns in relation to access to their children post-divorce. The desire to continue to assert control over women is certainly a factor for some men, as argued previously, but, as is discussed in Chapter Seven, it is often linked to feelings of pain and loss in a complex and changing world. Psychosocial analyses, such as those of Day Sclater and Yates (1999), which have a clear understanding of gendered emotional dynamics, seem important here also (see also Collier and Sheldon, 2008). The work of those such as Hollway (2006) highlights the importance of attending to biographical experiences of being fathered, as well as fathering, in ways that can be lost in more structural approaches. It allows us to ask crucial questions about why some men remain trapped in anger, whilst others are able to move on respectfully.

The scepticism about the possibility or desirability of innocent knowledge is well founded given how often feminist and anti-oppressive social work and social literature has seemed to promote its pursuit (Featherstone and Green, 2008). White (2006: 38) draws from Hall to express important sentiments:

> It is incumbent upon those of us who are educators to become tricksters, not so that we can stand outside and reject the settlements that others have left for us, but 'because the only theory worth having is that which [we] have to fight off, not that which [we] speak with profound fluency'.

Aims and structure of the book

The aims of the book are to:

- trace the emergence of ways of thinking about fathers in different disciplines;
- bring together in one book voices from disciplines that do not always speak to one another;
- identify the opportunities and dangers posed by policy and practice developments and debates;
- identify some of the learning by the author that has emerged over the last decade of evaluating services seeking to include fathers;
- reflect throughout on the insights that feminist and pro-feminist perspectives can bring to our understandings and practices.

Chapter Two offers an overview of fathers, fatherhood and fathering in the context of exploring demographic trends. Chapter Three locates contemporary developments in a historical frame alerting us to the importance of understanding the specificity of our current claims. Chapters Four, Five and Six trace developments within three of the key disciplines within the social sciences, psychoanalysis, psychology and sociology. Contemporary political challenges and developments are explored in Chapters Seven and Eight. Chapters Nine and Ten explore a range of research and evaluation projects that the author has been involved with concerned with exploring contemporary attempts to develop father-inclusive services. Chapter Eleven offers some concluding thoughts. Although it draws from a range of theories, political developments and research from a number of countries, it is important to acknowledge that the analysis is limited by the location of the author.

Notes

[1] Devolution has intensified diversity in the trajectories taken by all four countries in the UK (especially Scotland). The author is based in England where the research into practice outlined in Chapters Nine and Ten was carried out. Many, if not most, of the policies the author will explore apply to England and Wales (but not always to Scotland and Northern Ireland).

[2] As outlined in Chapter Eight, it has been decided to make joint birth registration legally binding except in certain circumstances.

TWO

The contemporary context

Introduction

The purpose of this chapter is to offer an overview of the demographic features of the contemporary context in relation to fathers, fathering and fatherhood. How much are fathers doing with their children? What about housework? These are some of the issues considered here. Although most of the research highlights trends in the UK, experiences from other countries are also drawn on. The primary aim is to set the context for discussions in subsequent chapters in relation to theories, policies and practices.

Change, continuity and diversity

Changes in marital patterns have excited much debate and concern. In the UK, married couples are the main family type (in 2004, there were 17 million families and around seven in ten were headed by a married couple).[1] The number of married couple families, however, fell by 4% between 1996 and 2004. This decline occurred despite an overall increase of 3% in the total number of families (ONS, 2005).

Between 1996 and 2004, the number of cohabiting couple families increased by over 50% to 2.2 million. Nearly 40% had dependent children living with them. The number of lone mother families increased by 12% to 2.3 million. In 2004, nearly nine out of ten lone parents were lone mothers. Seventy-three per cent were more likely to have dependent children living with them than lone father families (50%).

In 2004, there were 7.4 million families with 13.1 million dependent children living in them. Most of these (66%) lived in a married couple family. One in four dependent children lived in a lone parent family. This is an increase from one in 14 in 1972. Although, as indicated, the vast majority are lone mother families, the number of lone fathers has increased threefold since 1970 to 178, 000 (ONS, 2005). In line with trends in other countries, children in families headed by lone fathers tend to be older.

In 2001, 10% of all families with dependent children in the UK were stepfamilies (defined as couple families with stepchildren or with step- and biological children to both parents). There is a tendency for children to stay with their mother following the break-up of a partnership. Over 80% of stepfamilies consisted of a birth mother and a stepfather. Stepfamilies were generally larger. Twenty-seven per cent of stepfamilies had three or more dependent children compared with 18% of non-stepfamilies (ONS, 2005).

In terms of age, cohabiting couple families are much younger than married couple families – this can be explained mostly by whether they have children living with them. Lone parent families are younger than married couple families and lone mother families younger than lone father families.

There are important variations in relation to ethnicity.[2] Among all families, those headed by a person of non-White ethnic background are more likely than White families to have children living with them. In 2001, nearly four out of five Bangladeshi families in the UK had dependent children compared with just over two out of five White families. Over 70% of Black African, Other Black and Pakistani families also had dependent children. The differences in the presence of a child reflect the young age structure of non-White ethnic groups and past immigration and fertility patterns (ONS, 2005).

Moreover, there are differences in relation to marital patterns. Families of Asian and Chinese origin who have dependent children living with them were most likely to be married and least likely to be lone parents. Mixed, Black Caribbean and White families with dependent children had the largest proportions of cohabiting couple families, and lone parent families were most prevalent among Other Black families – 64%. Over 45% of Black Caribbean, Black African and Mixed families were headed by a lone parent, compared with 25% of White families.

O'Brien (2004: 123-5) offers an overview of fathers in the European demographic context. Since the 1970s, a key demographic trend has seen adults having fewer children in the more affluent and industrialised parts of Europe. In the UK, the average number of children in a family declined from 2.0 in 1971 to 1.8 in 2004 (ONS, 2005). Married couple families were generally larger than other family types, with an average 1.8 children compared with 1.7 in cohabiting couple and lone mother families. Based on slightly less recent figures, many European countries now have fertility rates below replacement level and the EU fertility rate is 1.4 children per female (O'Brien, 2005).

Comparative analysis has shown that, in some European countries, living without children has become normative for significant parts of the life course (O'Brien, 2005). Jensen (2001) suggests that, while there is a general pattern of gender convergence in the desire for fewer children, international trends suggest that women now want children more than men do. However, Dermott (2008) notes that, although it is true that successful masculinity is not tied to the achievement of fatherhood, and that parenthood is less central to the construction of adulthood for men than women, it is not clear that fatherhood has lost all its significance. Only around 5% of people across the European Union expect to remain childless and the majority of people, both men and women, think that having a child is important. Dixon and Margo (2006) offer an analysis of the complex array of factors impacting on fertility patterns. They suggest there is a 90,000 annual 'baby gap' between the numbers of children that people would ideally like to have and those born in the UK annually.[3]

The ageing of the population continues to arouse considerable concern for policy makers. As far as European fathers are concerned, one consequence is likely to be a growing pressure to work more hours for longer periods in order to support families economically, a pattern already apparent in the US (O'Brien, 2005: 123).

In the latter part of the 20th century, marriage rates, particularly first marriage rates, have declined while cohabitation rates have increased across Europe. In some Nordic countries, Norway, Denmark and Sweden, cohabitation is becoming an alternative to marriage.

In the UK, the percentage of married men declined from 71% of all adults over 16 in 1971 to 53% in 2000. For increasing numbers of European men, marriage is no longer the prerequisite for fatherhood:

> One consequence is that the differentiation of the partnership context can influence the timing and onset of fatherhood. For instance, in many European countries, men who get married are more likely to have children at an older age than are men who cohabit, although this difference will tend to reduce as cohabitation rates become more normative. In addition, not all children conceived in nonmarital unions live in couple-headed households; some are children born to lone mothers or mothers with nonresident partners. The growth of nonmarital childbearing indicates a further movement towards the marginalization of biological fathers from the lives of their children. (O'Brien, 2004: 123-4)

The increase in divorce and re-partnering in the last decades of the 20th century has changed the nature of fathering.[4] Throughout their life courses, fathers are more likely than previous generations to experience more than one family type and, in the process, they usually cease to reside with the children of their first relationship, which increases the possibilities for marginalisation according to O'Brien (2004), although there is evidence of increasing contact between non-resident fathers and their children.

It is apparent that fathering is less likely to take place with a marital partner and their biological children than for previous cohorts. It is interesting to note the variation between countries in this respect. In Denmark, this household form constitutes 40.1% of households whereas, in Ireland, it makes up 74.3% (O'Brien, 2004).

For some socio-legal commentators, developments around reproductive technologies have opened up a fracturing or fragmenting of fatherhood. For most of the first half of the 20th century, there was a preference for keeping family 'irregularities' secret, which has now been reversed to some extent (Smart, 2007: 122-32):

> While it was once entirely normative to treat paternity as a matter of pragmatics rather than biological truth, it is now almost impossible to keep secrets about biological paternity; those who seek to do so are increasingly identified as being outside appropriate moral boundaries. (Smart, 2007: 122)

Until recently, the parents of children born through artificial insemination by donor were actively discouraged from telling their offspring about the nature of their conception. It was felt for long periods that it was in the child's best interests for the husband simply to claim paternity and, indeed, it was made lawful for husbands to register their legal paternity legitimately after the introduction of the 1990 Human Fertilisation and Embryology Act.

In 2005, amendments to the 1990 Human and Fertilisation and Embryology Act allowed adult children of gamete donors access to identifying information about their donor (Donovan, 2006). Diduck (2007) notes that knowledge of one's genetic origins is now considered not only to be in the child's best interests but also his or her legal right.

Ideas about paternity secrets have changed, therefore, with not only an emphasis on the child's legal right to know the truth, but also a growth in the belief that it is a psychological need. The emphasis on openness does not apply only to reproductive technologies, but also to adoption.

There has been a shift in practice and policy here too towards 'open' adoptions and the importance of children knowing their origins.[5] The practice of step-parent adoption has fallen out of fashion (a step-parent could adopt his wife's child by a previous marriage, thus legally excluding a biological parent). So now the idea of multiple parents is common, with many adults able to apply for 'parental responsibility'. Smart (2007) notes the possibilities and the vulnerabilities this can create for all concerned.

Sheldon (2005) argues that fatherhood is changing dramatically in the context of reproductive technologies. She bases this partly on discussion of a case where the legal response was a flexible one. It accorded specific rights on the basis of a child's perceived best interests, and allowed for the recognition of a man with no genetic links with a child, no existing social relationship with him or her and no ongoing relationship with his or her mother. An unmarried couple began a course of IVF treatment together arising from the man's infertility, but the woman failed to conceive and the couple split up. She got pregnant after a subsequent course of treatment. Although the child who was born had no genetic relationship to her former partner, he applied to be acknowledged as the child's legal father and to have contact. By this point the mother had a new partner and did not want the former partner to be a 'parent' to the child. Ultimately, on appeal, he was not granted legal paternity, although the judge in a lower court had decided in his favour. He was, however, allowed indirect contact with the child.

Sheldon (2005) is, to some extent, optimistic, arguing that the fragmentation of fatherhood separates fathering from fatherhood. Diduck (2007) is more cautious. She notes that, while it is potentially transformative of the heterosexual parenting paradigm to separate fathering from fatherhood, or doing from being, we must examine the pieces into which the law is currently fragmenting fatherhood. She argues that a:

> ... rediscovered deference to biological determinism in the form of respect for genetic 'truth' has been accomplished in law by linking it to both welfare and rights. Once again, gender issues loom large in these links ... disputed parentage was traditionally, and still is, virtually always about disputed paternity and so the 'universal principles' about a child's need to know his or her *identity* developed from responses to questions about a child's *paternity*. Adopting the gender-neutral language of identity or origins simply masks the

importance thus attributed to knowledge of paternal lineage.
(Diduck, 2007: 468, emphasis in original)

She locates the timing and context of the legal creation of the right
to know one's identity/paternity in the context of unprecedented
social change, characterised variously by risk, global uncertainty,
reflexive individualisation, confluence or chaos (see Chapter Six for
further discussion of these issues). There is an economic and political
expediency in finding new ways to tie people together as families
which is expressed in part as the desire to impose a father in every
possible arrangement (Diduck, 2007: 468). Indeed, it has been argued
that fathers' rights to establish paternity are being protected more than
the child's right to know his or her genetic parents.

Boyd (quoted in Diduck, 2007) argues that the law will accommodate
different types of fatherhood as a type of affirmative action for men
because of men's more fragile ties to children historically and the now
diminished capacity of marriage to protect them (see, for example,
the discussion in Chapter One about proposals to make joint birth
registration mandatory in England). However, maternity still continues
to be a unitary construction, which has implications for those who
co-mother, such as in lesbian couples.

Diduck (2007) argues that the genetic link is only one type of
biological connection and that there are three other components
identified by biologists: the coital contribution; the gestational
contribution; and the post-natal care contribution. A new hierarchy
of parenthoods has been created, in her view, with one consequence
being that little conceptual space is created for those such as the lesbian
co-mother.

However, it is slightly more complex than she allows for. For example,
the Human Fertilisation and Embryology Bill, going through parliament
at the time of writing, has aroused great controversy. As Riddell (2007)
notes, there is much for the religious right not to like in a bill tackling
saviour siblings and embryo research, as well as offering a chance to
amend abortion law. But a key issue uniting a range of constituencies[6]
has been the provision that clinics no longer need to consider 'the need
for a father'. At the bill's second reading, despite considerable lobbying,
the 'need for a father' clause has been removed.

The small amount of research carried out on same-sex parenting
suggests considerable complexity in relation to fathers, fathering and
fatherhood. Dunne's (1999) research with gay fathers, for example,
found the issue of diversity central in terms of age (ranging from
early 20s to late 70s), stage in family formation and, most importantly,

parenting context. Within a sample of 100 participants, she found 11 married gay fathers. Of those who were divorced, only a minority reported difficulties in access to their children. The majority remained involved in their children's lives, with 23% actively co-parenting and a further 23% as main carers. Both the extent of their involvement in parenting post-divorce and their positive relationships with ex-wives contrast with findings on divorced fathers more generally according to Dunne. It is, however, important to point out that her sample is small in the context of the overall numbers who divorce every year.

An interesting point was that 40 had become parents in non-heterosexual contexts and 14 were planning to do so. Thirteen were foster carers, 14 were fathers via donor insemination and four had become fathers via surrogacy or adoption. A key point from this study is that gay fathers represent a very interesting population of fathers because many are so actively engaged as parents. Dunne's assumption that they are managing to break up and co-parent more 'successfully' than heterosexuals needs more research. Mallon (2004) provides a more recent account of research from a US perspective, which is of some interest in that it offers insights into how a sample of gay men are parenting (see also Doucet, 2006a, whose work is discussed in Chapter Six).

Research about lesbian parents opens up other issues. For example, while this is often an area that excites great public concern in terms of the perceived difficulties for children (especially boys) in growing up without male 'role models', the research that has been done suggests that such families will have fathers and other male figures available in a range of ways (Golombok, 2000). Diduck (2007) argues that lesbian parent families have to work hard at a range of complex and contradictory tasks; to be recognised socially and to protect the welfare of their children. So, for example, they may want to be seen as a legitimate family and regard this as important to their child's welfare, but many also want father involvement, sometimes just for the sake of their children, though not always. As Diduck (2007: 476) notes in the case of one particular couple: 'Ms A and Ms C are entirely happy for Mr B to be recognised as D's "father" and for her to see him for regular contact. They do not agree to an order that, as they see it, recognises him as D's "parent".' Diduck (2007) explores some of the legal complexities in relation to both how women partners should be treated in law and the differing roles men can play as fathers.

To summarise, it is apparent that there is considerable complexity with patterns of change and continuity coexisting. The majority of children live with their married parents but significant minorities of children are not living with their birth fathers for a variety of reasons. Indeed Jensen (2001), writing in a Norwegian context, although exploring international trends, argues that changing family patterns have contributed towards 'the feminisation of childhood'. She offers the examples of the large numbers of children living with their mothers only and the lack of men working in nurseries and early years provision (this latter point is discussed further in Chapter Ten). Others attest to a variety of fathering narratives and a fracturing or fragmentation of unitary notions.

The next section looks at changing work patterns and the implications for the gender division of labour.

Work and care

Economic provision was seen as the central component of fathering and, indeed, good fathering for most of the 20th century (Dermott, 2008). Chapter Three examines this from a historical perspective, but the focus here is on contemporary developments.

It is important to note that, in British two parent households, men continue to contribute a larger portion of the family income than women (Dermott, 2008). After couples have children, the inequalities between men and women become more pronounced. The Fawcett Society[7] points out that mothers are at greater risk of poverty in the UK than in any other western European country. In the UK, it is often the event of having a child itself that puts women at risk of moving into poverty. One factor is that, despite it being illegal, 30,000 women every year lose their jobs as a result of becoming pregnant. Many more face disadvantage and reduced opportunities in the workplace. After having a child, many mothers become trapped in part-time, low-paid and low-status work. The gap in pay between men and women is the largest in Europe and it more than trebles when women reach their 30s as a result of the financial penalties associated with motherhood. Women often have to give up more responsible and better-paid jobs because the work is not flexible enough to be combined with caring for a child. Some groups of women face an even bigger pay gap – Pakistani women, for example, are paid less on average for full-time work than White women and substantially less than White British men.

However, as Dermott (2008) notes, providing money to support the family is no longer the sole preserve of the man. Britain is a one-and-a-half breadwinner rather than dual breadwinner society (Crompton, 2006: 90). Sixty-six per cent of households with dependent children in the UK have both parents in the paid labour force (O'Brien, 2005).

The situation of men as economic providers needs to be located within wider economic changes to employment. Crompton (2006: 5) identifies some of the key features of employment change in a global context that have led to increased competitive pressures and employment insecurity: the speed of transactions and information processing, neoliberal economic and political ideas promoting competition and deregulation, theories of organisation promoting the 'lean organisation', outsourcing and the ability to transcend national boundaries. While the traditional stable paths open to men have been eroded, women, including mothers, have been entering the paid labour force.

A range of analyses have explored the emergence of new patterns of division between men in the context of globalisation (see Pease and Pringle, 2002). In the UK there has been a significant loss of unskilled 'male' manual jobs in sectors such as manufacturing and mining, with certain regions suffering serious decline. As Ruxton (2002) notes, there was a large rise in the number of men of working age becoming 'economically inactive' (not employed, or recorded as unemployed) during the 1980s and 1990s. At the same time there was a significant shift towards a service sector economy, with skills more commonly associated with women in demand.

The 'new economy' is characterised by job insecurity, organisational structures and employment practices such as flexible working, home working and teleworking. A TUC report (2008) notes that, while the average job tenure for men in the top income quartile is 12 years, for those in the bottom income quartile it is seven years.

The growth of flexible capitalism has been regarded by some as making a contribution to the resolution of the tensions between employment and family life. The non-flexible career bureaucrat was enabled to work in full-time, long-term employment because he could rely on the unpaid work of a full-time homemaker (Crompton, 2006: 7). However, although the opportunities for flexible working can be presented by policy makers in terms of offering more opportunities for father involvement with their children, flexible employment, which is concentrated among women, is not usually associated with individual success in the labour market and flexible workers often tend to be in lower level positions. Crompton argues that facilitating flexibility is convenient for employers and such policies are relatively cheap. The UK business world has facilitated 'extreme flexibility' and, alongside the US,[8] has the highest incidence of evening and night-time work among employed parents.

Crompton's finding that it is problematic to combine employment success and caring is not new. The tensions are, she argues, greatest for two groups that have 'responded positively' to the competitive changes of reflexive modernity and seek advancement within increasingly individualised career structures: aspirant managerial and professional women and men in routine and manual occupations who want to move up the career ladder. While much of the contemporary discussion of the problems of combining career success and family responsibilities has focused on individuals in high-flying managerial and professional occupations, Crompton's qualitative data suggests that even a move off a lower rung of the occupational ladder will be associated with increased pressures on domestic life. Full-time employment and longer hours' working are required to move off the first rung of the job ladder. This means that, as mothers and carers, most women are simply not able to compete on equal terms with most men. Thus, despite formal gender-equality policies in respect of employment, men still predominate in higher-level jobs.

It has long been argued that fathers in the UK are more likely to be economically active and have higher employment rates than non-fathers (O'Brien and Shemilt, 2003). Recent research suggests that, by 2007, fathers' average hours in their main job had shown a slight decrease from 1998 and that they no longer worked the longest hours in Europe (O'Brien, 2008). However, 27% are still regularly working over 48 hours a week (48 hours is the EU Working Time Directive maximum). Indeed, it is important to note that the UK has negotiated to opt out from this (see further discussion in Chapter Eight). At the time of writing, economic developments are highly volatile and there is already anecdotal evidence of an increase in working hours for some men alongside unemployment for others.

O'Brien (2005) points out that the combined working hours of British parents is comparatively high in the European context. She also notes the importance of attending to diversity – lone father carers, for example, are far less likely than other fathers to be employed full time (55% as opposed to 87%).

In Dermott's (2006, 2008) research, when fathers were compared with non-fathers, the results were similar to previous research indicating that hours of work are longer for those defined as fathers. Looking at the data in a different way, fathers are also more likely than non-fathers to be working extremely long hours. However, age is also related to the number of hours worked and, when age is constant, a large proportion of the variation between the working hours of fathers and non-fathers disappears. Hours of work are also related to the form of economic activity, occupation, earnings and partners' working times. Self-employed men work longer hours than those classified as employees and men in professional and managerial categories. Men working longer hours are more likely to have partners who are working full time rather than part time or not at all (this may be evidence of a split between dual earner and no earner households).

Dermott (2006, 2008) argues that her research does not support arguments that some men wish to reduce their hours when they become parents, even if they do not actually do it. Rather her research supports previous survey material (O'Brien and Shemilt, 2003 and discussed below) indicating that satisfaction with work–life balance only reduces significantly when fathers work extremely long hours. Fathers do make an adjustment when a new child arrives but this reduction is not maintained through the child's years of dependency. As there is no reverse process, such as a dramatic increase in work hours when children are of a particular age, Dermott suggests that some may return gradually to their 'normal' working practices.

Overall, Dermott suggests that the relationship between paid work and employment is very different for mothers and fathers in the UK. She argues that fathers do not have shorter working hours than non-fathers and that they do not find this problematic. There is no evidence that fathers as a whole, or a significant sub-group, are adopting a 'female model' by taking on part-time and reduced hours. She notes that, while this does not necessarily undermine arguments for the existence of a different discourse around fathering (emphasising emotional and nurturing elements), it does clarify that this is not translated into alterations to working hours.

These findings do not necessarily support arguments for the continuing significance of the 'breadwinner' model of fatherhood, as there is very little difference in the working hours of fathers and non-fathers once other variables, especially age, are taken into account. There is a male model of employment that is complementary to a financially responsible one. A commitment to full-time paid work in order to have the ability to economically support children may be a prerequisite for starting a family, but it is also the typical pattern for men of working age in general. Unlike mothers and non-mothers, the part time–full time distinction does not apply to fathers and non-fathers.

Dermott suggests that fathers' behaviour will need to be thought about in ways that do not assume female models. Fatherhood has changed, but it has not become motherhood and does not provide the backdoor route to gender equality. Her conclusion is of considerable interest because it has been a key theme from feminists that gender equality cannot be achieved if men's behaviour in the 'private' sphere does not change. For example, there are very serious consequences for mothers who take the part-time route in relation to employment in terms of economic and career advancement and, further down the line, implications for pensions and older age poverty.

O'Brien notes that specific studies of fathers' preferences indicate a reluctance to reduce working hours in practice. As noted previously, her research with Shemilt (O'Brien and Shemilt, 2003) showed that satisfaction with work–life balance dropped significantly only when fathers were regularly working 60 plus hours a week and they showed a greater tolerance of long working hours than mothers. O'Brien and Shemilt also acknowledge that, while their research suggests a substantial unmet demand for flexible working conditions, in general, fathers' preferences are different from mothers'. Part-time work, for example, was not a favoured option (only 22%). Fathers were most likely to want access to flexitime (52%), a compressed working week (46%) and working at home (40%). A relatively low proportion of fathers were interested in undertaking a job-share arrangement (14%) or working reduced hours for an agreed period at a reduced salary (22%). By contrast, mothers were most likely to want access to flexitime (46%), term-time only working (42%) and part-time working (44%). A key issue was, while fathers wanted flexibility, they wanted no reduction in pay. Mothers preferred arrangements entailing greater reductions in discrete chunks of working time, perhaps linking with children's requirements, with the inevitable drop in pay.

A controversial debate was set in train by Hakim (1992, 2000) who argued that women made different employment *choices* to men because of their preferences. She argued there were three categories of women: home/family centred; work centred; and adaptive/drifters. This was contested by feminists who had tended to stress the role played by constraints (see Crompton, 2006). While not denying the importance of choice, a crucial question has to be the basis on which choices are made: 'as "choices" will be shaped (or constrained) by the context in which choice is being exercised' (Crompton, 2006: 12). Over time, the issues in relation to mothers have been addressed particularly in the context of government policies to encourage lone mothers into the paid labour force. Duncan et al (2003: 310), for example, have argued that they took decisions relating to care and employment 'with reference to moral and socially negotiated (not individual) views about what behaviour is right and proper'. These rationalities were deeply inflected by gender, class and ethnicity.

What about fathers' 'choices'? Comparative work on men's take up of paternity and parental leave, discussed further in Chapter Eight, would suggest that the policy framework, including levels of financial reward for men, is crucial in influencing fathers' behaviour (O'Brien et al, 2007). However, as indicated previously, the assumption that individuals behave as 'rational economic persons', choosing the course of action that is assumed to be in their best economic interests, has been criticised. Indeed, Barlow et al (2002) argue against what they termed the 'rationality mistake' in New Labour's early family policy. They argue that people seem to take decisions about their moral economy 'with reference to moral and socially negotiated views about what behaviour is expected as right and proper, and that this negotiation, and the views that result, varies between particular social groups, neighbourhoods and welfare states' (Barlow et al, 2002: 111).

Dermott's (2006, 2008) analysis seems to suggest that to focus on constraint is mistaken and indeed that fathers' stated preferences are unitary and fixed. Crompton (2006) argues, however, that, while it is indeed important to take normative and moral frameworks, as well as individual preferences, into account when looking at employment and family interrelationships, it is also important not to take an uncritical approach to either. She notes the work of the feminist philosopher Nussbaum in this regard. Nussbaum (2000: 114) argues that we need to 'conduct a critical scrutiny of preference and desire that would reveal the many ways in which habit, fear, low expectations and unjust background conditions deform people's choices and even their wishes for their own lives'.

Although it is indeed important to interrogate preferences, Dermott's (2006, 2008) research, while including a temporal dimension, also ignores how mothers' and fathers' preferences and behaviours over the life course can shift in complex ways. These debates are returned to in Chapters Six and Eight.

Fathers are doing what?

It is important to note the limitations of the research base and what it highlights in relation to the lack of clarity over what kind of relationship is defined as fatherhood or fathering (see Dermott, 2006). Large data sets such as the British Household Panel Survey focus on the household as the unit of analysis. Thus fathers who live with their children – whether they are lone parents or in partnerships, have a biological relationship, or are parents through adoption – are all easily accessible. As co-residency is key, it is possible to find out about fathers living with stepchildren or foster children. However, fathers who are not co-resident with their biological children are often invisible and these constitute a significant minority of fathers. Although we know that rates of contact between children and non-resident fathers are increasing, we do not know much about time use by non-resident fathers.

Moreover, there are serious methodological issues about how best to capture the way in which individuals spend their time and what meanings are attached to activities.

The British Household Panel research, which mainly relies on data from two-parent couple households, would suggest there has been a change in practices, although there are considerable debates about what should be measured and what counts. It is interesting, for example, that economic breadwinning is not usually seen as constituting a form of care (Lewis and Lamb, 2007). As O'Brien (2005) argues, this may cause difficulties for particular groups of men for whom this has been a source of pride or honour.

Most research has looked at three dimensions: engagement, accessibility and responsibility (Lewis and Lamb, 2007). These dimensions encompass the amounts of time fathers spend interacting with, being accessible to or making arrangements for the care of their children.[9] According to Pleck and Masciadrelli (2004), using time budget diary data with nationally representative data sets, most studies have shown increases in time devoted to childcare activities for successive generations of fathers (see also O'Brien and Shemilt, 2003). In the UK, for fathers of children under five years, absolute levels of involvement in child-related activities as a main activity increased from just less than 15 minutes a day in the mid-1970s to two hours a day by the late 1990s (Fisher et al, 1999; O'Brien, 2005). Fathers' involvement in the care of older children has also increased from just more than 15 minutes a day in the mid-1970s to 50 minutes a day by the late 1990s.[10] In terms of international comparisons, Canadian and American full-time employed fathers devoted about 1.4 hours to child-related activities in the 1990s (Gauthier et al, 2004). This is 30 minutes more than German and Australian fathers and nearly 50 minutes more than Italian fathers.[11]

A gender comparison of dual full-time earner couples has shown that men spend about 75% of women's absolute time on childcare and other activities with dependent children (three-and-a-half hours a weekday compared to women – nearly four-and-a-half hours). Thus there appears to be convergence, but not equity, in contributions to childcare time. There has long been concern that 'responsibility' (planning appointments with the dentist, for example, which do not involve direct interaction but may involve worry, motivation and attention) continues to be the domain of mothers (O'Brien, 2005). Paternal responsibility in two parent households, indicated by planning childcare arrangements, has been reported to be about 29% of maternal responsibility (it has risen but from a low base historically). As O'Brien (2005) notes, researchers are describing responsibility in action rather than an equal responsibility attitude, levels of which are high for both men and women.

Most research suggests that class position has some impact on fathers' contribution to childcare, although it is not a clear picture. For example, evidence from the US and Australia suggests that higher educated and more financially advantaged fathers are more involved with children (Dermott, 2008). Canadian research suggests that better educated mothers and fathers tend to devote more time to childcare (Gauthier et al, 2004). But, in the UK, different findings have emerged with some research suggesting that fathers in professional occupations do the least childcare and manual workers the most (Dermott, 2008). However, analysis of the UK Time Use Survey found that fathers in manual and routine occupations spent significantly less time in childcare than those in white-collar jobs. It is important to consider fathers' time use in the context of their partner's employment status.

Interestingly, there continue to be debates about whether greater involvement by men with children correlates with greater harmony between the involved partners with research offering a mixed picture of results (Lewis and Lamb, 2007). Men who choose to be involved fathers do not necessarily have a motivation to become equal partners (Dermott, 2008).

While there has been some degree of convergence in relation to childcare, housework does seem to be less amenable to change and involvement by men. Dermott (2008) suggests that, in her interviews with fathers, while it was rare for the fathers to consider that housework was split equally, this did not imply they did none, rather it was not considered within the remit of fatherhood. While it might be expected that in practice housework and childcare would often merge, for most of the fathers the two were considered separate entities. While for mothers routine responsibilities of home may overlap with those of being a parent, these men saw the obligations of fathering as lying elsewhere.

For feminist researchers, evidence such as this poses very important issues about what is going on in relation to fathers, fathering and fatherhood today. For example, Gatrell (2007) argues that men are engaging in 'cherry picking' the more pleasurable aspects of childcare, such as playing with or nurturing children emotionally, while women have to do the mundane but vital housekeeping.

Jensen (2001) suggests that at least one study found that it was easier for women to get older children to do housework than men. O'Brien notes that, even in dual earner couples where mothers worked 48 hours a week and more, they were still also mainly responsible for housework. Only in less than 20% of cases did male partners take on the 'main responsibility' for any household tasks (O'Brien, 2005).

More generally, there is ongoing interest in exploring how both men and women 'contract out' a range of domestic tasks including childcare:

> Much childcare and domestic labour now passes to third parties, whether statutory or market providers; or, increasingly, in certain parts of the country, and amongst some privileged social groups in particular, to migrant workers. Such a passing on of care and domestic labour does not mean that structures of power and inequality have faded away. Rather, they are being displaced within an increasingly global and mobile economy. (Collier and Sheldon, 2008: 136)

As indicated in Chapter One, research into chains of care is opening up the complexities of transfers of time, money and services across countries, ethnicities and classes.

Fathers, violence and abuse

Defining violence and abuse involves complex methodological, conceptual and political issues. As Hearn and Pringle (2006) note, it is customary to consider questions about men's involvement in taking care of children or their use of paternity leave and so on separately from considering their use of violence. It is important, however, to integrate these considerations, as they have done in their work with researchers in the Critical Research on Men in Europe network (CROME), which is returned to in Chapter Eight.

European domestic violence prevalence studies have shown about a quarter of women experiencing domestic violence over their lifetime and 6-10% in a given year. Moreover, there appear to be differences in different localities, although, as indicated previously, this is an area with considerable methodological difficulties, so comparisons between studies can be problematic (Hearn and Pringle, 2006). Eighty-nine per cent of those suffering four or more attacks are women and 26% of women have experienced violence from a partner. On average, two women a week are killed by a male partner or former partner. In 2003/04, nearly 40% of all homicide victims were killed by their current or ex-partner compared with about 5% of male homicide victims.

How much of this violence is carried out by men who are fathers? There seem to be few reliable figures here (Harne, 2005). As is discussed in Chapter Nine, violence by men to women is recognised as a very important issue on the caseloads of those dealing with child protection concerns and was an important finding of the research carried out in the Fathers Matter project discussed in Chapter Nine. Caution must, therefore, be exercised in relation to statements such as that found on the website for the Fatherhood Institute (2008a) suggesting that violence by fathers to mothers was something 'very few men do'.

One reliable prevalence study, which explored with young people their experiences of maltreatment, has been carried out in the UK (Cawson et al, 2000). Fathers were responsible for 40% of the physical abuse suffered by children, mothers for 49%. What is notable about these figures is that, given the gendered division of labour in households, the figures for men are so high. Sexually abusive activity was carried out mainly by known males, with only 1% of the sample abused by a father or stepfather (11% of the sample had been sexually abused overall).

Almost a fifth of the sample named their father or stepfather as someone they had been 'sometimes really afraid of' as a child (about a tenth of their mother or stepmother). When the researchers considered this issue alongside which parent the young people reported having close loving relationships with, they concluded 'that there is work to be done to improve the quality of fatherhood for a substantial minority of children' (Cawson et al, 2000: 94).

A brief look at the implications for practice

While Chapters Nine and Ten deal in detail with the issues in relation to practice, a number of points are drawn out here. It is well documented in the UK that those who come to the attention of statutory social services departments are from socioeconomically disadvantaged backgrounds (Featherstone, 2004).[12] It is also important to note that patterns of cohabitation (which are more likely to lead to relationship breakdown) and lone parenthood (primarily lone motherhood) are much more pronounced among those who are disadvantaged. Those who become fathers younger are usually from socioeconomically disadvantaged backgrounds also.

As Ryan (2006) notes, very few studies of the families of the children who come into contact with social services departments have focused on fathers. It would appear from the very limited evidence we have that non-resident fathers and father figures are disproportionately represented on social work caseloads when compared with the wider population (Roskill et al, 2008).[13] Ryan found that many of the men were likely to be unemployed, with poor mental and physical health, and there were high levels of conflict, including domestic violence, between men and women. Evidence collected from fathers about their own childhood experiences revealed a high number who suffered abuse and neglect.

There is a growing body of research on fathers characterised as 'vulnerable' in terms both of their impact on their children and of the implications for services (Burgess, 2007), which is clearly of relevance here and is explored further in Chapters Nine and Ten. Moreover, there is a growing interest in identifying and developing a research agenda around 'disabled' fathers, which is also of relevance (Kilkey, 2007).

Conclusion

The availability of divorce, growth in cohabitation rates and associated rise in lone motherhood can suggest a marginalisation of fathers. Some even talk of a 'feminisation of childhood' but it is not straightforward. There seems to be agreement that there has been an increase in childcare by fathers, although there are limitations to the research base. Moreover, questions do have to be asked about why there has not been a corresponding increase in doing housework. Reproductive technologies can fracture fathering from fatherhood – 'doing' from 'being' – in exciting ways, particularly for those developing families as same-sex couples.

Notes

[1] A family is defined by the Office for National Statistics (ONS) as a married/cohabiting couple with or without child(ren), or a lone parent with child(ren). Cohabiting couples includes same-sex couples.

[2] This term is contested and ambiguous (see Phoenix and Husain, 2007).

[3] However, they do not offer a gender breakdown.

[4] There has been a stabilisation and even decline in divorce rates, but that is linked to the decline in marriage rates.

[5] Little research has been done on adoptive fathers, although Clapton (2002) has researched birth fathers whose children have been placed for adoption.

[6] To the author's knowledge, however, the key fathers' organisations explored in Chapters Seven and Eight did not campaign directly on this issue.

[7] The Fawcett Society is a charity campaigning to close the inequality gap between men and women.

[8] This was a study of Britain, US, France, Portugal, Finland and Norway.

[9] Although original researchers such as Lamb were explicit that exploration of these dimensions should not lead to the ignoring of other important aspects, many subsequent studies have ignored breadwinning for example (see Lewis and Lamb, 2007).

[10] Time given to the direct care of children usually decreases as children age (O'Brien, 2005).

[11] The cross-national differences for mothers are smaller.

[12] See Chapter Nine for a discussion of the organisational, policy and philosophical contexts in which services are delivered to children and families.

[13] To the author's knowledge, there has not been a study that has compared the characteristics of those coming to the attention of child welfare services with those in similar socioeconomic circumstances, so this point could be misleading.

THREE

The historical context

Introduction

This chapter explores historical debates. An extensive literature exists outlining serious theoretical and methodological debates and disagreements. A 'bottom-up' perspective from a variety of sources has sought to point out the exclusions of the 'great White men' view of history, which are so often dominant. Poststructuralists such as Scott (1992) have questioned whether there are transparent stories from those previously excluded, which are awaiting excavation and, indeed, whether concepts developed in one era can be employed to understand behaviours in previous times. The role and subjectivity of the historian himself/herself has been highlighted. The use of history as a political tool to inspire, demonise or impose a particular political project has been the subject of ongoing debate.

It is worth noting the considerable methodological problems in doing historical work. It is not just about what is available, but also what weight should be given to different types of evidence. Coltrane and Parke (1998) argue that the historical documents relied upon are often self-reports from those who were literate. This runs the danger of being accounts of ideals rather than actual practices. They note Elder's (1978) arguments about the blurring of the actual–ideal distinction as a result of the use of literary sources from particular sections of the population and documentary sources representing ideals that have been mistakenly assumed to represent actual practices. However, this actual–ideal distinction may be an unhelpful one. Ideals and, indeed, the advice of experts tell us of the discourses that circulated, which is useful. Legal judgements and their study can be of great value in identifying key discourses, as we will see further on in this chapter.

There are important political questions that need to be continually addressed about the function of accounts from whatever source (see Burgess, 1997). What version of fatherhood is being performed, enacted or constructed into being and why taps into issues of power rather than questions of truth.

This chapter outlines debates about images, roles and responsibilities in previous times and the making of the 'modern' father, particularly though not exclusively through the law.

Images, roles, responsibilities

Coltrane and Parke (1998: 11-13), writing from an American perspective, suggest the following difficulties in relation to the available literature. First, they argue that it is incomplete. Men's lives have often been the sole subject of historical research. However, this has not been from a gendered perspective naming them as men and it is their 'public' lives that have been explored rather than their 'private' lives as fathers. Second, while the studies that do exist have attempted to correct previous errors of omission, there has been, especially in some of the early studies, a tendency to overgeneralise from limited sources and to posit overly simple explanations for complex multidimensional phenomena. This has been linked to an ongoing tendency to either romanticise or demonise fathers' roles in the past in order to make specific political points about the present. A further issue has been the assumption that most fathers acted the same in a specific era and that changes from one era to the next were both linear and progressive. This is linked to the tendency to stress change and ignore continuities in images, roles and responsibilities and to overgeneralise based on the experiences of specific classes and ethnicities (those who were White and middle class and in specific regions). While current work on fathers, fathering and fatherhood is beginning to develop much more nuanced and cross-cultural analyses (see, for example, Lamb, 2004) there remains much to be done. In the UK the historical work on law of Collier (1995) will be used to develop an understanding of developments since the 19th century, but there do remain limitations in the evidence available. In particular, there appears to have been an undue focus on European and American families of the 18th and 19th century, although, as we will see, there are some very important histories such as Stone's (1977) of the English family from 1500 onwards. There are serious gaps: cross-cultural histories and fathers and families in other than Christian religions.

A further concern here has been the tendency to use the 1950s as a baseline for assessing what is happening in contemporary lives. As Somerville (2000) has pointed out, this tendency has plagued family studies generally and it does need to be continually pointed out that the marital and child-rearing patterns of that period were a historical anomaly.[1]

Gillis (1997) argues that the history of fatherhood is as complex, uneven and convoluted as that of motherhood. I would also add that of childhood, where serious disputes have emerged about the historical evidence and how it should be read – see, for example, Aries (1962) and the critique of his work by Pollock (1987) and subsequent debates in James and James (2004). However, Gillis does suggest that, before the 19th century, when Europeans and Americans thought about family and home, they almost exclusively conjured up father figures. He contrasts this with later and contemporary developments where he suggests: 'Fathers occupy a very modest place in our symbolic universe – always on the threshold of family life, never at its centre' (Gillis, 1997: 179). He puts forward the idea, and this is linked to developments in Christianity, that, between the 16th and 19th century, fatherhood carried more symbolic, if not actual, weight than before or since. During this era patriarchs took on nurturing as well as protective qualities and, until the mid-18th century, it was even possible to imagine fathers giving birth. Stories about cases of pregnant men circulated widely at a time when male and female bodies were still seen as superior and inferior versions of the same thing rather than as fundamentally different. Regardless of paternity, being the head of a household endowed a male with the rights of fatherhood and, indeed, while becoming a householder usually coincided with marriage, batchelors could also be fathers because of their propertied status. There were, of course, important differences between classes of men. Richer households attracted the children of poorer men and poor men often failed to achieve the status of paterfamilias that was guaranteed to heads of households. Paternity by itself was not sufficient.

Fathers were not just symbolically central but were also actively engaged in nurturing and educating their children, overseeing wet-nursing, clothing and doctoring. Differences in class did impact on this. The search for work sent poor men into the households of richer ones and aristocratic fathers served long periods in the military or civil service. It was at the middle level that fathers took on a prominent role among, not only artisans and farmers, but also business and professional men who conducted much of their work from home. Marriage was a working partnership and a man's work was not allowed to interfere with his fatherly responsibilities.

'The centrality of father figures in the early modern period is attributable in part to the existence of a set of reproductive rituals that transformed genitors into paters in a way that has no contemporary counterpart' (Gillis, 1997: 183). However, as indicated previously, reproductive rituals were only a part of this; to become a pater in an ongoing sense was not available to those who were not heads of households. But it was believed that fatherhood began at conception and that the male knew when fertilisation had occurred. According to the Aristotelian notion of reproduction, which was dominant until the 18th century, the male was the more active partner in fertilisation, the giver of human life, supplying both reason and soul. Fathers were very involved with the pregnancy and couvade was common in all cultures – this refers to men regarding the pregnancy as theirs as much as the mother's. Gillis recognises that there is little direct evidence of couvade in the historical record, although he suggests that it was quite widespread in the rural and urban working classes.

While birth itself remained a woman's affair, men were centrally involved in the arrangements and, after the birth, the child often received its second birth from them through various ceremonies. Gillis (1997) argues that motherhood ended in early modern Europe and North America at just that point in a woman's life when we would now expect it to begin, whereas fatherhood began when we would now see it as ending. Men took their fatherly duties very seriously and, indeed, Protestantism defined fathering as work. Martin Luther himself said 'when a father washes diapers and performs some other mean task for his child, and someone ridicules him as an effeminate fool ... God with all his angels and creatures is smiling' (quoted in Gillis, 1997: 186). Clearly, as the quote suggests, there were tensions between a 'hands-on' version of fathering and a particular construction of masculinity, and this reminds us of the competing versions of masculinity, which intersect with fathering practices that need to be attended to.

Gillis (1997) suggests that all this was to change with the advent of the Industrial Revolution and political revolutions in the late 18th and early 19th centuries. His account is helpful in puncturing historical claims such as those asserting that it is a recent, rather unnatural, phenomenon to want men to be involved closely with the care of their children. It is equally helpful in puncturing stories pointing to a linear and progressive trajectory from father indifference/cruelty to the 'new man'. It suggests, as Coltrane and Parke (1998) point out, the need to attend to uneven and inconsistent trajectories in relation to fathers' involvement historically. It is also helpful in supporting those historians of children's welfare who argue against a reading of history that sees us moving away from cruelty to enlightenment.

However, despite counselling against nostalgia all through his book, Gillis (1997) can be read as an ode to a bucolic past brutally disrupted by the Industrial Revolution and political revolutions. While it is only fair to note that Gillis makes it clear that his desire is for a society of gendered equality where both men and women can be involved with children, his account of the period does neglect important issues about the power and control fathers wielded in ways that are not to be mourned for. Stone (1977) in his book *The Family, Sex and Marriage in England 1500-1800* paints a complex, nuanced but ultimately much more pessimistic picture of paternal roles and behaviour, and his work will now be explored although, given the dauntingly massive enterprise it represents, this can only be sketchy.

Stone's book is an attempt to chart and analyse what he considers massive shifts in world views and value systems that occurred in England over a period of some three hundred years, shifts that expressed themselves in changes in the ways members of families related to each other, in terms of legal arrangements, structures, customs, power, affect and sex. 'The main stress is on how individuals thought about, treated and used each other, and how they regarded themselves in relation to God and to various levels of social organization, from the nuclear family to the state' (Gillis, 1997: 3).

He argues that, in the 16th century and for a millennium before, the characteristic type of family, especially among the social elite, was the open lineage family. This term is chosen by him because of its two characteristic features: its permeability to outside influences and members' sense of loyalty to ancestors and living kin. In terms of the concerns of this book, some key points are as follows: life itself was seen as cheap and death came easily and often, so it was seen as unwise to become too emotionally dependent on others. Romantic love was perceived as a form of mental illness by theologians and moralists, although it flourished in court circles. This does not mean that this was what everyone thought, but, according to Stone (1977), affective relations generally were rather cool and those that existed were widely diffused rather than concentrated on members of the nuclear family:

> As a result, relations within the nuclear family, between husband and wife and parents and children, were not much closer than those with neighbours, with relatives or with 'friends' – that group of influential advisers who usually included most of the senior members of the kin. (Stone, 1977: 5)

Relations with children were not, therefore, particularly close. Richer families put their children out to wet-nurse and when they returned home the dominant advice after the Reformation certainly was that the will of young children should be crushed by physical force as the only way of containing Original Sin. Most children of all classes left home between the ages of seven and 14.

The second type of family that first overlapped with and then replaced the open lineage family over a period of about a century and a half (and then only in certain social groups) was what Stone (1977) calls the restricted patriarchal nuclear family. This type began in 1530, predominated until 1640, ran until at least 1700 and saw the decline of loyalties to lineage and kin as they were replaced by more universalistic loyalties to the national state and its head, and to a particular sect or church. Boundary awareness became more exclusively confined to the nuclear family, which became more closed off from external influences either of kin or the community. At the same time both state and church actively reinforced the pre-existent patriarchy in the family, and there are signs that the power of the husband and father over the wife and children was positively strengthened, 'making him a legalized petty tyrant within the home' (Stone, 1977: 7). This formulation by Stone stands in stark contrast to that of Gillis (1997). Stone does argue that, after 1640, a series of changes undermined this patriarchal emphasis while continuing the decline of external pressures on the increasingly nuclear family. The result was the evolution among the upper bourgeoisie of a third type, the closed domesticated nuclear family, which evolved in the late 17th century and predominated in the 18th. This family was the product of the rise of affective individualism:

> It was a family organized around the principle of personal autonomy, and bound together by strong affective ties. Husbands and wives personally selected each other rather than obeying parental wishes ... More and more time, energy, money and love of both parents were devoted to the upbringing of the children, whose wills it was no longer thought necessary to crush by force at an early age ... Patriarchal attitudes within the home markedly declined, and greater autonomy was granted not only to children but also to wives. (Stone, 1977: 7-8)

This was not diffused widely until the late 19th century and it did go into reverse for a century. But it is important to note that, by 1750, in the middle and upper sectors of English society, key features of the 'modern' family were established: intensified affective bonding of the nuclear core; a strong sense of individual autonomy and the right to personal freedom in the pursuit of happiness; a weakening of the association of personal pleasure with sin and guilt; and growing desire for physical privacy.

However, as Stone (1977) points out, and as has been noted previously, it is important to eschew notions of linear or cyclical change. First, there are, and have been, ongoing differences between groups. Second is what he calls the temporal stratification of cultural values and the slowness and irregularity of cultural change. Thus one set of values and their corresponding behavioural changes are already obsolete and generating their opposite a little before they reach their heights. Third, is the multiplication of possible mixes in cultural values, as a result of which it is extremely unlikely that the particular combination adopted by a social group in one period will be exactly repeated in another. Finally, wider societal changes such as literacy and printing and geographical and social mobility render cyclical or linear patterns impossible.

Stone (1977) does suggest that the power of the father between 1500 and 1700 was absolute or monarchical. However, as McKee and O'Brien (1987) note, his portrayal of the brutality and absolutism of pre-modern fathers has been criticised as generalising from evidence drawn from a literate elite, thus misrepresenting working people's experience and being too monolithic in its neglect of affection, love and mutuality.

Poster (1978), exploring 16th- and 17th-century family structures, suggests, for example, there were differences between aristocratic and peasant forms and experiences. His account of aristocratic families is compatible with Stone's in that he suggests that mothers and fathers rarely bothered with their children and that they were in the hands of servants from the moment they came into the world. Children were thought of as little animals and certainly not as objects of affection. However, peasant fathers were not as omnipotent as aristocratic fathers, being liable to sanction from the community: 'Nothing could occur in individual families of any importance that was not known by the village and supervised by it' (Poster, 1978: 185).

Burgess (1997, 2005) is keen to showcase historical evidence of men's involvement with their children and, indeed, suggests such evidence has either been systematically suppressed or misrepresented. She also wishes to counter what she sees as dominant myths of fathers' cruelty through the ages and points to the historical evidence that there has been a running debate since the 17th century between those who have recommended breaking a child's will and those whose attitudes have been liberal even by today's standards (which are complex anyway).

Whatever the complexities of the debates, there is agreement that parental and especially paternal rights have over time given way to parental duties (McKee and O'Brien, 1987). This did not happen in a uniform or universal way and it was 'uneven, chequered and gradual'(McKee and O'Brien, 1987: 16).

In the next section we explore some key developments in 19th-century law, exemplifying such change and signposting gendered and generational battles, which continue today.

From rights to duties to responsibilities: fathers 'unmade'

As has been extensively documented, in most of Europe and America, the Industrial Revolution meant that, for many, the office and factory replaced the household as the point of production. This was by no means a uniform shift. Rural economies continued to dominate in large parts of the world with all members of the family involved in some way or other in family farms and businesses. Indeed it was in one such household that the author grew up in the West of Ireland in the 1950s and 1960s. Allied to a recognition of the complexities here is the importance of eschewing notions of a 'before and after' shift, with 'before' entailing patriarchal fathers ruling over extended families (either kindly or cruelly depending on perspective) and 'after' the nuclear wage-earning father who was a companionate husband, distant breadwinner and occasional playmate to his children. As Coltrane and Parke (1998) note, while this captures something important about general shifts, its simple assumption of unidirectional linear change can be misleading. However, at the end of the 19th century, it was common among key classes that more husbands and wives spent their days in separate worlds with men outside the home in paid work. It was then that the predominance of the father as breadwinner became entrenched in many sectors. When households were organised as economic units, it was harder to make this specific claim for men.

Tosh (2007: 195) argues that, from the 1830s to the 1870s, there were two quite complex processes going on. Didactic writers were almost at one in declaring that bourgeois men had not only time for a domestic life but also a deep and compelling need for it. However this was strikingly at odds with the direction that industrial society was taking. Intensely homosocial leisure pursuits flourished alongside a call to the hearth, which was observed widely and the balance between patriarchal and companionate marriage was struck in many different ways.'Fatherhood encompassed every variant from the almost invisible breadwinner to the accessible and attentive playmate' (Tosh, 2007: 195).

Pleck and Pleck (1997), exploring the US, categorise 1830–1900 as the era of the 'distant breadwinner'. At the turn of the 20th century fathers were encouraged to develop companionate marriages in the sense of being more devoted and emotionally connected with their wives. In the US, certainly, this development coexisted with a movement for 'involved fatherhood' where fathers were encouraged to take part in household tasks and that was concerned with involvement rather than authority. Some writers suggest that the Depression period marked a point in the development of a model of fatherhood where it became possible to value identities that were less concerned with breadwinning (Dermott, 2008). However, it was not until the 1970s that a major transformation in ideas and practices occurred as a result of the effects of the post-industrial economy changing gender relations and cultural processes emphasising individual reflexivity over authority.

Much has been written, based on legal judgements, about the move away from the 'common law' empire of the father as a succession of legal reforms brought increased rights to the mother. However, in the UK, such rights were not fully legalised until the 1970s (see Fox Harding, 1991; Collier, 1995; Smart and Neale, 1999).

The Agar–Ellis case in England is often referred to as an illustration of the belief that to reject the jurisdiction of the father over the child was to set aside the whole course and order of nature. Collier's comments are of importance here. He argues that this case presents us with a historically specific construction of masculinity in law, but it is a judicial construct, an ideal. This fatherhood only ever applied to the lives of some fathers and was not straightforwardly diffused through the social order.

The Agar–Ellis case involved a number of court hearings in the 1870s and 1880s and concerned an English upper-class family where there was a dispute between the estranged parents about the religious upbringing of their three children. The Protestant father, having promised the Catholic mother that they would be brought up as Catholics, changed his mind and, in the face of resistance from the children, started court action to have them made wards of court. As Fox Harding (1991) notes, the courts refused to have regard to the children's wishes and the following famous statement was made in relation to paternal rights by one judge:

> The right of the father to the custody and control of his child is one of the most sacred of rights. No doubt the law may take away from him this right or may interfere with his exercise of it, just as it may take away his life, or

> his property or interfere with his liberty, but it must be for
> some sufficient cause known to the law. (Quoted in Fox
> Harding, 1991: 43)

As the quote makes clear, paternal rights could be interfered with in
some cases. Indeed, in 1817, the poet Shelley's atheism and intention
to bring up his children without religion was regarded as grounds to
deprive him of custody. Furthermore, Fox Harding notes other cases
of immoral conduct or where the father was judged guilty of the
abandonment of parental duty.

However, there was a perception generally of paternal rights as of
a kind with other basic civil liberties (Fox Harding, 1991). Over time
this was to be challenged and writers have highlighted a number of
factors in this. Protection of the rights of married women was one such
factor. Fox Harding notes that, at various points in the 19th century,
legislation granted some restricted rights to married women in relation
to their children. The 1839 Infants' Custody Act gave married mothers
restricted custody and access rights in cases of marital separation
and later legislation further extended maternal custody, access and
guardianship rights. By 1886, the mother had the right to apply for
custody of, or access to, a minor child up to the age of 21, and rights to
appoint a testamentary guardian and act jointly with the one appointed
by the father (Fox Harding, 1991: 44).

Seeking the greater protection of children was also a key in driving
legislative changes. Laws restricting child labour and introducing
compulsory education were all resisted, however, because they were seen
as an unacceptable intrusion into family life and paternal responsibility.
Indeed, children's labour was considered the property of the father.
Such campaigns as those against child labour and child cruelty took
place in the same period as that of the Agar-Ellis case and suggest the
complexities and tensions of the time.

Gordon (1986, 1989), discussing the work of child welfare reformers
and charity workers in Boston at the turn of the 20th century, suggests
that they were strong advocates of social control. Many of them
were women and involved in what has become known as first-wave
feminism:

> Indeed, in part organised feminism was a liberal reform
> programme, a programme for the adaptation of the family
> and the civil society to the new economic conditions,
> because consciously or not, feminists felt that these new
> conditions provided greater possibilities for the freedom

and empowerment of women. Child protection work was
an integral part of the feminist as well as the bourgeois
programme for modernizing the family. (Gordon, 1986:
75)

However, of course, this was very double-edged, offering supports to
mothers as well as rendering them vulnerable by opening up their
mothering to scrutiny. Lewis (1992), discussing the work of women
charity workers, suggests that many were motivated by a concern
for the plight of the working woman and very critical of men who
did not fulfil their side of the gender division of labour by providing
financially.

Smart and Neale (1999: 34), discussing the erosion of father right
as the prime consideration in custody cases, attach great significance
to the gradual ascendancy of the counter-discourse of maternal love.
This discourse was a combination of a new notion of child welfare
and an assertion of the importance of the kind of love and care
only a mother could provide. The importance of a child's need for
emotional warmth and care was asserted over the need for discipline
and moral instruction. The establishment of a 'child welfare science'
further validated this view. This science is explored further in the
next two chapters. Science rather than sentiment was central to what
Smart and Neale suggest was a modern welfare principle. This was
introduced formally into legal practice in the 1925 Guardianship of
Infants Act. At this point, the welfare of the child was established as
the paramount consideration of the court, although this did occur
in the context of a fault-based divorce law where an adulterous wife
could be found to be an undesirable mother. Father right was, they
argue, replaced by the 'tender years' doctrine and this doctrine was to
become a virtual orthodoxy in the 1950s and 1960s. In this process
the role of the father seemed to dwindle into insignificance and the
courts, for example, did not concern themselves with the quality of
the father–child relationship.

Indeed, by the 1970s, there was a clear preference in divorce cases for
the idea of a 'clean break' for all concerned, which meant, in practice,
that birth fathers were encouraged to move on and set up new families.
The first of the organisations concerned with the rights of birth fathers,
Families Need Fathers, was established in 1974 in the wake of the 1973
Matrimonial Causes Act (see Chapter Seven).

Outside the legal arena, at the turn of the 20th century, according
to Lewis (2002), there were concerns that families at both ends of the
social spectrum failed to conform to what was seen as an ideal, the male

breadwinner model family, although of course it was those in the poorer sectors of society who were scrutinised most harshly. The characteristics of the stable family included the firm authority of the father and the cooperative industry of all its members, the wife working at home and the husband wage-earning. There was, also, a connection made between the stable family and the national importance of maintaining male work incentives (Lewis, 2002: 127).

The establishment of the welfare state in the UK post-World War Two was based on a strong male breadwinner model with social policies prioritising men's roles as workers, citizens and ex-soldiers rather than fathers (see Lewis, 1992, 2002; Williams, 1998). This contrasted with policies for women casting them as wives and mothers. This, of course, does not mean that this is what actually happened in families, as a range of studies attest (McKee and O'Brien, 1987).

As has been documented extensively, and is discussed further in the next chapters, child psychology played a role here alongside maternalist health and welfare measures. '[M]en's role as fathers was deemed to follow largely from their engagement with the discipline of paid work in the public sphere, and until recently, prescriptions for paternal activity were vague and general rather than specific' (Williams, 1998: 65). As the next two chapters suggest, the gaze in relation to ensuring the welfare of children was turned towards mothers. Indeed, it could be argued that a key impetus for the re-emergence of feminism at the end of the 1960s was to contest the responsibility that women carried for the welfare of children and the restrictions this placed on women.

Collier (1995) argues that fatherhood has, from the late 19th century to the present day, been 'modernised' in law and, in this process, it has in important respects been rendered safe. However, he suggests that: 'this reconstituted paternal masculinity remains bound up within discourses which both continue to construct fatherhood as involving specific claims to power and authority within the family ... and separate out this "safe" paternal masculinity from other "dangerous", extra-familial masculinities' (Collier, 1995: 175). He argues against a reading of history that sees the diminishing of fathers' legal rights as necessarily meaning a weakening in the power of men generally.

Collier argues there has been a reconstitution or modernisation of the power of men and masculinity. The separation of work and home in liberal thought and legal discourse reconstituted the domestic as the source/symbol of comfort and renewal for men, but it did so at the same time as there was an institutionalisation of public masculinities in the public domain that entrenched men's power (Collier, 1995: 211).

Fatherhood in law was itself transformed as men in the private domain came to be defined less as fathers and more as husbands (see also Hearn, 1992). However, the masculinity of the man of law embodied ideals of class and respectability that did not relate to the lives of all men with the demarcation of the safe and dangerous. There was a desexualising of the father that was to be challenged dramatically by the emergence in the 1970s and 1980s of feminist and child survivor campaigns around sexual abuse, but which became located for many decades in the 'other'.

This construction of safe familial masculinity came under pressure from a range of fronts. The construction rested on a detached breadwinner model, which was never fully accessed and became more and more challenged by women's entry into the workforce. It rested on the expulsion of other categories of men in terms of sexuality – the homosexual is one example. Again this is now challenged. More positively, as time has gone on, it has not resonated with the desires of at least some men to be more involved in the care of their children. At the same time there has been a growth in discourses from a range of sources constructing father presence as desirable and natural for the well-being of children particularly.

Collier (1995) sees the law as just one regulatory system within a network of powers that regulate the family, and part of a form of rationalisation concerned with the transformation of the subjectivities of both men and women implicating domestic reproductive and conjugal politics (the traditional area of family law) as well as the world of work and public politics. Discourses of both public and private masculinities are indivisible and must be understood one in terms of the other (Collier, 1995: 70).

Whether the law does or does not embody a formal equality between men and women is not the only question of importance: 'It now becomes a question of the relation between law and how we actually *experience* ourselves as men and women, male and female' (Collier, 1995: 86, emphasis in original). This is important in the context of the issues raised in Chapter Seven in relation to fathers' organisations today and what has been called their 'yearning for law' – a yearning onto which is displaced all sorts of anxieties.

Collier (1995) suggests that one effect of the developments outlined by Smart and Neale (1999) and explored previously has been to politicise fatherhood and to bring men's involvement in childcare into the public domain. The emerging welfare principle thus fractured the basis of the father right of Agar-Ellis through providing an alternative and child-centred moral imperative – in effect bringing fatherhood into the public and political domains. Do families need fathers and, if they do, why? The next chapters look at some of the key developments in psychoanalytic and psychological thought that have sought to address such questions.

As Collier notes in more recent work (Collier and Sheldon, 2008), while there was no golden age of fatherhood as an experience or institution that enjoyed a fixed unitary character, the idea of fragmentation captures something new in recent social shifts. Such shifts have already been outlined in Chapter Two and their theorisation is the subject of the next chapters.

Conclusion

Historians, such as Gillis, have emphasised the dominant role that fathers have played in children's lives and suggested that, as men's economic roles have increasingly drawn them outside the home and into the marketplace, women have extended their sphere of domestic influence. Others, such as Collier, caution against seeing this as a diminution of men's power. There has been a shift away from paternal rights to paternal duties, however, and we will see in Chapters Seven and Eight how such a shift is being played out in contemporary policies and practices. The emergence of the father as breadwinner was a feature of the transition to industrialisation but has come under pressure in the latter part of the 20th century.

A key point from this chapter is that it is not possible to read history as supporting a straightforward picture of fathers' roles and responsibilities and the importance of acknowledging complexity and diversity. This is important as it is often invoked alongside biology to support a story of a desirable past where men and women both knew their places and stuck to them!

Note
[1] Somerville is making this point in relation to the UK and the US.

FOUR

Freud and his legacy

Introduction

This chapter explores how fathers have been constructed within psychoanalytic thought. In particular, the feminists who engage with psychoanalysis continue to develop thinking on fathers in interesting and contested ways.

As outlined in Chapter One, this chapter and the following two need to be viewed as interrelated. While this chapter tells about how fathers have been constructed psychoanalytically, and Chapters Five and Six concentrate on psychological and sociological perspectives, feminist and pro-feminist theorists are involved in all. Moreover, there is increasing evidence of a psychosocial approach being developed by a range of researchers from differing disciplinary backgrounds. Poststructuralist approaches are a critique of, and an attempt to move beyond, the individual–social divide of disciplines such as sociology and psychology. Insofar as they use psychoanalytic approaches, and not all versions do, they will be dealt with here.

The 'daddy' of them all

> But this turning from the mother to the father points in addition to a victory of intellectuality over sensuality – that is, an advance in civilisation, since maternity is proved by the evidence of the senses while paternity is a hypothesis, based on an inference and a premise. Taking sides in this way with a thought process in preference to a sense perception has proved to be a momentous step. (Freud, 1939: 361)

As Frosh (1997: 37) notes, the above quotation supports a reading of psychoanalysis as a discipline of rationalism, of clear-headedness and, in the rationalist world view, there is little doubt that fathering is preferred to mothering: 'Mothering is so *messy*, after all, so full of bodily functions … Children stop you thinking; everyone knows that they turn your brain to porridge' (Frosh, 1997: 37, emphasis in original).

But Freud is also the 'king of irrationality'. Through his work on the unconscious, he dethroned the I as master in its own house. Rather he established us as people who are seldom in charge of our thoughts, actions and dreams. Moreover, as Connell (1995), a contemporary theorist on masculinity, argues, he 'let the cat out of the bag. He disrupted the apparently natural object "masculinity", and made an enquiry into its natural composition both possible, and in a political sense, necessary' (Connell, 1995: 8). That he opened more doors than he, or his more conservative followers, felt able to walk through is central to the ongoing debates and disagreements about psychoanalysis for those of us concerned with transforming gender relations and challenging hetero-normativity. However, it is important to emphasise that he opened the door to the vital understanding that one is not born but rather *made* a man or woman via complex and tension-ridden processes. This is central to his utility for those who seek to unmake destructive and oppressive masculinities.

Freud, alongside the other early psychoanalysts, saw the father as the central figure in the child's life and the castration complex as the major organiser for emotional growth (see Etchegoyen, 2002: 20). From around the age of three, the child wishes to have an exclusive relationship with the parent of the opposite sex, which places him/her in a position of rivalry with the other parent. Freud thought that the recognition of sexual difference had significant, but not identical, consequences for boys and girls. '[T]he girl accepts castration as an accomplished fact, whereas the boy fears the possibility of its occurrence' (Freud, 1924: 178, cited in Ethchegoyen, 2002: 23). The castration threat finishes the Oedipal conflict for the boy as he is forced, through fear, to abandon his desire to possess the mother in rivalry with the father. An important point here is that the father requires the son to renounce the mother as the love object and acknowledge paternal authority. This is returned to further in later sections as this process raises vital questions in relation to men's capacities as fathers. A central issue explored further below, particularly by feminists such as Benjamin (1995) and Hollway (2006), is whether the boy renounces or repudiates the mother.

The relation to the Oedipal father was central in Freud's philosophical and anthropological writings over three decades. Much of it was concerned with the father as threat and there was less emphasis placed by what has become known as classical psychoanalysis on a more positive relation until recently (see Target and Fonagy, 2002, and discussion below). The father represented the outside world and its morality and was seen by Freud as a crucial link for the child to gain autonomy from the mother and achieve differentiated selfhood and sexual identity. For many classical psychoanalysts the stakes could not be higher here:

> Then the father comes along, representative of reality, and says 'no' to all this: 'no' to the boy possessing the mother, 'no' to the girl having her own penis, 'no' to home. The child – or at least the male child – gets pointed outwards: here is reality; to this you have to succumb; prepare yourself in this way for the worlds of war and work ... this function of the father is necessary for the mental health of the child and the social polity. Without it, the individual collapses back into regressive narcissism, avoiding the world and searching for the illusory consolations of the womb. At its worst such a collapse can result in a failure to tolerate difference of any kind, and consequently a relentless hunting for sameness – for the purity of the same as represented in fascist mythology. (Frosh, 1997: 39)

After World War Two there was a shift in perspective within psychoanalysis with an increased, if not almost exclusive, emphasis on the mother–child relationship. Melanie Klein, Anna Freud and Margaret Mahler were all concerned with exploring the baby's early dependence on the mother and conflicts over separation and individuation (Hollway, 2006). Bion, Winnicott and Bowlby continued this and, of course, the latter is particularly associated with attachment theory, which is highly influential today and influences some contemporary work on fathering (see Lamb and Lewis, 2004).

It is beyond the scope of this book to address this work in any depth but the interested reader is directed to sources such as Frosh (1987) for a very readable account of psychoanalytic theory and Gomez (1997) for a similarly readable account of object relations theory where many of the above are often situated.

However, it is necessary to give a brief account here of the work of Klein as it is relevant to understanding some of the feminist theories on mothering and fathering that have developed. Bowlby's work will be explored in the next chapter because his position within psychoanalysis is contested. His emphasis on what 'real' parents do, or do not do, as distinct from the psychoanalytic emphasis on fantasy or phantasy makes him more acceptable to the psychologists covered in the next chapter.

It's really mummy who counts

Klein started work as a psychoanalyst at the time of World War One and was still practising and developing her ideas until she died in 1960 (see Mitchell, 1986).

Klein's starting point is the newborn baby who inhabits a chaotic environment where the boundaries between self and others have yet to be established and there is no sense of the mother as a separate person. In Klein's view the body was the vehicle of mental life and the raw material of primitive experience (Gomez, 1997: 36). At any particular moment, this unboundaried world can be dominated either by the good breast, which fulfils the baby's need or the bad breast, which withholds. The experience is one of being either completely loved or persecuted. The urge to make sense of chaos leads the baby to order his or her experience by splitting or dividing it into good or bad. Splitting remains an integral part of the defensive repertoire, although most of us broadly go on to develop the capacity for ambivalence and the ability to see and accept the good and the bad as part of the same person (what is known in Kleinian terms as 'the depressive position').

A key point is that every object the child relates to has an internal representation and, as we will see below, this insight is central in the work of those theorists today who want to counter overly rational approaches to gender relations and parenting. For example, children have both an external or real father who does or does not do things *and* an internal father. As Lupton and Barclay (1997) note, and as will be explored in greater depth in the work of Hollway (2006), sociologists and psychologists generally do not agree with, and integrate the notion of, an 'internal' father in their analyses of what influences boys and girls.

'Return' to the father

The focus was on the mother–child relationship and infantile dynamics particularly post-World War Two. However, the French writer, Jacques Lacan, continued to emphasise Freud and the importance of the Oedipus complex (see Grosz, 1990, for a very readable account of his life and work). From the 1930s onwards, he addressed the role of the father as a specific presence in psychoanalytic theory (Etchegoyen, 2002). He shared Freud's view about the fundamental importance of the Oedipus complex and was not concerned with preverbal, pre-Oedipal experiences. However, there are important differences between Freud and Lacan. For Lacan, the unconscious is structured as a language and it is the father who introduces 'the law of the language system' fracturing the illusory link between mother and child: 'Language is what distinguishes the Subject from the Other' (Frosh, 1997: 29). Lacan was, therefore, concerned with the study of unconscious language structures, rather than instincts or the development of the ego as an organ of adaption to internal and external reality:

> Making it all linguistic, Lacan emphasises the paternal 'no' in a literal way: the name ('nom') of the father is experienced as a no ('non'); speaking from his place as father, the father's voice is heard as one that breaks into the cosy illusions of narcissistic absorption and announces the creation of a cultural subject, the child as social being. At the developmental moment in which the father speaks, the infant is taken out of the register of the Imaginary (where a fantasy of wholeness predominates) and into the Symbolic, subject to all the demands and constraints of the linguistic and cultural order, but also capable of entering into transactions with others – of being a social self and of communicating as such. (Frosh, 1997: 41)

His theory focuses on symbolic processes and is an outright rejection of the biological. The 'Law of the Father' constitutes culture. Oedipal repression creates a system of symbolic order in which the possessor of the phallus (a symbol distinct from an actual penis) is central. Gender is a system of symbolic relationships and not of fixed facts about persons: 'The subject ... can only assume its identity through the adoption of a sexed identity, and the subject can only take up a sexed identity with reference to the phallus, for the phallus is the privileged signifier' (Segal, 1990: 85).

Lacan's structural linguistic approach goes back to Freud's theories of phallic monism (Ethchegoyen, 2002: 31). Castration becomes the organising mental event, which places the individual in the Symbolic order. The role of the father is of prime significance for mental health and for the insertion of the individual in the human order and in culture. For Lacan, the father's symbolic castration and prohibition against incest transcends individual experience. It belongs to the human order and separates humans from the animal kingdom.

While some feminists see Lacan's work as phallocentric, others use his work to challenge phallocentric knowledge (Grosz, 1990). Grosz argues that a feminism interested in subjectivity, knowledge and desire cannot afford to ignore his work, but she also recognises that Lacan's views can be accepted only at great cost because his position is clearly antagonistic to a feminism that is committed to equality between the sexes. Indeed, Lacan publicly scorned strategies for undermining or transforming existing structures of sexual difference.

His indifference to historical processes and material realities limits his utility for others (see Segal, 1990). While Segal does not wish to deny the importance of language, the primacy Lacan attaches to it is unconvincing and too determinist. A Lacanian analysis does not address the possibility of the transformation of masculinity, rather 'the identification of the problem is as far as we get' (Segal, 1990: 90). She further argues (Segal, 1999) that the popularity of Lacan in feminist theory has proved the most acutely paradoxical of all of feminism's flirtation with psychoanalysis.

Grosz, in more recent work (Grosz, 1994), suggests that it is time to rethink the value of a discourse of desire that fails to account for, or acknowledge, the existence of an active and explicitly female desire and, particularly, the desire for other women that defines lesbianism. Furthermore, as Segal (1999) notes, feminists such as Juliet Mitchell have moved towards Klein, while not wholly abandoning Lacan (although see Cornell, 1998, for a Lacanian inspired reading of some contemporary men's despair and the difficulties with responses offered by fathers' groups in the US).

Hollway, too, in earlier work (1989) used Lacan, but in her latest work (Hollway, 2006) refers little to him. Rather she draws from Klein, Winnicott and Britton (this work is explored further later).

The feminist return to mummy and daddy, or maybe not?

While some feminists turned to Lacan, others turned to looking at the relationship with the mother. The best known is Chodorow (1978). In *The Reproduction of Mothering* she argued that the gendered division of care taking was a key factor in the creation and perpetuation of male dominance. The key to understanding why men and women develop as they do, as well as why men continue to dominate women, lies in the fact that women, not men, mother. In a society where women are devalued, women's relations with their sons and daughters cannot help but develop in contrasting ways. Mothers experience their daughters as less separate from themselves and girls, in turn, retain their early and intense identification to their mothers. Moreover, they grow up with a weaker sense of boundaries, although with a greater capacity for empathy and sensitivity towards others. Boys, by contrast, are pushed to disrupt their primary identification with the mother. They must repress or deny the intimacy, tenderness and dependence of the early bond with the mother, if they are to assume a masculine identity. Being mothered by women generates conflicts in men about their masculinity, conflicts heightened because of men's lack of involvement in caring for children. They have to develop their identity in the absence of their father and this is fraught with anxiety, because masculinity remains abstract in such a context. Men need to become involved with women in care taking in order to change matters. However, as has been noted over the years, given the implications of Chodorow's analysis of how boys are raised, it is difficult to see why or how they could. This work has been extensively criticised by feminists for sociological reductionism, universalism and its privileging of care taking as *the* locus of producing and reproducing male domination and female subordination:

> For each sex there is a direct continuity between the self and the social environment, with neither the anguish and the loss, on the one hand, nor the threat of annihilation and engulfment, on the other, seeming to play such a significant part in the experience of the child … it loses its grip on what seemed to be the strength of classic psychoanalytic accounts of sexual difference: their stress on the unstable nature of sexed identity, and its uncomfortable failure to conform to social expectations. (Segal, 1999: 191)

Chodorow has revised and developed her position. In later work she emphasises complexity and variation – there are many individual masculinities and femininities (Chodorow, 1995). Moreover, she accepts that 'real' relationships do not map onto either the positions taken up or the possibilities of change in those positions, thus underscoring the importance of the unconscious and fantasy.

The contemporary feminist theorist Hollway (2006) has used a range of theorists, but owes a considerable debt to Klein and what are known as the post-Kleinians to explore how boys develop and whether and how fathers can care for children. She writes from within what can be called an 'emerging' perspective, that of psychosocial theory. The term psychosocial has been well known in social work and applied to practice for many decades, although much of what is developing under its rubric today seems very different from how it has been used previously (see Froggett, 2002: 31–47, for an account).

Hollway (2006) contests what she sees as the widespread substitution of the term parent for mother. She sees it as signifying a huge ideological and political shift to the 'principle that fathers should be involved in parenting beyond their traditional breadwinner roles, even to being the primary caretakers of infants and young children ... it claims, in its gender neutrality, that the sex (and gender) of this carer is unimportant, even irrelevant' (Hollway, 2006: 83).

She challenges the views of those who consider that changes in the external world, in this case in gender relations and positions, will be reflected in an unproblematic way in gendered subjectivities (she singles out feminist socialisation and social learning theorists as particularly culpable here, see Chapters Five and Six of this book). She argues that the psychoanalytic emphasis on the importance of the inner world and its salience, particularly in the early development of the baby, challenges assumptions that changes in the external world will translate in a straightforward way. Children's experience of their parents is the product of a constant encounter between the external world and their internal world where it is mediated by the psychic processes triggered by desire and anxiety. There is a constant dynamic tension between the real and the fantasy parents in children's experiences. 'Boys' and girls' gendered self development is affected by identifications with both their parents differently in every phase, as well as by the parents' relationship and the parents' identifications with their own parents and their sons and daughters' (Hollway, 2006: 85).

Given the centrality of Hollway's belief that a person's capacity to care owes a great deal to their early relationship with primary carers, a key question for her is what features of boys' growing up might affect their caring capacities as fathers. She argues that, while much has been made of girls' penis envy when they confront the fact that they are not boys, it is important to remember the point made by psychoanalysts, such as Karen Horney, that boys have to give up something very valuable as well – the capacity to bear children. Both boys and girls have to come to terms with loss and this begins at a time when they are also confronting issues of separation from the primary caregiver. The coincidence of the challenges – recognition of loss and separation – is important for gender development.

There are many possible pathways through to adult development for individual boys and girls, although it is the boy that is of concern here. He, like the girl, begins in helpless dependency on the mother from whom he must separate. This is neither a sudden achievement nor a smooth process. It interacts with recognising and coming to terms with the loss of the characteristics that he cannot be or become. These, such as the ability to bear a child, are embodied in the mother on whom he has been dependent and from whom he is now separating.

His identifications with his mother, which until this point have not been constrained by knowledge of his own gender and the lack/loss this entails, now become problematic:

> Is he going to have to give up everything that he cherishes of his mother in order to grow up like a boy? Has he come to terms with the frustrations and satisfactions that both emanate from the same mother? ... Can he, at least part of the time, see his mother as a separate entity, a subject in her own right, and not just an extension of his own wishes? (Hollway, 2006: 87)

Such questions reflect Hollway's debt to Klein. But she also argues that the internal processes they refer to intersect with the actions of his 'real' mother and 'real' father. For example, how does the real father treat the mother – with respect or domination? As indicated previously, Hollway highlights an important concern also shared by Benjamin (1995). They both argue for the importance of recognising the distinction between *repudiation* and *renunciation* of the mother by boys. To repudiate means the defensive rejection of the aspects of her that he sees as unattainable. In Kleinian terms it means a splitting between what is masculine and feminine, and a rejection of the feminine and of her capacity, *and indeed his*, to care. In renunciation the boy is functioning in the depressive position, which means being able to hold the good and bad parts of the masculine and feminine in himself and the other, and so permit identification with the mother's caring and his own capacity to care. It is important to note that these are not constituted as stable positions, but 'rather potential modes of organisation of experience which oscillate depending upon current anxieties and realities as well as the build-up of meaning during a whole life history' (Hollway, 2006: 88).

A key point is that mothers and fathers *cannot* fill identical positions in early childcare. The early experience of the mother as creating the baby in her body is crucial and, therefore, the father does represent separateness in a way the mother never will. 'Perhaps, we can conclude that, while fathers can perform the maternal and paternal functions (and mothers both these functions too); in the internal world of the child these will never be entirely interchangeable as long as the infant is born out of the mother's body' (Hollway, 2006: 90).

Hollway concludes that, if boys are to grow up with the capacity to care as fathers, much depends on whether they succeeded as boys themselves in retaining their positive identifications with maternal capacities to care for them, while at the same time coming to terms with being boys.

There is much of value in Hollway's approach. The approach to equality, promoted by many political campaigns, not only ignores gendered inequalities, but also can be understood as a defence against acknowledging limitation. Men can neither give birth to, nor breastfeed, babies. Thus women have a bodily connection to children that men simply do not. For Hollway, this needs to be seen as akin to a floor onto which experiences and meanings are built, although she does not see it as predictive. Indeed, the feminist research on mothering suggests many possible permutations in how mothers respond to this connection, with some mothers finding the lack of bodily separation a frightening and painful assault (Featherstone, 2000). Further, as we will see in Chapter Six, fathers spoke of the importance of their bodies, not only as limitation, but also as possibility. All of the fathers and mothers did see the mother as having a deeper bond with the baby because of the bodily connection (Doucet, 2006a, 2006b).

As Hollway (2008, personal communication) acknowledges, the psychosocial approach or 'turn', as it is also called, is still an emergent perspective. A key issue is that the 'social' needs further theorisation in Hollway's analysis. While the stress on the biographical is very important, it is crucial that this is integrated with an interrogation of fathers' practices in terms of class, ethnicity, sexuality and so on, and within competing discourses of masculinity. Doucet (2006a), for example, notes how class mediated women's perceptions of fathers' bodies in relation to their ability to be safe caregivers (see Chapter Six).

The South Asian fathers, who were part of the consultation mentioned in Chapter One, were located in highly specific sites where their complex shift patterns obliged an array of fathering and parenting practices. These practices were not simply 'chosen', but were located within moral, economic and cultural concerns about 'the right thing to do' in a particular deprived locale. These points are returned to when discussing different perspectives in relation to understanding men and masculinities in Chapter Six.

Recent developments in 'mainstream' psychoanalysis: refinement and critique

In recent British and American psychoanalytic thinking, fathers appear in different ways but remain important (Ethchegoyen, 2002: 33). Contemporary Kleinian thinking focuses on the significance of the parental couple as a complementary pair and as an organiser of perception and thinking. The role of the father as a separate significant figure is not discussed in detail. There has been a conceptual shift over the nature of the Oedipal conflict and its resolution, and the work of Britton (1989), drawn on also by Hollway, is central here. The recognition and acceptance of the creative, sexual relationship of the parental couple, which produces a baby, provokes feelings of envy and jealousy in that baby. However, the internalisation of the Oedipal triangle creates a mental space where the child is able to have differentiated relationships with each parent, while recognising their relation to each other, a relation excluding him/her. This developmental move creates a capacity for self-reflection and for seeing ourselves in relation to others.

Target and Fonagy (2002: 45) have critically considered psychoanalytic thinking on the father in the context of acknowledging the complexities and diversities in family life today. They argue that psychoanalysts, over the past quarter of a century, made significant assumptions of homogeneity of family structure, individual behaviour and interpersonal relationships. However, they argue that there is a paradox or dialectic in these generalisations. The nuclear family of western society is, to a considerable degree, structured by gender roles. By contrast, the focus of psychoanalytic interest is invariably on deviations from such social norms that might explain, and arguably underpin, the individual differences at the heart of psychoanalytic clinical interest. This dialectic has been part and parcel of psychoanalytic writing from its earliest days, with psychoanalysts attempting to provide general developmental theories on the basis of exceptions from these theories as presented in their clinical practices. They argue that theorising around fathers is a key case in point, with generalisations made about the role of the father that are not integrated with observations of actual fathers with their children.

Target and Fonagy (2002) critically reconsider classical psychoanalytic ideas. In relation to the Oedipal father they make some well-known criticisms. Freud's reading of the legend is selective and open to a range of readings rather than a universal truth. Moreover, the universal presence of a vengeful or hostile/censorious father needs to be contextually located. Certain aspects of this myth may have as much to do with contact patterns of the largely absent father in Victorian days. Target and Fonagy conclude that the predominantly negative view of the father in classical psychoanalysis could be less to do with a cross-cultural universal than with a specific type of fathering practices.

Moreover, in arguments that are highly compatible with those of the psychologists in the next chapter, and indicate their commitment to attachment theory, they reject the separate and distinct role assigned to the father and suggest that evidence does not support such highly differentiated contributions in terms of either mother or father. 'The father's and mother's roles may not be identical in terms of the child's psychic organisation, but nor are their roles as clearly distinguished as some psychoanalytic writers have assumed' (Target and Fonagy, 2002: 51).

They note that psychoanalysts often seem to hear the words 'absent father' to infer a range of child psychopathology. They note in particular the literature on homosexuality. Indeed, one of the more troubling aspects of classical psychoanalysis is that homosexuality is treated as a pathology with roots lying in distant fathers with whom sons failed to make a successful identification (see Butler, 2000, for an account particularly in the context of exploring Lacanian responses to contemporary demands by gay people in relation to marriage and parenthood).

The next section looks briefly at some of the poststructuralist writers who have engaged with psychoanalysis.

Poststructuralists: deconstructing the father?

Henriques et al (1998) were concerned primarily to expose the limitations of traditional psychology and sociology and the individual–social divide that they exhibit. They suggest psychoanalysis has the following strengths (Henriques et al, 1998: 205-6). First, in contrast to the rational subject of psychology, psychoanalysis gives space to our fundamental irrationality and the extent to which our will or agency is constantly subverted by desire. Second, the assumption of a unitary subject is undercut in psychoanalysis by its focus on unconscious processes. Third, where psychology divides cognition from affect, in psychoanalysis these processes are undercut in complex ways. Fourth, it provides an account of the continuity of the subject, of the past implicated in the present, and a view of development that is in contrast to either biological or social determinism.

In summary, they suggest that it profoundly challenges any attempt to separate the individual and the social and to think about this individual in terms of its consciousness of self or a unitary capacity for rational action. In relation to gender they challenge the assumptions of versions of sociology and psychology in relation to gender roles that people are socialised into or learn (see Chapters Five and Six). An important point to make here is that this has implications for research practices and places those who are psychoanalytically informed at odds with many research practices within sociology and psychology. Researchers such as Hollway and Jefferson (2000) argue for the importance of methods of researching that recognise the role the psyche plays in producing defended subjects whose accounts must be interpreted.

The belief that psychoanalysis can be employed in the service of progressive political purposes is long-standing (see Frosh, 1987; Segal, 1990, 1999). From Henriques et al's perspective, examination of the unconscious is an essential precondition for understanding our resistance, as well as the possibilities for change:

> Psychoanalysis supports the view we have developed of subjectivity as produced through contradiction and conflict, a subjectivity whose machinery is not entirely accessible because of the subterfuges of the unconscious. But we do not consider the subject incapable of change as if it were produced and positioned in an originary moment and held constant in the vice of refractory desires. So we need to move beyond what psychoanalysis offers, whilst positively utilizing its lessons. In particular there remains the task of outlining the disposition of power-desire-knowledge complex, wherein subjectivity is intricated. (Henriques et al, 1998: 225)

Doing so, for these authors, involves reworking Lacan's analysis of the positioning of subjectivity in the structure of language, and interrogating the historical specificity of unconscious processes and their relation to bodies of knowledge and regimes of power:

> [T]he infant's separation from the mother and its production as a subject can be seen in terms of successive moments of transformation and its insertion into discursive practices. These are culturally and historically specific, but also changeable, and to some extent, idiosyncratic. Such practices are always already locked in power-knowledge relations, and the production of desire is inextricably intertwined in them. (Henriques et al, 1998: 225-6)

Lupton and Barclay (1997) use poststructuralist and psychoanalytic theory in research with a small number of first-time fathers in Australia. The stories elicited from the men ranged across an array of subjects

– relationships with their fathers, work, beliefs about parenting, equality – and covered the period before and after birth. They elicited some expected responses: for example, the tension for many between being an involved father and work demands. These are played out differently in different welfare regimes and socioeconomic and cultural contexts. Other features highlighted such as the affective, embodied, sensual dimension of parenting and its implications for fathers are perhaps less well rehearsed in the literature on fathers (see Chapter Six and Doucet's research [2006a, 2006b]) but those features do not necessarily need a psychoanalytic analysis to uncover. Indeed there is a considerable sociological literature on emotion and the body.

An interesting point that is more likely to be uncovered by a psychoanalytic perspective is that, for most men, fathering did challenge their sense of being in control. Furthermore, as part of their defence against the unconscious anxieties first produced in infancy in the process of individuation from the mother, both men and women could seek recourse in taking up the gender-differentiated discourses available to them (Lupton and Barclay, 1997: 146). Thus both men and women could revert to highly differentiated ways of parenting, even if that was not their plan. Lupton and Barclay's study found a complex intertwining of acculturation and personal biography at work in how the men and women in their sample approached parenting. This involved:

> ... an interplay of aspects peculiar to couples' immediate situations, such as the nature of their paid work, their infant's behaviour and disposition, the availability of support from their family or friends and individuals' experiences with, and observations of, their own parents, with broader sociocultural trends, such as the range of dominant discourses circulating on how a 'good' father and 'good' mother should approach and conduct parenting. (Lupton and Barclay, 1997: 151)

While this seems an impressive list, missing are discussions of the internal father, the murderous impulses of the child towards the parents and so on.

This study seems to fit, to an extent, with the emergence of what Henwood and Procter (2003: 338) call a progressive psychosocial transformation, which seems of importance to a range of scholars interested in fathers from a variety of disciplinary backgrounds:

> Drawing on psychoanalytic arguments, it illuminates how gendered family dynamics – and especially their role in

producing polarized masculine and feminine identities – can, while appearing to be 'normal', habitually undercut people's human strengths and foster vulnerabilities in their lifelong experiences of self and others ... This perspective highlights the seductiveness of relations of power, dominance and subordination between men and women in families, while questioning the associated splitting apart of human qualities such as emotional literacy about relationships and personal self-care. Fathers have been identified as potentially helpful agents of change if they adopt positions that foster their children's (and partner's) fluidity and choice in the face of rigidly prescribed roles. (Henwood and Procter, 2003: 338)

This is explored further in the next chapter when looking at Henwood and Procter's research with first-time fathers, and reinforces the points made at the beginning of the chapter about the interdisciplinary nature of much important contemporary work on fathers today.

Before concluding this chapter, it is important to note that many welfare practitioners are not currently trained in psychoanalytic thinking. Chapter Nine highlights recent developments in psychosocial theory in relation to social care and social work.

Conclusion

It is not so much the future of psychoanalysis that anyone should worry about, but rather the finding of languages for what matters most to us; from what we suffer from or for, for how and why we take our pleasures. (Phillips, quoted in Segal, 1999: 199)

Segal, a socialist feminist, suggests that feminists still need psychoanalysis, as it provides the fullest account to date of the complex and contradictory nature of subjectivities formed through desire and identification. Its treatment of fathers is absolutely central to what she calls, however, its phallic logic and conservative family romance. And yet!!! There are examples of using psychoanalysis to destabilise, to disrupt the authoritarian vengeful father and to envisage and support fluid and non-oppressive possibilities for men and women. This is obvious across disciplinary boundaries as we saw in this chapter and consider further in the next chapters.

FIVE

Psychological perspectives

Introduction

As anyone who has worked in a university department containing psychologists knows only too well, there is no one psychology, but different, often highly conflicting, types – for example, behaviourism, social psychology, critical social psychology – with feminists involved in many of the areas. Developmental psychology's status is not clear. As Burman (1994) notes it is considered by some not to be a domain or type of psychology but rather a perspective or an approach encompassing all other areas of psychology. Developmental psychology's main focus has been to study child development and, in that context, the role of mothers and, in more recent decades, fathers and it has been a key aspect of the training of many child welfare practitioners (see Chapter Nine).

This chapter does not aim to offer an overview of psychology as a whole. Rather it explores the literature on the 'conditions of historical possibility' for psychology. It then focuses on developmental psychology, and particularly contemporary developments. An important aim of the chapter is to critically engage with the research that appears to have become influential with policy makers.

More 'critical' psychologies are discussed in terms of the potential they offer for challenging oppressive gender relations and identities.

The background

As Hollway (1989: 88) argues, it is of central importance to appreciate the foundational belief at the end of the 19th century that psychology is a science.[1] Thus, through its methods, progress towards knowledge is guaranteed. She notes that this begs a supplementary question, which takes us onto the terrain of philosophy: 'what is the character of that knowledge and how can we know that science guarantees its truthfulness?' (Hollway, 1989: 88). She argues that this question has not often been posed because psychology, in seeking to establish itself, cut itself off from its roots in philosophy and theology and aligned itself with the spectacular developments in biology that were emerging. This was, for better or ill, in order to achieve control over the human behaviour of others, a point that is explored further later.

It is beyond the scope of this chapter to discuss in any depth the extensive literature about the status of science generally, and specifically the issues posed for knowledge about the social world. However it is useful to provide a brief synopsis. In the social sciences, the view that there is a reality that, given the right scientific procedures, can be explained, and the opposing view that there may be many plausible explanations for the same phenomena, have been characterised as realism or objectivism and relativism or social constructionism (see Taylor and White, 2000). For the realist or objectivist we can come to know a world that is separate from, and independent of us, through careful observation of it. The laboratory is often seen as the ideal setting for this disinterested study. While the natural sciences contain the most proponents of this view (although there are, and have been, ongoing debates within the natural sciences), it has also been found within social sciences, particularly, though not exclusively, within psychology. Taylor and White (2000) offer as examples the laboratory explorations of attachment behaviours in young children and experiments into conformity and obedience. While realism is often associated with quantitative approaches – the measurement of particular behaviours and so on – it is also to be found in qualitative approaches (for example, in naturalistic ethnographic approaches). These are underpinned by a correspondence theory of truth. We can see things as they really are if we use the right methods.

By contrast, those within a social constructionist frame argue that the things that exist are represented and constructed through language as a set of concepts and ideas (Gergen, 1994) and moreover all of us, researchers included, come to know about and articulate these things through language. Most social constructionists do not deny there is a 'real world' of pain, loss, poverty, hunger and so on, but they are concerned with how we come to know about and construct this world, or more accurately worlds, and indeed to stress the multiplicity of perspectives that may attend such constructions. This is of crucial importance in terms of the understanding of fathers, fatherhoods, motherhoods and childhoods.

It is argued by a host of critics of psychology that its claims to science are premised on the constitution of *the individual* as an object of science. A central concern here has been the way a specific notion of the individual has emerged under certain historical conditions and the related theorisation of the relationship between the individual and society. As we saw in the last chapter, it is argued that psychology and sociology exemplify an unhelpful individual–society divide. It is important to note that there is a long history of attempting to rethink the relationship between the individual and society within psychology. But Henriques et al (1998) argue that there has been a tendency towards an a priori assumption of a pre-given psychological or biological subject who is either capable of processing the information contained in the interaction or of internalising the social description of its actions.[2] Categories such as child, mother or father are neither biological givens, nor are they simply social constructs according to them. The relational character of their mutual effects needs to be stressed.

It is contended that modern psychology is important in producing many of the apparatuses of social regulation that affect our daily lives (Henriques et al, 1998: 1). Psychology, because of its insertion in modern social practices, has helped to constitute modern individuality. It is productive, regulating, classifying and administering. By producing explanations as well as identifying problems it contributes also to specific political positions. Burman (1994: 14), for example, argues that individual psychology in late 19th- and 20th-century Western Europe reflected and translated social preoccupations with population control and mental abilities into policy recommendations, prescriptions on infant and child management and education.

It is perhaps most helpful in terms of illuminating some of the above points to turn now to writings within developmental psychology.

Developmental psychology: truth or norm?

> Developmental psychology is premised on a set of claims to truth which are historically specific and which are not the only or necessary way to understand children. (Urwin, 1998: 154)

According to Burman (1994), developmental psychology arose in the 19th century to answer particular questions related to evolutionary theory and anthropology as well as philosophy. It participated in social movements explicitly concerned with the comparison, regulation and control of groups and societies, and is closely identified with the development of tools of mental measurement, classification of abilities and the establishment of norms and, as indicated previously, it was associated with the rise of science and modernity. Burman is among those who suggest it contributed to a specific gendered model of practice – the privileging of the rational over the emotional, the male disinterested observer over the emotional mother/female. Objectivity was prized and men/fathers were seen as having the necessary rationality and detachment.

Charles Darwin's study was the first and was published in 1877 (but based on notes made in 1840). His interest was in the relative contribution of genetic endowment and environmental experience (Riley, 1983; Burman, 1994: 10). He was concerned with identifying that which is reflex or instinctive as opposed to that which is acquired through experience, and with the theory of 'cultural recapitulation', according to which embryological development echoes the evolution of a species. According to this theory, the development of a child repeats the development of adult human cultures, proceeding in stages from the primitive to the civilised (Riley, 1983: 44).

His was a prototype of the form studies were to take. As Burman (1994) notes, it was characteristic to depict the infant as a biological organism abstracted from the familial and material environment. It was motivated by the quest to discover the origins and specificities of the adult human mind and was related to similar ventures in anthropology, with the child of the time equated with the 'savage' or 'undeveloped'. Additionally, the apparently bizarre behaviours of both primates and babies were seen as relevant to the understanding of neurotic and pathological behaviour. A conception of development emerged, which was that of individual and evolutionary progress and involved taking steps, under direction, up an ordered hierarchy (Burman, 1994: 11). However, it is important to note that Darwin was more equivocal than those who followed him. It is also interesting that his work was to reinforce pre-Darwinian versions of biology, focusing on heritability rather than variability. 'Child study "societies" soon flourished, observing children, weighing and measuring them, documenting their interests, states, activities' (Burman, 1994: 11).

These psychological studies were a reflection of wider anxieties at the time about the 'quality' of the population, particularly those considered unstable and unruly. 'Pauperism', for example, was seen as a trait rather than a set of circumstances. But Walkerdine (1998) argues that political motivations cannot be said to have caused in any simple sense the way the science of the individual developed. Politics and psychology were mutually implicated making each other possible.

Nor is there a simple story about how the discipline 'progressed', with conflicts about the relative role of heredity vis-à-vis education, for example (Burman, 1994: 19). Behaviourist ideas became popular from 1910 onwards and environment in a wide sense became the focus of attention. Thus child training was accompanied by improvements in sanitation and social reforms. Testing and classifying became not only central activities but also the way that psychology was able to construct itself as useful or legitimate. It, in turn, legitimated classifying and regulating and was thus important in social control in very complex ways:

> The technologies of description, comparison and measurement of children that underlie the descriptive knowledge base of developmental psychology have their roots in demographic control, comparative anthropology and animal observation that set 'man' over animals, European man over non-European, man over woman, as well as politician over pauper. (Burman, 1994: 19)

Burman suggests, however, that what became central and uncontested, but is a site of central paradox, is that the natural course of development has to be carefully monitored, supported and even corrected in order to emerge appropriately. That which is designated as natural or spontaneously arising is in fact constructed or even forced.

As Taylor (2004) notes, much of the underpinning knowledge for childcare practice is based uncritically on developmental psychology. Thus, assumptions about what is the 'normal' course of development for children and what is required from parents to foster such a course have often been unquestioned, and there is little engagement by practitioners or policy makers with the critical literature profiled in this chapter.

Before moving on to look at more contemporary developments, it is also worth highlighting the emphasis that emerged on 'description'. As Hollway (1989) notes, much of this type of psychology kept theory and method separate, and, in so doing, not only obscured the theoretical presupposition behind the methods used, but also acted to foreclose alternative understandings of 'why we are as we are or do what we do'. An interesting argument advanced by Burman and Hollway among others is that the drive towards rationality in psychological models of development can also be understood in psychoanalytic terms as a defence against anxiety – what is repressed or left out may be the complexity and chaos of the research process, for example, and the omission of which also meets unconscious needs for control and certainty.

The child, the mother and attachment anxieties

It is generally agreed that developmental psychology constituted the woman as mother, alongside the child, as its object of concern and intervention until recent decades. This is partly attributable to the influence of attachment theory. As we saw in the last chapter, psychoanalytic perspectives for a large part of the 20th century were very focused on the mother–child relationship and, while attachment theory occupies a very uneasy position to psychoanalysis, it did share this mother–child preoccupation.

Bowlby's work is, of course of central importance here. His first book chapter, 'Personal aggressiveness and war', written with Durbin in 1938, drew heavily on notions of innate human aggression, which was justified by drawing analogies with the behaviour of apes (see Riley, 1983: 92-3). In 1940 he wrote his first book *Personality and Mental Illness*, which was an account of 65 patients at the Maudsley Hospital and added the influence of 'early surroundings' to the genetic component in mental disturbance. These influences included the separation of the child from the mother, the impact of parental disturbances and the experience of being fostered. In a paper published in 1940 he condemned the lack of attention paid to the role of environment in the analytic literature. By environment, though, he meant the mother and her behaviour. At this stage he was not arguing that mothers ought never to leave their children. Moreover, he was arguing that, while most mothers were reasonably good, 'the mothers of neurotic children are frequently bad, in the sense that they have very strong feelings of hatred and condemnation towards their children, or else make inordinate demands from them for affection' (quoted in Riley, 1983: 94).

Riley notes, however, a difference in Bowlby's clinical papers and his more sociological papers of that time. In the latter, he wrote strongly about the dangers posed to younger children if they were evacuated without their mothers. While it is often believed that his major preoccupations about mothers and children remaining together and the dangers of group care were fostered as a result of the damage he observed because of evacuation, Riley suggests they were formed before evacuation actually took place. The research for which Bowlby was probably best known, on 46 juvenile thieves, was not published until 1946, though mentioned in the 1940 article noted previously. His aim was to prove by clinical demonstration his conviction that separation of the child from its mother or mother substitute was inherently traumatic.

As Walkerdine and Lucey (1989) note, while it is Bowlby who is often singled out for abuse, a far wider movement took up what became known as attachment theory. Experiments such as those by Harlow in 1958 in the US on rhesus monkeys were to be influential and, in 1959, Bowlby organised a conference at the Tavistock Clinic in London where this work was presented. Harlow set himself the task of scientifically proving that mothering is natural, normal and inevitable and that this love was not sexual.

Thus was to emerge an ethology that stressed the evolutionary necessity of mother–infant interaction and was a rejection of what was seen as the negativity of Freud's theory of drives and the social Darwinism of the time, which stressed the inevitability of aggression and war:

> In this formulation, it will be noticed, there is no reference to 'needs' or 'drives'. Instead, attachment behaviour is regarded as that which occurs when certain behavioural systems are activated. The behavioural systems themselves are believed to develop within the infant as a result of his interaction with his environment of evolutionary adaptedness, and especially of his interaction with the principal figure in that environment, namely his mother. Food and eating are held to play no more than a minor part in their development. (Walkerdine and Lucey, 1989: 53)

As Walkerdine and Lucey (1989: 141) note, attachment theory lent itself to a form of environmental optimism, with a strong post-war movement that tried to produce the possibility of social reform through the agency of the mother. Indeed, the project of social democracy created natural mother love as an object that was to be the bedrock of its policy (see Rustin, 1996, for a fascinating discussion of attachment theory in context).

The critiques of Bowlby, Bowlbyism and attachment theory are extensive and beyond the remit of this chapter to recount in detail (see Riley, 1983, for an interesting discussion). What is important to note are the issues in relation to the role of fathers. According to Daniel and Taylor's (2001) review of the literature, attachment theory has, in recent decades, been refined and developed to incorporate the potential, not only for primary attachment to the father, but also for multiple attachment figures. They argue that the main message that emerges from current attachment theory is that it does not matter who the attachment figure is, at long as there is at least one. Their concern is primarily with exploring the implications for practice with fathers in health and social care. A key insight from the recent attachment literature, which opens the door to fathers caring is that the capacity to care is increasingly understood as a developmental capacity – it is not just innate or biological.

Others suggest that the research on attachment used measures that placed men in a poor light relative to mothers (Lamb and Lewis, 2004). Lamb and Lewis argue for, and welcome, what they term 'more patrocentric research themes' (Lamb and Lewis, 2004: 292). It is also interesting to note that reviews of parenting practices, informed by attachment theory, suggest similarities between parents rather than the unique qualities of mothers or fathers (see O'Brien, 2005, and the discussion later in this chapter).

The 'role' of the father in child development: beyond developmental psychology

Lupton and Barclay (1997) suggest that much of the research by psychologists (including developmental psychologists) on fathers:

> ... confines the experience ... to an individualized, largely asocial context, with little recognition of the 'external world' and relationships beyond the mother-father-infant triad. While the 'social context' is occasionally acknowledged in this literature, this generally relates to such factors as the nature of the father's marital relationship, his orientation towards his career or his relationship with his own father. (Lupton and Barclay, 1997: 47)[3]

It has to be added here that the question of power relations and understandings of fathers as *men*, so central to the research explored in the next chapter, is seriously neglected.

They also note the emphasis within some of the social psychology literature on the 'transition to fatherhood' and 'father role', which tends to focus on personality-based differences in men's adaptations to becoming a father and their relationship with other family members (Lupton and Barclay, 1997: 46). Methodologically, the preference in such research is for scales to measure personality traits and so on. As is explored in a later section, this is by no means the case for some of the work emerging from social psychologists such as Henwood and Procter (2003).

In this next section, developmental psychology's evolution is explored and, while the concerns of Lupton and Barclay are legitimate, it is clear that it is internally differentiated, with many leading researchers concerned with understanding the 'social' and in looking at differing welfare and cultural contexts (see the edited collections by Lamb, 1997, 2004; Lewis and Lamb, 2007). As indicated in Chapter One, it is clear that employing disciplinary boundaries is problematic, and it is particularly the case for researchers such as Lewis whose work on fathers has spanned social policy and sociology (see, for example, Chapter Six).

Lamb (1997) traced research over the previous 40 years (the majority of it in the early decades, particularly from the US). He identified three traditions: correlational studies, studies of father absence and father involvement. He notes that, between 1940 and 1970, the father as a sex role model was considered most important and most studies concentrated on sex role development, especially in sons. The design of these early studies was simple, and indeed crude. Researchers assessed masculinity in fathers and in sons, and then determined how strongly the two sets of scores were correlated. There was no consistent correlation, which Lamb notes was puzzling to the researchers and led them to the question – if fathers did not make their boys into men, what role did they have?

A host of studies on other areas suggested that paternal warmth or closeness appeared beneficial, whereas paternal masculinity appeared irrelevant. It is interesting to note that, if one accepts the premises underlying this research, as far as influences on children are concerned, Lamb suggests that very little about the gender of the parent appeared distinctly important, although there continued to be researchers who argued for the crucial importance of distinctive maternal and paternal roles.

Segal (1999) suggests that, within psychology before the 1960s, stereotyped sex differences were mostly either simply assumed or, when measured, assigned to biology. Following Maccoby and Jacklin's research in 1974 it became equally routine, as well as routinely challenged, to point out that there were more similarities than differences between the sexes and to assign recorded psychological differences to environmental processes. A host of feminists emerged looking at this area in order to argue for similarities, but others argue that the search for sex similarities endorsed a way of looking at the world that remained trapped in the deliberations generated by polarised gender categories (Segal, 1999: 153).

The second research tradition noted by Lamb (1997) concerned studies of father absence and divorce. Again this was very strongly represented in the US. It was suggested in this literature that boys growing up without fathers had problems in the areas of sex role and gender identity development, school performance and so on.

Researchers and theorists first sought to explain the effects of father absence by noting the absence of male sex role models. It was assumed that, without a masculine parental model, boys could not acquire strong masculine identities or sex roles and would not have models of achievement with which to identify. However, many boys without fathers seemed to develop 'quite normally' so far as sex role development and achievement were concerned. Lamb pointed out that: 'In sum the evidence suggests that father absence may be harmful, not necessarily because a sex-role model is absent, but because many aspects of the father's role – economic, social, emotional – go unfulfilled or inappropriately filled in these families' (Lamb, 1997: 11). Is it the absence of a second parent and the loss of men's generally higher earning power that is important, as well as the absence of the support two parents can give each other? (See Golombok, 2000, for a discussion of this.) The other important issue is what psychologists often call in a very coy and problematic way, 'marital conflict' or 'hostility'. There seems to be a consensus that this adversely affects children and outcomes are related to whether it continues post-separation or not, although there is often a worrying lack of precision about what such conflict or hostility encompasses. (See Chapter Seven for further discussion in relation to compatible difficulties with some of the definitions of domestic violence currently used by feminists.)

The research on the outcomes of divorce continues to be contested today and indeed Daniels' (1998) edited collection notes many of the key debates that centre around the absence of fathers and outcomes for children. It has moved away from a focus on boys, although that still emerges. This research is increasingly multidisciplinary (see Golombok, 2000; Featherstone, 2004). An interesting development in more recent years is that the emergence of financially secure lesbian mother families has offered new possibilities for research purposes.

The debates have been highly politicised and imbued with assumptions about the desirability or otherwise of particular family arrangements. In the US, debates became encoded with racial subtexts from the 1960s onwards with the publication of Daniel Moynihan's report on Black families, which suggested that their structure (women headed) was central to their failure to achieve economically (see

Featherstone, 2004, for a further summary and Chapter Eight for discussion of contemporary debates).

As Smart and Neale (1999) note, the popular and research debates have often been stuck within a discourse of 'harmism' – divorce causes harm and there has often been insufficient consideration that it is a process, not an event, and is associated with an array of complex variables. Moreover, as many researchers have noted, outcomes can be misleading, giving little sense of the variability of the journeys that have been taken. There is a preference for qualitative work partly for that reason and there is a strong research tradition now, exploring with children themselves what their views are of changing families (see, for example, Dunn and Deater-Deckard, 2001).

Impact of father involvement on children

In terms of 'involvement', the research has been dominated by exploration of three different dimensions. These are: the amounts of time that fathers spend interacting with, being accessible to, or making arrangements for, their children. However, it is increasingly argued that this is too restrictive a focus and indeed was never intended to obviate the need to explore other important aspects of fatherhood, such as breadwinning (see O'Brien, 2005; Lewis and Lamb, 2007; and Chapter Two).

According to O'Brien (2005: 11-13), the literature on fathers' impact is now extensive and shows that children are at risk from, or benefit from, the life histories both parents bring to their parenting. Traditionally, psychological research had not recorded paternal behaviour and had relied on maternal accounts, making it difficult to discover if fathers had any independent influence on children's development. In addition those studies that began to explore paternal factors often failed to control for the level and quality of maternal involvement experienced by the same children, making it difficult to assess the relative contribution of fathering and mothering to child outcomes. A recent systematic review of studies where maternal involvement had been controlled for, and where data had been gathered from different independent sources, has found a beneficial impact of 'positive' father involvement in children's lives (Pleck and Masciardrelli, 2004). These studies have moved beyond time use indicators. 'There is little evidence for a linear relationship between amount of time invested in children and good child outcomes' (O'Brien, 2005: 12).

O'Brien argues that what counts as positive depends to some extent on the theoretical models of the researchers and the age of the child, but there are certain commonalities: activities likely to promote an emotionally secure environment and well-being in its broadest sense such as warm, responsive and sensitive interaction, monitoring and guiding behaviour to set limits, spending time to listen and talk about the child's concerns, encouraging age-appropriate independent action and caring for the child's physical welfare. It is important to note, however, that researchers such as Phoenix and Husain (2007) have critically interrogated this consensus in the context of exploring differing parenting practices among differing minority ethnic families. Moreover, Walkerdine and Lucey's (1989) study was a classic in exploring the ways in which particular expert discourses were imbued with class-based assumptions.

A key point made by many researchers is that:

> Father involvement cannot be separated from the network of family relationships within which it is embedded. The *couple relationship* is a key one, setting the scene against which parents negotiate and balance their family and employment roles and responsibilities. Research suggests that high paternal involvement is 'grounded' in harmonious couple relationships. (O'Brien, 2005: 9, emphasis added; see also Pleck and Masciadrelli, 2004)

This is important in alerting us to the dangers of abstracting father involvement or activities from the overall relationship context in which they operate. As outlined in Chapter One, this is a danger with government policies. For example, it is of concern that the research by Pleck and Masciadrelli (2004) is used as part of the justification for making joint birth registration a legal requirement by the government (DCSF and DWP, 2008). This is an inappropriate use of research that stresses the importance of 'positive' father involvement, which may not be achieved by forcing mothers and fathers to legally register the birth of their child.

According to the research, the quality of fathers' relationships with their children is more vulnerable than mothers' to the negative effects of conflict between partners, and lower marital quality is more consistently associated with negativity by fathers to children (than negativity by mothers). This has been explained by stressing the vital mediation role mothers play in facilitating men's parenting. The average father is more reliant on their partner's interpretation of children's behaviour than the average mother. This is often referred to as maternal gatekeeping. Moreover, men's attempts to become more involved in childcare are contingent on maternal beliefs and mothers' assessment of its benefits. The issue of maternal gatekeeping is returned to in discussions of the research by Doucet (2006a) in Chapters Six, Nine and Ten.

There is a body of work showing the importance of fathers at different stages of children's lives and there are some emergent findings (see also Lamb and Lewis, 2004; Lewis and Lamb, 2007). O'Brien (2005) suggests that studies assessing the impact of father involvement in the early years on later child outcomes confirm the importance of early paternal investment in caring. Moreover, analysis of British cohort studies is beginning to show continuity in paternal involvement over time (Flouri and Buchanan, 2003).

In later years, fathers' occupational status is a significant predictor of educational attainment. However, income is insufficient on its own to secure successful educational outcomes:

> [H]igher levels of attainment were predicted by a combination of psychological and socio-economic factors: parental couple stability, material resources, occupational status, child educational aspirations, and parenting style ... Being able to talk to mum about 'things that matter' emerged as a significant parenting factor for higher attainment at both GCSE and A level. Talking to father was also significant but to a lesser extent. (O'Brien, 2005: 18)

Flouri (2005) applies a process model of parenting, which has a systemic framework highlighting the interacting influences of five different factors on father involvement: contextual factors, father's factors, mother's factors, quality of the co-parental relationship and child's factors. Her findings suggest that no universal claims can be made about the impact of father involvement on children. Rather, studies show that certain aspects of father involvement in certain groups of fathers are associated with certain outcomes (both positive and negative) in certain groups of children.

Moreover, Lewis and Lamb (2007) stress the importance of understanding that all family relationships are highly interrelated and that it is difficult to single out individual relationships as unique determinants of child development. They note that the quality of the father–child relationship may be simply a marker of all the relationships within these families, rather than that fathers make some magical contribution.[4]

While the bulk of the research is about the impact on children, there is research on fathers (from a range of sources in psychology). It is argued that fathers differ from non-fathers in being more connected to wider generational relationships. Fatherhood status has been independently associated with psychological and physical well-being, except for men who lived away from their children who were lower on psychological well-being and life satisfaction. However, there is a need for more research because it may be that men who are already connected to kin and have high work motivation are more likely to become fathers (O'Brien, 2005).

Hawkins and Dollahite (1996) have drawn attention to the important generative effects for fathers who are highly involved with their children, and there is a literature on generativity and interest in thinking about this in the context of working with marginalised and vulnerable men (see Ferguson and Hogan, 2004).

To summarise, there are many criticisms, theoretically and methodologically, to be made of the research on father involvement and outcomes (see Lupton and Barclay, 1997). There continues to be a need certainly to locate and interrogate concepts such as father involvement, for example, rather than see it in terms of an individualised set of practices engaged in by disembodied fathers. The coyness of the language around marital conflict and hostility is of real concern in some of this research. What is meant by conflict and hostility? When can it be considered violence or abuse?

However, this is a vibrant field conceptually and methodologically. Researchers such as O'Brien (2005) and Lewis and Lamb (2007) urge the necessity of multidisciplinary and cross-cultural approaches to the study of fathers and for more theoretical and methodological sophistication. A key point of interest is that the findings of most sophisticated researchers do not lend themselves to universalist assumptions about the impact of fathers and father involvement on children and that seems important in the current policy and practice context, as outlined briefly in Chapter One. The research does not support simple (simplistic) assumptions that father involvement is good for children. Moreover, the importance of the relationship between the parents is stressed.

'Critical' psychologies

Segal (1999) notes that many feminist psychologists have turned away from the mainstream preoccupation with gender difference research (explored further in the next chapter) and quantitative approaches and the study of individual attributes, and have focused instead on the conflicts and difficulties accompanying the acquisition of normative gender and sexual identities in girls:

> The dominant theoretical explanations they favour make use of learning theory and cognitive theory, but in line with a more general social construct framework which pays close attention to social context and meanings. (Segal, 1999: 154)

For example, Segal argues that the work of feminist psychologists such as Carol Gilligan[5] has been crucial in exposing how stereotypes of 'femininity' can undermine women's confidence and dictate gendered performances that *confirm* rather than *contest* existing meanings and social practices (Segal, 1999: 155). However, Segal is also troubled by much of this work, as it seems to focus unduly on women facing problems. When it does focus on men it is simplistically focused on exploring issues such as why men conform, as in not talking for example, and does not explore how a reformed masculinity might increase rather than reduce men's power. Indeed she notes the work of Connell (1995) who suggests that refashioning masculinity has been an important way of men maintaining power (see discussion in Chapter Six).

Segal argues that social construction theories lead us to expect the successful moulding of identities and behaviour, but psychoanalytic reflections point us towards the continued failure of psychic life to reflect consciously learned norms. On a methodological level this suggests the need to collect thick data, rich enough to expose the fragility, contradiction and context-bound resistance or compliance within gendered experiences and performance:

> Insofar as gender is seen as consistently internalised, the worn out biological/social polarity has not been transcended to embrace any richer psychological hermeneutics attempting to encompass the contingent, precarious, often contradictory processes through which the social becomes embodied ... Identities are indeed social, but they are also exceedingly complex – both psychologically and in terms of their socio-cultural framing. One problem with social construction theory is that it has tended to erase the nuances of subjective conflict and ambivalence. (Segal, 1999: 157)

Social psychologists such as Henwood and Procter (2003: 340) investigate: 'how men perceive themselves and evaluate the changing sociocultural scripts of fatherhood and masculinity on becoming fathers'.

They suggest their findings contribute to an emerging, although far from unitary, corpus of social-psychological research on fatherhood and masculinity that is seeking, in various ways, to read experiences and accounts given for their constitutive values, gendered or other socially constructed meanings: 'Along with other proponents of such works we have sought to step outside taken-for-granted assumptions about men's sense-making and foster analyses of the potential complexity of paternal subjectivity' (Henwood and Procter, 2003: 352).

They suggest that at the point in their lives at which they were interviewed (just prior to and after the birth of their first baby) the men expressed no lack of purpose or clarity about the role as fathers. Nor did they directly express any sense of personal insecurity about what it means to be men. Rather they seemed to welcome the changing nature of men and masculinity and their new father role:

> This enabled them, with striking consistency, to flesh out
> a wide range of reasons for the importance they attached
> to the status of fatherhood, its sociocultural characteristics,
> and their own transition to fatherhood. Without exception,
> and with great clarity, interviewees related the importance
> of fathers to the very particular and changed character of
> the landscape of contemporary manhood and fatherhood.
> (Henwood and Procter, 2003: 342)

They showed a clear preference for a new involved fatherhood because it contrasted with the previous dominant model of a breadwinning, disciplinarian and authority one. Masculinity, as in being 'big and macho', was not counterposed to caring. Indeed a man might most display or perform masculinity through caring.

In findings that are compatible with that of Lupton and Barclay (1947) – discussed in Chapter Four – they note the tensions and difficulties when they sought to find a way of living as a new father and confronted the work–life balance, equality and care in gender relations and personal autonomy and leisure.

A very important point made by Henwood and Procter (2003), and one shared by the author, is the importance of not engaging in reductive analyses of the men's practices as fathers:

> The fact that the interviewees in our study expressed a
> range of emotional and psychological investments in, and

ways of valuing, fatherhood makes it difficult to assimilate their talk of tensions in living the new father ideal to any single interpretive frame. Analyses of struggles for masculine hegemony clearly have their place in investigations into what is going on in family life. But to reduce to an exercise in power and domination the efforts of our interviewees to bring together – or their expressions of regret or frustration at not bringing together – different facets of their lives would seem to overlook their expressed *desire* to take up a care-taking and not just a providing role. (Henwood and Procter, 2003: 351, emphasis in original)

However, as Henwood and Procter conclude, while the model of new, involved fatherhood is undeniably a pre-eminent part of the contemporary social context and is having a considerable impact on family life, it is necessary to keep a socio-historical perspective, and to recognise that models and ways of living fatherhood are constituted out of a nexus of sometimes fixed, and sometimes fluid, discursive practices and meanings.

Conclusion

Psychology is indeed a broad church. It has generally attracted considerable criticism from those interested in changing gender relations. It has proved influential in popular and powerful discourses, and is part of the professional training of many welfare practitioners. While 'old' arguments in relation to boys needing male role models continue to be used, also evident are 'newer' arguments suggesting father involvement promotes good outcomes for children. Careful exploration of the work of researchers suggests that such arguments cherry pick from the data.

This chapter explores how differing fields of psychology are developing and shifting, and the interest in working across disciplines. There is work being carried out by those who locate themselves within critical or social psychology which has much in common with some work highlighted in Chapter Four on psychoanalysis and in Chapter Six on sociology, suggesting a growing tendency for researchers to use interdisciplinary approaches.

Notes
[1] The status of psychoanalysis in this respect has also been hotly debated since Freud.

[2] It is important to note this may be too simplistic and, as will be discussed further later in this chapter, there is considerable evidence of developments in psychology that differ from either of these characterisations.

[3] As they acknowledge, this is not the case for all writers within this tradition.

[4] They stress that they would make the same point in relation to mothers.

[5] Carol Gilligan's work has been enormously influential in scholarship from a number of disciplines that have emerged around the 'ethic of care'. Doucet's (2006a) analysis of fathers and fathering is located within this field.

SIX

Sociological perspectives

Introduction

As sociologists engage more with the diversity and complexity of fathers, fathering and fatherhood exciting possibilities appear to be emerging for future research.

This chapter explores key themes in a journey from the rigidity of role models to contemporary work around intimacy, the 'meaning' of children, the body, and feminist and pro-feminist work particularly in relation to masculinities. The latter highlights how crucial it is that individual practices by men as fathers, including the kinds of knowledge they draw on, are located within wider social relations.

The 'role' of the father

European sociology had its origins in the social upheavals and intellectual aspirations of the 19th century with its foundation as a discipline usually attributed to Comte (Marsh et al, 1996). His establishment of the Positivist Society in 1848 was rooted in his concern to search for order and progress. Like psychology, sociology was formed in a period where the superiority of the methods used by the natural sciences was accepted and it was hoped that such methods could also be used to study the social world. Furthermore, like psychology, sociology has been, and continues to be, a broad church. However, most of what is taught today is at a considerable remove from concerns with measurement and testing, unlike psychology. Therefore it has not been judged necessary to explore its very early history, as has been done with the subjects in previous chapters.

The concept of role is one of several that have a dual origin in sociology and psychology, as we saw in the last chapter (Rogers and Rogers, 2001). Sex role research generally has its origins in 19th-century debates about differences between the sexes (Connell, 1995). In a project founded on resistance to demands by women for emancipation, a 'scientific' doctrine of innate sex differences stimulated research into such differences. This gave way to sex role research. The use of the concept of 'role' provided a way of linking the idea of a place in the social structure with the idea of cultural norms. This work dated from the 1930s and, through the efforts of anthropologists, sociologists and psychologists, the concept had, by the end of the 1950s, become a key term in the social sciences.

According to Connell (1995) there are two ways in which the role concept can be applied to gender; the roles are seen as specific to definite social situations, and the more common approach in which being a man or a woman means enacting a general set of expectations that are attached to one's sex. In this approach there are always two sex roles in any cultural context. Masculinity and femininity are interpreted as internalised sex roles, the products of socialisation or social learning. This concept mapped smoothly onto the idea of sex differences and the two notions have been consistently conflated. Although sex roles can be seen as the cultural enactment of biological sex differences, this does not have to be so. Sex role theory does allow for change in that the agencies of socialisation can transmit different expectations, and indeed sex role theory blossomed within second-wave feminism and sex role research became a political tool to demonstrate how key agencies of socialisation socialised men and women into stereotypical and oppressive roles. Some of those who became involved in Men's Liberation too saw sex role research as helpful in demonstrating the oppressiveness of sex roles (Connell's critique of sex role research is returned to in a subsequent section).

A key figure in the development of sex role theory in the 20th century was the sociologist Talcott Parsons. He dominated American sociological writing on parenthood, courtship and the family from the 1940s to the 1960s. His theory of structural functionalism saw social organisation emerging through a form of social evolution in which social practices and customs evolve because they benefit social cohesion. As Poster (1978: 80) points out, Parsons collapsed abstract principles into concrete capitalist practices making institutions appear universal and necessary. He defined the structure of the family in relation to its basic function of socialisation and argued that two structures were essential – a hierarchy of generations and a differentiation of socialising figures into 'instrumental' and 'expressive' roles. The Parsonian father was the instrumental leader of the family while the mother was the expressive leader: 'Women alone can provide the expressive function. Boys alone can be oriented to achievement in the adult world because they undergo a more difficult process than girls of shifting identifications from Mama to Papa' (Poster, 1978: 83).

Parsons argued that bringing up children in the mid-20th century required attuned and dedicated specialists and this role fell to women. As Jamieson (1998) notes, he felt it was no longer appropriate to provide children with detailed rules – young people had to be self-directing, autonomous and robust to cope with rapid social change. The loss of traditional authority was an intrinsic aspect of the transition from pre-modern to modern and a corollary of greater intimacy between parents and children. Parsons identified this greater intimacy as the new basis for parental control: 'In his ideal-typical family mothers manipulate their children rationally and emotionally with their power resting in threats of withdrawal of love, rather than appeals to traditional authority' (Jamieson, 1998: 65).

Functionalism has been out of favour in sociological scholarship for some decades. However, in the US, contemporary and influential writers on fatherhood such as Popenoe (1998) are influential. Popenoe echoes Parsons in emphasising the importance of fathers and the instrumental role they play in contrast to mothers' expressive role. Fathers do things differently and their play with children is particularly important in promoting 'self-control' among children. However, as we will see later, this seems a strange assertion to make about men who are considered to need such strong cultural regulation themselves:

> Fathers are important to their sons as role models. They are important for maintaining authority and discipline. And they are important in helping their sons to develop both self-control and empathy towards others, character traits that are found to be lacking in violent youth. (Popenoe, 1998: 41)

While Popenoe acknowledges the important contribution that fathers make as economic providers and second parents, he also argues that they bring a unique array of parenting qualities to the parenting role – as protectors and role models. He disagrees that they should become more like mothers and thinks they have a distinctive role to play. However this is confusing because he immediately slips from saying they are unique to stressing the importance of emphasising their uniqueness as otherwise: 'Already viewed as a burden and obstacle to self-fulfilment, fatherhood thus comes to seem superfluous and unnecessary as well' (Popenoe, 1998: 41). He does not specify by whom fatherhood could come to seem superfluous – fathers themselves, mothers or children?

Popenoe invokes biology as destiny:

Men are not biologically as attuned to being committed fathers as women are to being committed mothers. The evolutionary logic is clear. Women, who can bear only a limited number of children, have a great incentive to invest their energy in rearing children, while men who can father many offspring, do not. Left culturally unregulated, men's sexual behaviour can be promiscuous, their paternity casual, their commitment to families weak. (Popenoe, 1998: 35-6)

Given the centrality and weight attached to the desirability of fathers, it is noteworthy how unstable and unreliable actual men are considered to be, and the importance attached to the need to regulate them. Furthermore, what is often left unconsidered in such arguments is that it is women who are both expected to do the regulating and be regulated (see Cornell, 1998, for further discussion of this strand of thinking).

Stacey (1998) argues that, in the US, the ruling paradigms of 1950s' sociology such as structural functionalism have lost prestige and power in the academy. However, while functionalists, such as Popenoe, have more or less abandoned academic sociology, they have created independent institutions through which to disseminate their views: 'The gap in the degree of prestige that functionalist sociology enjoys in popular, as compared with professional, domains is also considerable and growing' (Stacey, 1998: 187). There is not currently a parallel process going on in the UK, although we will explore some of the developments in the 1990s in Chapter Eight, supported by cultural commentators concerned with the growth of fatherless families.

Sociology and family journeys

Smart and Neale (1999) argue that the study of family lost its core significance to sociological thought after the decline of functionalist thought (see the overview in Allan, 1999). There were writings from critical psychiatrists such as Laing and Esterson (1964) and Cooper (1971) and Marxist theorists such as Zaretsky (1973). Moreover, feminists, throughout the 1970s and 1980s, wrote extensively about how to theorise the family, the connection with capitalism and:

[C]onceptual and theoretically informed empirical work and arguments raged as to whether or not 'the family' was the site of gender oppression and, if so, how it reproduced

gender inequalities. Yet, in spite of the immense energy of
this work, mainstream sociology remained unaffected at a
theoretical level. (Smart and Neale, 1999: 2)

As they note, the 'family' did become interesting again to mainstream
sociologists in the mid-1990s. Before exploring this it is important to
note the kinds of issues that were explored, particularly by feminists, in
the 1970s and 1980s and continue to be built on, and inform current
work on, families and specifically fathers.

There have been ongoing conceptual and empirical explorations of
the gendered division of labour within the home, and the connection
with gendered inequalities in the world of waged work. Some of the
earlier work was concerned with analysing how women's unpaid work
could be theorised in relation to capitalism and patriarchy, and with
developing appropriate political strategies (for example, Wages for
Housework has been a controversial strategy adopted by some feminists)
(see Bryson, 1999, for a review). However, qualitative work in the 1980s
was often concerned to explore the meanings attached to activities,
partly in an attempt to understand the irrationality of the division of
labour in the light of changes in women's employment patterns. Lewis
(2002: 136) outlined a host of studies that suggested that gendered
meanings influenced the allocation of work. For example, Hochschild
(1989) found that American women working full time would often
try and do more housework in order to bolster their husbands and
assuage their own guilt. She also found what she called an 'economy of
gratitude' where the wife invested more in household work and both
expected and valued support from her husband, which she interpreted
as 'sharing'. A profoundly unequal situation was understood as equal.
Backett (1982) in the UK showed how far women were prepared to
go to interpret their husband's words and behaviour favourably. In later
research Lewis (2001) herself found that, while there was little evidence
that men had changed their behaviour, their changing position in
the job market during the 1990s seemed to have produced a change
in mentalities such that men were more willing to acknowledge the
tensions arising from the gender division of labour: 'This more open
acknowledgement may have served the same role as myth for couples
in the 1970s and early 1980s in serving to defuse conflict' (Lewis,
2002: 136).

The other area that feminists opened up to scrutiny was men's
violence to women within and outside the home and, indeed, the
interconnections between both. In the 1970s, this work was often
linked to theorising how patriarchy had developed and worked, but

it was also, from the outset, highly practical in terms of developing support services such as refuges for women and their children. It has developed an extensive body of scholarship that is often applied to seeking changes to policies and practices (for example, this will be apparent when looking at debates about changes to contact post-separation in the UK in recent years).

Family practices and intimacy: what about fathers?

Morgan's (1966) book *Family Connections* was a very influential intervention in sociology. He used the term 'family practices' to challenge the fixed assumptions tied to notions of 'the family':

> He uses this in order to challenge the idea that 'the family' is a thing. Rather it is a variable set of relationships which change and are modified and so the term 'practices' emphasized fluidity. More than this the term 'practices' allows us to conceptualize how family 'practices' overlap with other social practices (eg, gendering practices, economic practices and so on). Moreover, while 'practices' are historically and culturally located, they allow us to imagine the social actor who engages in these practices and who may choose to modify them ... Morgan ... speaks of the auto/biographical turn in sociology, which has started to recognize the importance of the individual to the construction of histories and cultures. (Smart and Neale, 1999: 21)

This 'turn' towards studying practices rather than 'the family' as an institution has led to a considerable scholarship. Partly as a result of seeking to understand changes in the nature of personal and social relationships and differing types of commitments/ties as well as an interest in generational issues, there is now also an extensive sociological literature on intimacy. Gabb (2008) offers a very helpful discussion of themes within this field, specifically focusing on family intimacy.

The book by Giddens, *The Transformation of Intimacy*, published in 1992 can be seen as a key (if controversial and contested) intervention into making fashionable the understanding of relationships between men, women and children within sociology and also in bridge building between popular/populist and sociological concerns. The work by Giddens on intimacy needs to be located within his work on self in late or high modernity and, while it is beyond the scope of this chapter to give anything other than an outline, it is important to do so in order to understand his argument (see Giddens, 1992: 32-4; also Cassell, 1993: 303-15).

The self becomes a reflexive project in the context of a changed social order. In former cultures where things stayed more or less the same from generation to generation, a changed identity such as when an individual moved from adolescence was clearly staked out. However, in contemporary conditions, the altered self has to be explored and constructed as part of a reflexive process of connecting personal and social change. Giddens notes, for example, that an individual has to develop a new sense of self after marital separation as part of a process of pioneering innovative social forms such as modern step-parenting (the very term parenting is, he notes, itself a relatively recent invention helping to constitute what it describes). This reflexive mobilising of self-identity is not confined to life crises but a general feature of modern social activity in relation to psychic organisation:

> This focus on the self, the production of narratives of the self (as a way of giving meaning to modern life) and the search for ontological security among massive (global) social change, brings Giddens directly to the spheres of intimacy and personal life while still understanding these fields in relation to wider concepts like globalization, post-industrialism, history or chaos. (Smart and Neale, 1999: 7)

He argues that there is a new form of intimacy epitomised in concepts such as the pure relationship and confluent love. By pure relationship he means:

> ... a social relationship ... entered into for its own sake, for what can be derived by each person from a sustained association with another; and which is continued only in so far as it is thought by both parties to deliver enough satisfactions for each individual to stay within it. (Giddens, 1992: 58)

Confluent love refers to 'active, contingent love, and therefore jars with the "for-ever", "one-and-only" qualities of the romantic love complex' (Giddens, 1992: 61). He sees women as central to the changes going on, although he acknowledges that male power epitomised in, for example, the sexual division of labour in the home has not altered substantially. As Gabb (2008) notes, Giddens sees mutual disclosure between adults as a fundamental site for constructing intimacy and, moreover, sees the transformation of intimacy as reflecting a widespread democratisation of the interpersonal sphere.

Smart and Neale (1999) argue that Giddens does not deal much with children in his book in 1992 and what little he says sits ill with the ideas about the reflexive self. Children are depicted somewhat as objects, or burdens, or the source of strain. The concept of the 'pure relationship' where one can end a relationship, once it becomes unsatisfactory, ignores the impact of having children. He also seemed, in that work at least, to be ignorant about the trend towards ongoing parenting after divorce and indeed the policy consensus of its desirability (see Smart and Neale, 1999; and Chapter Seven). However, he does suggest that the loss of traditional authority (also noted previously by Parsons and often bemoaned by conservatives) means that parents must be able to defend their control 'in a principled fashion' (Giddens, 1992: 109).

In his book in 1998 on *The Third Way*, which is a very explicit intervention into political debates and must be located in the context of his taking on a public role as a New Labour adviser, Giddens argues all is not well with marriage, family and the state of children. He considers what effective political strategies could improve matters and what ideal state of the family should be striven for:

> First, and most fundamentally we must start from the principle of equality between the sexes, from which there can be no going back. There is only one story to tell about the family today, and that is of democracy. The family is becoming democratised, in ways which track processes of public democracy; and such democratization suggests how family life might combine individual choice and social solidarity. (Giddens, 1998: 93)

Giddens (1999) argues that there are three main areas in which emotional communication, and therefore intimacy, are replacing the old ties that used to bind together people's personal lives – in sexual and love relationships, parent–child relationships and friendship. In terms of parent–child relationships, he argues these cannot and should not be materially equal: 'Parents must have authority over children, in everyone's interests. Yet they should presume an in principle equality' (Giddens, 1999: 63). He advocates a democracy of the emotions, but stresses this does not imply lack of discipline or absence of respect. It simply seeks to put discipline and respect on a different footing. In a democracy of the emotions children can and should be able to answer back.

So, if the family is becoming democratised according to him, and this is a good thing, what does he consider is 'not well' as noted previously? It is not made clear. He suggests that the protection and care of children is the single most important thread that should guide family policy. It needs to be safeguarded by parenting contracts that endure post-divorce and support for fathers to stay involved post-divorce. Here he explicitly contests the view of those who see men as intrinsically feckless and irresponsible and the necessity to lock them away in marriage. He suggests (based on one piece of research, which he does not reference) that there is a very thin line between those who remain involved with their children and those who do not.

His thesis that disclosing intimacy is increasingly the key organising principle of people's lives is strongly contested by Jamieson (1998). She made what has become a now familiar criticism that his work is inadequately empirically located. However, as Smart (2007) notes, we can see work such as his as anticipatory theorising and be wary of literal readings as the most fruitful or generous way of assessing the value of the ideas.

However, empirical interrogations are, of course, of great importance. In terms of researching fathers there seems to have been an increase recently. Dermott's (2008) research on contemporary fathering practices uses the work of Giddens and Jamieson as starting points to consider themes that are prominent in discussions of intimacy: sexuality, reflexivity, equality, fragility and communication, as well as the meaning of time in order to explore fatherhood. Only a brief summary can be offered here. However, it is important to remind ourselves of the findings from her research, outlined in Chapter Two.

Overall, Dermott suggests that the relationship between paid work and employment is very different for mothers and fathers in the UK. There is no evidence that fathers as a whole or a significant sub-group are adopting a 'female model' by taking on part-time and reduced hours. She notes that, while this does not necessarily undermine arguments for the existence of a different discourse around fathering behaviour, (emphasising the emotional and nurturing elements), it does clarify that this is not translated into alterations to working hours.

Dermott argues that her research does not support the suggestion that some men wish to reduce their hours when they become parents, even if they do not actually do it. Rather her research supports previous survey material (O'Brien and Shemilt, 2003) indicating that satisfaction with work–life balance reduces significantly only when fathers work extremely long hours. Unlike mothers and non-mothers, the part-time/full-time distinction does not apply to fathers and non-fathers.

Fathers' behaviour will need to be thought about in ways that do not assume female models. According to Dermott, fatherhood has changed, but it has not become motherhood and does not provide the backdoor route to gender equality. She argues that, as intimacy involves a focus on creative personal relationships, conceptualising contemporary fatherhood as an intimate relationship allows for an emphasis on the aspects of male parenting that fathers themselves view as most significant – emotions, the expression of affection and the exclusivity of the reciprocal father–child dyad. Contemporary fatherhood is centred on a personal connection at the expense of participation in the work of childcare; because caring activities flow from an emotional connection rather than in themselves constituting the fathering role, the practicalities of 'intimate fatherhood' are fluid and open to negotiation. Dermott argues that this helps to understand the apparent, and often very irritating, gulf between conduct and culture where men continue to do less care while professing a strong commitment to being 'involved' with their children.

Dermott's research findings assume a rather unitary and fixed set of meanings being attached by men to intimacy with children. Women's perspectives on what they might want from such men are also missing from the research. Her work leaves us with the important issue already raised by Gatrell (2007). Are men 'cherry picking' the nice bits and leaving women with the mundane housekeeping roles? However, where does earning come into this? As Dermott and a range of others ask, is economic provision not also a form of care? Demott's work also leaves us with important political questions about how much social policies can and should be used to change mothers' and fathers' behaviour. This is returned to in Chapter Eight.

Research by Doucet (2006a, 2006b) with fathers who self-identified as primary caregivers for their children in Canada offers insights into the current diversity of fathering practices.[1] In her book entitled *Do Men Mother?* Doucet (2006a) argues that a key finding was that fathers relied on mothers to define their fathering. Some of the men were caring full time in a context of loss of the relationship with the mother. 'Interviews were haunted by the unseen presence of the child's mother. Perhaps most notable is how the majority of fathers' interviews open with a remark about the child's mother' (Doucet, 2006a: 216). A related point was that the men did not identify as mothers or refer to the work as mothering.

Moreover, the relational losses felt by men when their marriage broke down were stronger than she expected. 'It is as though hegemonic masculinity, with its emphasis on autonomy and self reliance, collapses in those moments of crisis to reveal the hidden influences of connection, relationship and interdependence' (Doucet, 2006a: 217). These specific points are of interest when considering the issues raised by men who join fathers' groups in the next chapter.

The overwhelming picture painted by both mothers and fathers was that mothering and fathering have much in common, but gender differences play out in several ways. One arena, play, is considered below. Doucet employs the concept of 'borderwork' to capture the constant emphasis on gender differences. Two recurring instances of borderwork were: gendered responses to the child who is hurt or has fallen down, and deeply held beliefs in the intimate connection between mother and child. In relation to the first point, there was a tendency to identify differential responses by mothers and fathers to children's distress when falling. Further, most fathers believed that fathers and mothers have a different connection to their children and that the one held by the mother is stronger, vaster and more profound. Yet there was also evidence of significant movement and flow that disrupted this binary picture. Ethnicity, social class and sexuality mattered more than gender in some contexts, for example. A further point, which has already been raised in Chapter Four, relates to maternal gatekeeping and highlights its complexities:

> Finally, what emerges as particularly interesting in this study is the idea of women moving over and creating spaces for men. Metaphorically, the image of borders (borderwork) and gates (gatekeeping) can be joined here. It is women, however, who lead in taking down this gender border, or opening the gate, so that men can also participate fully in parenting. This idea of opening and closing borders or gates provides for a more dynamic concept of maternal gatekeeping, and the recognition that while it may occur in particular spaces and times, *it does shift and change and even disappear*. (Doucet, 2006a: 232, emphasis added)

This raises important questions in relation to the differing possibilities open to women to 'make' men into fathers or to 'stop' men from fathering. Chapter Nine explores mothers' and fathers' accounts of the role of services in facilitating father involvement, which suggest that services can play an important role in supporting mothers who want more father involvement, although they often do not do so. Doucet's research also suggests a much less fixed and unitary approach on the part of men, and indeed women, on what men wanted from their caregiving.

Doucet (2006b) was also interested to recover what she considers largely invisible links between theoretical and empirical understandings of fatherhood, caring and embodiment. She makes three key arguments: fathers speak as embodied subjects in caregiving; the care of children is social and occurs not only between carer and cared-for but within larger sets of social relations within which it is perceived and judged; and these social venues draw attention to how space and embodiment constantly intersect. Fathers speak about themselves as embodied agents with their emphasis on play with infants and young children, most highlight their active and outdoor approach to caregiving and they point to how their experiences as fathers is fundamentally different from that of mothers because of perceived embodied experiences.

In terms of the second point about social spaces, the overwhelming majority of fathers spoke about having felt a watchful eye on them at some point. They highlight an area that is of considerable relevance for social care practices and will be explored further in Chapters Nine and Ten – the implications of men moving through women-centred spaces, going for coffee in women's homes and their daughters having sleepovers.

There were factors that might minimise the visibility of embodiment. For example, one man who was a doctor reflected that his professional status appeared to render him less threatening, so that class seems to matter. Having a woman act as a bridge and vouch for the man to other women helped. Being known over time and in the community (for example, a gay bookshop owner who adopted a child) also helped.

Doucet (2006b) concludes that, while many studies on gender and domestic labour assume that men and women are interchangeable disembodied subjects within and between households, her research emphasises how mothers and fathers are embodied subjects who move through domestic and community spaces with intersubjective, relational, moral and normative dimensions framing this movement. These dimensions are not fixed but contextually negotiated and renegotiated.

Doucet critically locates her analysis within a discussion of themes that have emerged from a literature on men and masculinities. Key themes from this literature are now explored.

Men, masculinities and fathers

According to Connell (1995), the first attempt to create a social science of masculinity had at its core the idea of a male sex role, as explored previously. However, although those interested in changing roles have used this, Connell suggests it has little to commend it to those interested in change. For him, male sex role theory is reactive, it does not generate a strategic politics of masculinity and is power blind. It has been argued that much of the first wave of critical writings by men in the social sciences was indeed 'power blind' (Whitehead, 2002) and that this situation changed with the publication in *Theory and Society* of an article by Carrigan et al (1985). They argued for an understanding of masculinity that recognised dominant interpretations and definitions of masculine as embedded in and sustained by a range of male-dominated institutions such as the state, education, the family, the workplace and so on. It was neither a product of functional sex roles nor a psychological innateness of the self. Masculinity was a vital component in the armoury of male dominance, informing the gender system while legitimising and reinforcing male power. Carrigan et al connected the institutional aspects of male power with the practices of men, arguing that there was a dominant form of masculinity called 'hegemonic masculinity'. Connell (1995) went on to develop the analysis further in his book on *Masculinities*. He noted the importance of recognising multiple masculinities in the context of the interplay between gender and other social divisions.

Hegemonic masculinity is not a fixed character type always and everywhere the same. 'It is, rather, the masculinity that occupies the hegemonic position in a given pattern of gender relations, a position always contestable' (Connell, 1995: 76). Connell identifies categories: subordinated, complicit and marginalised. Gay men are the most conspicuous form of subordinated masculinities. In terms of complicit masculinities, Connell argues that normative definitions of masculinity face the problem that not many men actually meet the normative standard; this also applies to hegemonic masculinity. The number of men rigorously practising the hegemonic pattern in its entirety may be quite small. Yet the majority of men gain from its hegemony, since they benefit from the 'patriarchal dividend' – the advantage that men in general gain from the overall subordination of women (Connell, 1995: 79). Masculinities that are constructed in ways that realise the patriarchal dividend, without the tensions or risks of being at the front line of patriarchy, are complicit in this sense.

While hegemony, subordination and complicity are relations internal to the gender order, the interplay of gender with other structures such as class and 'race' creates further interplay between masculinities. Marginalisation is always relative to the authorisation of the hegemonic masculinity of the dominant group. Connell (1995) points out, for example, that in the US particular Black athletes may be exemplars for hegemonic masculinity, but the fame and wealth of individual stars has no trickle-down effect. It does not yield social authority to Black men in general.

The concept of hegemonic masculinity has been influential over years, as well as critiqued extensively and subject to revision (see Featherstone et al, 2007).

Scholars from within the men and masculinities field express important concerns about the scholarship concerned with fathers. For example, Hearn (2002: 245) argues that 'debates about fathers and fatherhood need to be more explicitly gendered and more explicitly about power'. He notes that, for example, the notion of patriarchy, while subject to ongoing critique, is an important notion for fatherhood scholars to engage with. It has shifted from the literal meaning of the rule of fathers or the father to that of the social, economic, political and cultural domination of men more generally. There has been particular attention paid to the historical movement, from private patriarchy with men's power located in the private domain as fathers and husbands, to public patriarchy with men's power primarily in public domain organisations as capitalist and state managers and workers (see Chapter Three and Collier's [1995] analysis). This is of particular interest in the context of men as policy makers, managers and workers (see Chapter Ten).

Morgan (2002) notes, however, that to characterise matters in terms of a shift from private to public is too general to take us very far in analysing current debates, although it has some utility in that it directs us towards understanding wider issues and forces such as the marketplace and state policies. Too often the issues are reduced to individual men's wishes or behaviours rather than the construction of fatherhood/s. Morgan notes that one of the merits of a concept such as patriarchy is that it encourages looking beyond the particular topic and seeing wider connections. He suggests that, just as our understanding of fathers is enhanced by looking at significant others outside the immediate father–child dyad, our understanding of fathering is increased by considering practices that might seem at some distance from this relationship. One example is sexuality with, for example, links made between concerns about fatherhood and the construction of the sexualities of young men. Most of the discourses around fatherhood have been implicitly or explicitly discourses about the construction and privileging of heterosexual identities. This is of interest when we consider the fathers' organisations profiled in the next two chapters.

Morgan (2002) suggests that discussions of fathering and fatherhood should be located within debates about declining patriarchy, hegemonic masculinities, individualisation and reflexivity. In relation to the first theme he draws attention to what has been termed the 'end of patriarchalism' (Castells, 1997). This does not mean that gender either as difference or structured inequalities has become irrelevant. Rather it refers to a weakening of the determining character of gender. Individuals' life chances are now less clearly determined by their gender and the possibilities for challenging the relevance of gender are considerably increased. Morgan argues that the 'loosening' of the gender order constitutes part of the background against which current debates about fatherhood are taking place. But concerns and tensions about the practices of fathers also contribute to the loosening of the gender order. On the one hand there are assertions or reassertions of fathers' rights in the face of apparent challenges to, and undermining of, what might be seen as their traditional authority. In some cases these may take the form of an active assertion of the special claims of biological fatherhood. On the other hand we have moves towards a more active or positive understanding of fathering and pressure on governments and employers to reorganise working practices. As we will see in the next chapters, these positions are exemplified in particular organisations (certainly in the UK).

Morgan draws on two of Connell's (1995) key themes, hegemonic masculinity and masculinities in the plural. The idea of hegemonic masculinity suggests that, despite plurality, there remain deeply embedded notions of what it really means to be a man. In relation to fatherhood, Morgan suggests this can be seen in the continuing stress on fathers as responsible and providing. He notes, for example, that this idea continues to be strong in the US despite the continuing uncertainties of the labour market where there continues to be a deterioration in the position of the male breadwinner. It is important to note the complexities here and to recognise Lewis and Lamb's (2007) note of caution about making general claims across and within categories and countries.

An important aspect of recognising masculinities in the plural is endorsed by looking at the accounts of a small number of marginalised young fathers from Black and minority ethnic backgrounds in London (see Featherstone and White, 2006, and Chapter Nine, for a fuller account of this research and the implications for services). The economic provider discourse was almost entirely absent from such accounts. See also Chapter Ten for an analysis from Ferguson and Hogan (2004) on young fathers and 'protest masculinity'.

As indicated above, Morgan (2002) also draws on theoretical discussions around individualisation. Beck and Beck-Gernsheim (1995, 2002) are among those sociologists who have located the meanings attached to having or not having children within a wider frame. Linking with Beck's earlier work (*Risk Society*, 1992), they explore individualisation in a context of globalisation with its risks and opportunities. For Beck and Beck-Gernsheim, individualisation 'consists in transforming human "identity" from a "given" into a "task" – and charging the actors with the responsibility for performing that task and for the consequences (also the side effects) of their performance' (Beck and Beck-Gernsheim, 2002: xv). In their work they emphasise the notion of contradictions and the way individuals try to manage these (see Smart and Neale, 1999: 13-19, for the discussion from which this section draws). While often linked with Giddens, and there are similarities, there are important differences. Rather than the rather cool notion implied by the 'pure relationship', which can seem to imply a rather rational moving on when the relationship no longer meets the person's needs, the love between adults is seen as desperate and needy but vulnerable and temporary:

> Traditional bonds play only a minor role and the love between men and women has likewise proved vulnerable and prone to failure. *What remains is the child.* It promises a tie which is more elemental, profound and durable than any other in this society. The more other relationships become interchangeable and revocable, the more a child can become the focus of new hopes – it is the ultimate guarantee of permanence, providing an anchor for one's life. (Beck and Beck-Gernsheim, 1995: 73, emphasis added; see also Jenks, 1996, for compatible analysis from a sociology of childhood theorist)

The implications of the above are significant but may differ for men and women. Jensen (2001) argues, for example, that children have lost their economic utility and become less important to men. Women may and can choose to have children without a partner. Beck and Beck-Gernsheim (1995) suggest, however, that children remain important to both, with a trend for both mothers and fathers to want to keep them post-divorce. As we will explore in the next chapter, this is of some interest in terms of understanding those who become involved with groups advocating the rights of fathers. Certainly, based on their empirical study of parenting by men and women post-divorce, Smart and Neale (1999) suggest that there is much that is compelling in their analysis. They agree that men's anger about custody laws and their willingness to challenge mothers legally can be seen as part of a wider process of individualisation through which there develops a yearning for a permanent bond that only children can supply. 'However, it is a weakness in the thesis that the authors do not differentiate between the *perception* of a child as provider of permanent unconditional love and the actuality of parent–child relationships' (Smart and Neale, 1999: 17-18; emphasis in original). They ask pertinently whether it is their distance from day to day life care that provides an idealised vision of this form of love. This may, however, be too simple. It is possible that the perception of children as sources of unconditional love may coexist with experiences of difficult behaviour by actual children.

Smart et al (2001) locate their research with children within a well-established literature of childhood studies (see, for example, James and James, 2004). A key development has been the recognition of the social construction of childhood, the deconstruction of universal or normative assumptions about child development and the exploration of actual children's lives, crucially through research with them rather than on them. As we saw in Chapter Four, sociologists and critical thinkers within psychology and psychoanalysis have pointed out the ways in which certain kinds of knowledge have produced, as well as described, the 'normal child' or 'normal' child development.

What Smart et al (2001) in their study with children do suggest, which is of interest, is that divorce can be a most significant catalyst in bringing into being 'new forms of childhood'. They argue that previous research supports the argument that kinship in the UK has always been substantially personal and flexible, and based more on the degree of liking and affection between kin than positional relationship. The ties between children and parents have, however, always been regarded as an exception to this and have been seen as less flexible and less voluntaristic than those between other kin. Changes in family structures and attitudes seem, however, to be bringing about more optionality in the parent–child relationship – at least for some children:

> It is noticeable how often the children and young people
> in our samples spoke of 'liking' or 'not liking' individual
> parents. They may have felt that their parents held a unique

> position in their lives which could not be taken over in any absolute sense by other adults, but they no longer felt bound to them in the same way. We found that respect and liking significantly influenced the commitment as well as the closeness they felt towards them. (Smart et al, 2001: 84)

While their arguments are of interest, there are a number of points to be raised here. First, Jamieson (1998) points out that, while parent–child relationships are assumed to be the most durable, they are not and have never been beyond alienation and breakdown, so is there anything new going on? While Smart et al (2001) would appear to welcome optionality, there is a pessimistic view that children and young people are over-powerful and parents correspondingly disempowered. It is probable, however, that this is quite complex and certainly the latter view neglects the economic, social and policy changes in transitions for young people, which can mean establishing 'independence' is complex for many (Fawcett et al, 2004).

What do we know of children's understandings of their relationships with fathers? As we saw previously, Giddens (1992) argued that there was a general move towards disclosing intimacy in relationships. There is research evidence from young people themselves to cast some doubt on this thesis in relation to fathers. For example, Cawson et al's (2000) study of nearly 3,000 young people's experiences of family life found that a fifth were 'sometimes really afraid' of their father or stepfather (see Chapter Two). Frosh et al's (2001) research with boys aged 11-14 found that they saw their mothers as more sensitive and emotionally closer to them than their fathers who were seen to be more distant and detached. A substantial minority articulated a sense of 'loss' when talking about relationships with fathers.

Solomon et al (2002: 965) argue from their research that the twin ideals of intimacy and democracy necessarily clash in parent–teenager relationships:

> While both parents and their teenage children subscribe to the discourse of openness and honesty as the route to both intimacy and democracy, there are tensions within the concept of openness because both parties have opposing goals in the trading of information. For parents, information gain means the retention of power and control, while for teenagers, withholding information from their parents ensures their privacy, power and identity.

They suggest that Giddens' views on democracy in the family are important and influential. They derive from and support a strong ideal image of the family that is particularly persuasive for the parents of teenagers as they strive to parent successfully and in a context of greater perceived risk. Teenagers aim for greater emancipation and autonomy. Solomon et al suggest that families with teenagers not only are some way off from democratisation, but also will remain so because of the structural and psychological power imbalances between parent and child:

> For the parent, information gain means the retention of power and control, and the gaining of intimacy at the expense of democracy; for the teenager, the withholding of information is the means by which they gain privacy, power and identity, but at the expense of intimacy. (Solomon et al, 2002: 966)

While this research was not just about fathers, there were some interesting insights in relation to fathers. For example, there was evidence of 'competitive intimacy' in situations where daughters had chosen fathers to talk to about periods and sex. However, relations were usually constructed in terms of shared gender identity and common experience. There is research to suggest that a shared gender identity may be problematic for boys seeking to discuss difficulties such as bullying with their fathers, with some evidence that particular constructions of masculinity are used to invalidate expressions of vulnerability or anxiety (Featherstone and Evans, 2004).

Finally, as indicated previously, Morgan (2002) uses the concept of reflexivity to refer to the increased monitoring of the self and of a wide range of individual practices. Of particular relevance is the monitoring of interpersonal relationships within families and households. The monitoring comes from within and from outside. Morgan suggests that, in contexts where there is a stress on the rights and obligations of fatherhood, the monitoring, while not absent, will be less central. As long as they pay up, fathers are left alone, which was the situation of the post-war welfare state. Where there is a stress on fathering, there is a much more critical and reflexive examination of routine practices. As is explored further in Chapter Eight, developments under New Labour would suggest there has been a shift, but it is very limited. Another aspect of reflexivity is that there is wider reflection on the state of the society in which these practices are taking place. This wider process is extremely limited currently in the UK.

Dermott (2008) has looked at the internal monitoring men do and suggests that, while the transition to fatherhood is often associated with rethinking relationships, priorities and men's sense of self, these reflections are more likely to result in individuals seeking out commonly available patterns of behaviour. As she notes, context is important here. Doucet's (2006a) respondents spoke of how certain environments, such as spaces usually occupied by mothers, obliged care-taker fathers to engage in complex interpersonal moral negotiations about space and gender and what was 'appropriate'. Non-resident fathers and gay fathers too are obliged to engage in a range of ways with habit, convention and their own biographical investments.

Morgan (2002) concludes that individualisation, the undermining of at least some aspects of the gender order and reflexivity are some of the key features impacting on intimacy and domestic relationships. It may be possible, therefore, to identify very loosely a threefold division in terms of opportunities for individualisation and the construction of personal biographies for men as fathers: the first group are well advantaged, the second less stable and the third face the collapse and erosion of old certainties without having access to the opportunities provided by new models. Certainly, Stacey (1998) argues for the urgency of paying attention to those men who seem poorly equipped, because of class and ethnic disadvantage, to deal with the hazards and opportunities posed by a changing landscape.

While most researchers from within the men and masculinities field stress the importance of engaging with diversity among men, McMahon (1999) argues, from a materialist feminist perspective, that it is in the material interests of men as a group to resist women's demands for change in power relations. Exploring the domestic division of labour within the home, he treats men as a category with interests that they consciously seek to advance or protect. Such interests lie with their concern to keep their existing privileges, which correlate with continuing to ensure that women take care of them and their children. Indeed, he suggests that, by resisting the expectation that caring should be shared, men are taking care of themselves in time-honoured fashion: 'The figure of the New Father combines the narcissistic consumer and the male nurturer in a way which flirts with the feminisation of men, but manages to neatly reinstate gender difference and male right' (McMahon, 1999: 116). All that has changed is the imagery but not the practice. McMahon makes important observations but he is stuck in an approach that does not allow adequately for complexity and differences between men and is caught up in a 'grand theory' approach to all men. It also seems increasingly important to deconstruct what men are doing in the home, as Chapter Two suggests – they may be doing more childcare but not housework, for example.

Interestingly, Gatrell (2007) argues from her research with married cohabiting couples, where mothers are professionally employed and there are pre-school children, that some fathers seek to enhance their paternal role and become very actively involved with their children because of fears about the erosion of male hegemony. She notes previous sociological work on gender and power within marriage that suggested that in many heterosexual relationships men still hold the balance of power because they earn more. However, in couples where women are professionally employed, it is more difficult for men to maintain the level of power previously associated with the male breadwinner role. She argues that, while there is recognition that children become a site for gendered power struggles post-divorce, her research indicates that this may also be happening in couples where mothers' professional status has destabilised the traditional balance of power.

Sociology and fathers: future directions?

To conclude, Carol Smart (2007) has argued that sociology has been frosty about looking at love and has had problems discussing emotions,[2] so it is probably no surprise that many sociologists have been, at best, extremely ambivalent about the subject matter of Chapter Four, psychoanalysis. Moreover, a considerable literature that is extremely critical of developmental psychology has emerged in the field of childhood studies, led often by sociologists.[3]

However, as already indicated, sociologists too have not been immune to, and indeed have been actively involved in, developing a psychosocial approach to studying issues such as intimacy (see, for example, Roseneil, 2006). The research by Lupton and Barclay (1997) on fathers has already been explored in Chapter Four. All these projects explicitly use versions of psychoanalysis.

While avoiding any mention of a psychosocial project, and certainly of psychoanalysis, Smart (2007) draws attention to the importance of the following when studying what she calls 'personal life': memory, the importance of cultural life, the significance of emotions (both positive and negative) and how family secrets work and change over time. It has already been noted in Chapter Two that family secrets were often secrets about paternity and it is likely that future work on fathers will engage with many of the other issues raised by Smart. As outlined in Chapter Two, the evidence of the continuing diversity and complexity of practices will encourage analyses that explore fathering biographies across generations (see, for example, Brannen and Nilsen, 2006). The psychosocial approach will continue to develop exploring how individual life-histories unfold and will offer valuable pointers towards understanding why men vary in their responses to changing social conditions.

Building 'big' frameworks has been under concerted attack for some time, partly prompted by postmodernism.[4] But, as the work from the men and masculinities scholars highlights above, it is absolutely crucial that individual practices by men as fathers, including the kinds of knowledge they draw on, are located within wider social relations.

Conclusion

The strength of sociological approaches lies in the linking of individual practices to wider practices at a range of levels. There is also generally a much stronger emphasis on power relations and understanding, and linking fathers' practices to men's power and practices, than in the psychological and much of the psychoanalytic literature. This chapter has traced the journey from Parsonian rigid roles (still powerful in some contexts) to research on whether some men today are actually mothering. It has also highlighted, and in some cases explored, sociological research into the multiplicity of sites in which men are constructed as fathers. In the next chapters attention now focuses more explicitly on interrogating specific sites in relation to the roles of fathers' groups and 'the state'.

Notes

[1] The research sample was 118 fathers and 14 heterosexual couples. The category of primary caregiving father was disaggregated into single fathers and stay-at-home fathers, along with a few shared caregiving fathers and fathers on parental leave. There were nine gay fathers, four aboriginal fathers, 15 fathers from visible minorities and diverse representation across social class, as measured by income and education levels.

[2] There is a body of sociological work on emotions now, and indeed Smart argues that it was always an aspect of sociology, but it has not always been a topic either of interest or study.

[3] This field is interdisciplinary.

[4] Although there has long been an important strand of sociology devoted to the 'micro', such as conversation analysis and ethnomethodology (see Taylor and White, 2000).

SEVEN

The politics of fatherhood: contemporary developments

Introduction

This chapter explores one of the most visible and controversial aspects of fathering today – the emergence of many men who seek to articulate claims as fathers.[1] It concentrates on the UK with a limited exploration of international developments. The chapter is based mainly on an exploration of the academic literature, although a survey of websites conducted specifically for the chapter does inform some of the thinking.[2] As other chapters have done, it draws briefly from the author's own research, which is explored in more depth in Chapters Nine and Ten.

Categorising the politics of masculinity: where do fathers fit?

A number of writers have constructed typologies of masculinity politics as expressed in social movements (see Featherstone et al, 2007: 26-8). Clatterbaugh (1990) identifies the following: pro-feminist men (both liberal and radical versions); men's rights approaches that see men as having lost out to feminism; conservative men arguing for continuity with 'traditional' models of masculinity; men in search of spiritual growth (often called mythopoetic); and socialist men and those gay and Black men who emphasise inequalities between men. Connell (1996) suggests the following: masculinity therapy; the defence of patriarchy; queer politics; and transformative politics. Messner (1997) has constructed a model of 'the terrain of the politics of masculinity'. This can be used as a tool to assess the politics of groupings and interventions along the following axes: whether they are concerned with the institutional privileges of men, the costs of masculinity, or differences between men.

Attempts at categorisation are helpful and, in particular, Messner's has been usefully employed (see, for example, Scourfield and Drakeford, 2002, on government policies in the UK). However, as we will see in our discussion of a piece of research with young Black and minority ethnic fathers in the public law field (Featherstone and White, 2006), and in Chapter Nine on practice interventions, there is messiness and complexity attached to what fathers say and do, and what workers say and do. This is not captured in neat typologies, although they do serve to clarify key themes.

It is usual for those involved in the politics and scholarship of men and masculinities to locate activities 'in the name of fathers' within a conservative frame and view them with suspicion This suspicion is understandable but does mean that the articulation of a progressive politics in this area is precarious (see Flood, 2004, however and Collier and Sheldon, 2008). Given the symbolic weight and often the centrality of fathering practices for everyday lives, this is problematic. It also means that, to some extent, men and masculinities scholars have vacated the field and left a vacuum for the conservatives to fill.

There is a broad and contested literature on what constitutes a social movement, as Collier and Sheldon (2006) note. They suggest that the term 'fathers' rights movement' should be deployed with caution and, indeed, a further note of caution is needed about assumptions that there is a fathers' movement either within one country or internationally.

It is crucial to stress the importance of understanding the differing legal, political and cultural landscapes within which activists around fathering operate. The renegotiation of fathers' rights and responsibilities is culturally specific. For example, Rhoades (2006) documents the apparent influence that organisations emphasising fathers' rights had on the conservative administrations headed by John Howard for 11 years in Australia (although they did not achieve some of their key goals).[3] Certainly, the author's own experience of spending time in Australia discussing issues around fathers with academic colleagues made her aware of the differences between her own political context and theirs. Overall, it is apparent that dialogue across a range of countries on these issues can be fraught with difficulties because of the very real differences between organisations, governments, welfare regimes and cultures.

Collier and Sheldon (2006), in their edited collection, explore fathers' rights activism and law reform in Canada, the US, the UK, Australia and Sweden. They recognise that this is by no means a comprehensive choice of countries and website searches conducted for this chapter found activity in France, Germany, Holland, Italy and Japan. They argue that, while there has been previous activity in relation to fathers' rights (see Collier, 1995; and Chapter Three of this book), the last 30 years has seen a marked intensification of activity in this area with more militancy and higher media and political profiles. However, there have been differences in differing political contexts. For example, the UK media has seemed eager to publicise organisations such as Fathers 4 Justice (F4J), whereas similar activity was ignored in Sweden (see Eriksson and Pringle, 2006).

In the UK,[4] according to a website search conducted for this chapter in January 2008, there appeared to be 23 organisations of differing statuses intervening in public arenas, speaking either as fathers or about fathers and demanding various changes. The most long-standing, Families Need Fathers, is considered here as well as a brief discussion of F4J. A further organisation, the Fatherhood Institute, is explored in the next chapter as it has emerged from the policy context developed by New Labour and, unlike those in this chapter, its focus is not on private law. Moreover, it did not emerge from the concerns of men experiencing separation/divorce, as many of the others appear to have.

Families Need Fathers (FNF) is a well-established organisation. It was formed in 1974 just after the 1973 Matrimonial Causes Act when the notion of a 'clean break' was promoted as desirable legally and psychologically (see Chapter Three).[5] FNF (2008a) describes itself as a social care organisation, the only organisation, on a national basis, helping parents whose relationship with their children is under threat (as a result of divorce or separation). It has a charter with a pdf link, which is actually a Father's Day Manifesto 2004 (FNF, 2008b).[6]

The charter is brief with ten points. Over half of these call for changes in the name of the child, one of which is that the United Nations Convention on the Rights of the Child be incorporated into domestic law. The others call for changes for parents with the gender-neutral term used throughout. The changes called for refer almost exclusively to the arena of divorce and separation. There is one brief reference to policies in relation to work and care, and the call is for them to be shared equally by both parents.

In the FNF's Father's Day Manifesto 2004 the language used is slightly different. For example, it calls for the ending of gender discrimination in social attitudes towards parenting policy in relation to the family and the family justice system, and calls for family-friendly entitlements to be available to both parents equally. It is noted that fathers' involvement with their children is increasing rapidly and this should be encouraged until it equals the care provided by mothers. Child benefit and tax credits should be shared according to the costs that fall on each parent, rather than being given automatically to one parent. The clause 'equality between spouses' in the European Convention on Human Rights should be ratified and included in UK legislation.

It is important to note that there is no talk of fathers' rights. In its construction of itself as a charity lobbying in the way charities 'traditionally do for changed social and legal attitudes', FNF could be seen to denote its distance/difference from the activities of controversial organisations discussed later, such as F4J. Moreover, its self-designation as a social care organisation is significant to note also.

Women are called upon to establish moral credibility in a variety of ways. The website highlights that many of the supporters and volunteers are women and that FNF works closely with its sister organisation MATCH (Mothers Apart from Their Children). Moreover, the endorsements received by two influential women are noted, the president of the family division of the High Court and Britain's 'most respected' agony aunt and trustee of a government-founded institute.

The Manifesto talks of equal treatment for both parents within the arena of separation and divorce. Although it suggests shared parenting, there are no specific references to how much that should be (for example, 50/50) but shared residence is promoted (although no specific formula is suggested). It calls for the sharing of benefits including cash benefits. In the FNF account, good fathers are concerned with the welfare of their children and, above all, the rights of children to see both parents. FNF also aligns itself with child-centred welfare practices and concerns to offer children more voice.

F4J, which describes itself as a civil rights group, was founded in 2002, closed briefly in 2006 after allegations that members had been involved in a plot to kidnap the son of the then Prime Minister Tony Blair and closed again on 5 September 2008. The website home page indicated that it was closing because of a personal decision by its founder Matt O'Connor. At the time of writing it is unclear what other men involved with F4J plan to do.[7] There continues to be a website developed by The Real Fathers For Justice an earlier breakaway from the original.

This organisation courted and achieved considerable publicity for a variety of very public protests from 2002 onwards (see Collier, 2006, for an in-depth exploration). It set itself against a range of predictable targets such as the courts and the welfare professionals but also characterised other fathers' organisations as 'poodles' with a misguided belief that letter writing would achieve change.

At the time of writing there is still a website for the organisation F4J and a document entitled *Blueprint for Family Law in the 21st Century* is available. This is considered to provide the foundation on which 'a truly fair, just, open and equitable system of family law can be based. A foundation of rights, intertwined with responsibilities, built for the 21st century that genuinely puts children first'.

The *Blueprint for Family Law* proposes three strategies to reduce conflict for children and their families in contact disputes and rebuild public confidence in the 'discredited' family justice system. First, mediation should be mandatory for all couples. Second, the starting point after separation should be to maintain where possible what the status quo was before separation. Children currently have no right in law to see their parents. The principle of shared parenting creates a level playing field where conflict can be reduced, as opposed to the current 'winner takes all' scenario, which generates maximum conflict. Third, the document calls for 'open justice'.[8] It suggests that the three principles should be the foundation on which to build a new Bill of Rights for the Family.

Again it is notable that it does not use a language of fathers' rights but of children's or family rights. Indeed, this is a tendency noted throughout the examination of the many organisations that have sprung up in this area.

According to Collier (2006), there is no one fathers' rights perspective or agenda in the UK, and, within a loosely based coalition, there is a diversity of approaches and political views. FNF represented the 'beginning' of contemporary fathers' rights politics in 1974. There have been shifts in strategy and focus linked to wider social, demographic, legal, cultural and economic changes. Collier charts a historical shift in the focus of grievances, a move from central concerns around property and finance in the 1970s and early 1980s to, by the late 1990s, a growing focus on child contact and residence arrangements. While, as outlined in the next chapter, financial issues do remain significant in relation to child support, currently there is a heightened focus on the father–child relationship.

A body of writing has emerged exploring developments in other countries. For example, Flood (2004) provides an overview of Australian developments, the overwhelming majority of which seem focused on fathers and family law decision making post-divorce. Flood is highly critical of the politics of many of the organisations, seeing them clearly as part of a backlash. However, he does caution against dismissing the experiences of personal pain motivating many of those who get involved and urges dialogue with such men. Rhoades (2006) from Australia also offers a fascinating account of the processes of consultation and discussion in relation to changing the law around post-separation parenting. She notes the way in which men in government and activist men were able to work together and seemed to share some experiences. Nonetheless it is important to note that the demands of the fathers' rights activists did not completely win the day in what was, for them, a congenial political climate.

Boyd (2006) documents developments in relation to family law in Canada. Eriksson and Pringle (2006) outline developments in Sweden that are located within a paradigm of fostering gender equity between men and women in relation to earning and caring. However, they counsel that the Scandinavian model appears less able to address the difficulties of sexual violence by men (this is returned to in the next chapter on policy).

Gavanas (2002) explores some of the developments in the US. She identifies a fatherhood responsibility movement, supported by successive US governments, and encompassing those encouraging marriage and those seeking to support 'fragile' families. There are also fathers' rights organisations. Divisions in relation to class and ethnicity are apparent. For example, White middle-class men are more likely to be in fathers' rights organisations, whereas the fatherhood responsibility movement is concerned with those who are poor and from minority ethnic populations. Gavanas suggests that there are difficulties in defining the fatherhood responsibility movement within masculinity politics because most say their goals and concerns are not specific to men but may also benefit women and children. Indeed most point out that they are primarily about children. The links with religious organisations and philosophies are also very strong in the US.

Why are men getting involved?

This section considers why men appear to be getting involved in these organisations. It also interrogates the claims they make in order to assess whether these developments can be assessed straightforwardly.

Why are men getting involved? The first answer is perhaps obvious – there are more men living apart from their birth children (Collier and Sheldon, 2006). Bradshaw et al (1999) explored the difficulties with estimating numbers of non-resident fathers, although there is agreement that the numbers increased very significantly in the 1980s and 1990s (this is important in terms of understanding the impetus for child support legislation discussed in the next chapter). They suggest that the best way to think about the scale of the experience of non-resident fathering is to note that it is estimated that between a third and a half of all children will experience a period of not living with both natural parents during their childhood: 'Each one of these children will have a non-resident parent and in most cases it will be the father' (Bradshaw et al, 1999: 4).

Second, 'at the very time when fatherhood becomes less secure, then cultural, economic and legal imperatives are reframing the debate about what it means for men to become "good fathers" and more "involved" parents' (Collier and Sheldon, 2006: 11-12). Collier and Sheldon alert us to the important and often overlooked point that many activists are steeped in the discourse of the new father. Good fathers fight for their children in a context of discourses stressing the importance of children retaining contact with both parents post-separation/divorce:

> Crucial to these arguments is the idea of the father as an active presence in his children's lives, an idea that mirrors a growing concern across western governments about how to facilitate forms of 'active' desirable fathering. (Collier and Sheldon, 2006: 12)

Indeed, Collier and Sheldon note the tendency on the part of activists to distinguish the good father from the 'deadbeat' or reckless father. Certainly, in the experience of the author, there can be considerable irritation on some activists' part when the problems posed by men who, for example, are violent to women and/or children are raised. This may not simply be about them wanting to deny such men's existence, but rather not wanting to be put in the same category. It may signal a desire to promote themselves as good fathers rather than deny there are 'bad' fathers. But, as explored later, there are important difficulties with their attempts to bifurcate in this way.

Collier and Sheldon (2008) argue that a model of the responsible divorce has emerged in which law is seen to have a central and distinctive role in encouraging behaviour modification. Men and women should behave responsibly and cooperate for the sake of their children. Moreover, Collier and Sheldon note the centrality of the father figure to a new paradigm of post-divorce family law. Such prescriptions have entered the vocabularies of both parents and are interpreted in ways that reflect gendered lives and rationalities. Collier and Sheldon also make the very important observation that negotiating the transition from a situation in which parents may have colluded in maintaining a belief in gender equality in parenting prior to separation would itself appear to be a source of anger on the part of many men. As was noted in Chapter Six, research evidence suggests that, when some women in couples are asked about the division of labour in their homes, even profoundly inequitable settlements can be presented as otherwise. However, separation can be a result of or expose the fault lines in this construction. Thus men who believed the 'myth' may be asked, at a time of great pain and upheaval, to take on the implications of a reconstructed narrative.

It is perhaps not surprising at a time when more men identify with the idea of the father as carer that the perceived loss of that role should prove so painful. Furthermore, it is not surprising that the idea of co-parenting contained in law might itself serve to fuel conflicts between separating parents in cases where it is perceived to be the product not of cooperation, but of legal coercion (Collier and Sheldon, 2008: 166).

Crowley (2006) researching fathers' rights organisations in the US suggests that, contrary to popular perception, the desire to change public opinion is only one of the many reasons men choose to join such organisations. As important, if not more so, are their needs for emotional and legal assistance in the context of divorce/separation. This can be located within Giddens' (1992) work on the mobilisation of diverse sets of resources in order to author our lives and the possible absence of other sources of support for men. Certainly, it has already been suggested that men may see the state and state services as feminised (see further discussion later in the chapter) and may not feel able to approach more 'traditional' sources of support. There are interesting parallels here with the second-wave feminist emphasis on developing refuges and helplines run by women for women because of suspicion about the state.

Some psychosocial analyses are very important in helping illuminate why some men get involved in such groups. The emphasis in this literature on exploring life stories can also help understand why many can seem to get so stuck in anger. As Day Sclater (1999) argues, divorce involves engaging with, often overwhelming, feelings of loss and can be likened to bereavement. Profound emotions are mobilised in contexts of loss. The emphasis on adults behaving cooperatively fails to acknowledge the psychological coping strategies that both men and women need to mobilise to cope with the emotions that are involved in loving and losing. Conflict is routinely attributed to the nature of court processes. However, this obscures the powerful emotions that are being mobilised. In emphasising the vulnerability of children, not only do adults' needs get lost but children too become lost as individuals and appear solely as objects of adults' concern. Moreover, the psychological experience of loss can jar with the powerful rhetoric of the harmonious divorce and deny the space to articulate adult feelings of pain and hurt (see also Collier and Sheldon, 2008).

In work with Yates, Day Sclater noted that divorcing men and women routinely made gendered interpretations that raised questions about the psychological investments that men and women make in disputes about divorce (Day Sclater and Yates, 1999). This flies in the face of the gender neutrality of family law and its central concept of parental responsibility.

There were common themes among the accounts of men and women, and aspects of the divorce experience shared by men and women. There were also places where they diverged. The central theme uniting the mothers' narratives was a tension between the welfare and independence discourses, which women sought to resolve in a range of ways and which required considerable emotional work. The problems were primarily relational ones with their own needs and financial issues secondary.

By contrast, the theme uniting the fathers' narratives in this study was a strong sense of vulnerability and loss, overlaid from time to time with angry appeals to justice and rights in order to salvage something for themselves. All felt a profound sense of injustice towards women in general. While both made interpretations of the welfare discourse they differed. For some men it presented them with an opportunity to pursue a rights-based discourse, for some it was inseparable from financial issues. Women, as indicated previously, tended to prioritise relational issues. As Day Sclater and Yates (1999) note, both men and women were doing gender in relation to post-divorce parenting.

Decoding their calls and claims

The law is seen as central to the disadvantaging of men and part of a wider feminisation of government. There is a belief that laws provide the solution as well as constitute the problem and, as has often been noted, a 'yearning' for law (Collier, 2006). As already noted, while 'rights talk' is employed by activists, it is by no means dominant, certainly on organisations' websites. However, it is important to note that accounts such as those produced on websites do particular work in terms of establishing credibility and moral authority. Its absence is not that surprising, therefore, given that it is apparent to anyone doing work in the family policy arena that mobilising 'rights talk' can serve to construct one as invalid, selfish and unconcerned with children's welfare, and is particularly problematic in the legislative and policy climate in the UK. Parents are constructed in terms of their *responsibilities* and this has intensified under New Labour since 1997 (see Chapter Eight). But it would be unwise to see rights talk as absent either. It often coexists with other discourses around welfare (children's) and in a context where women are assumed to have gained their rights. Moreover, the welfare of children can be conflated with the rights of fathers.

It is important to note that research, in other very diverse contexts, is uncovering 'rights talk'. In a focus group with young fathers from Black and minority ethnic backgrounds, a language of rights was used to cover a much broader set of concerns than those relating to separation and divorce (Featherstone and White, 2006). For example, rather than using a language of racial discrimination, the young fathers suggested that, in the UK, unlike the US, men had no rights. The state was perceived as on women's side providing them with financial support through the welfare state (this links with other men's perceptions of the feminised private law system). By contrast, they perceived the state was interested in them only for child support purposes or where they suspected them of domestic violence. Many of the accounts from the young men depicted a world split into powerful, unpredictable women, good, vulnerable children and powerful, unpredictable services, staffed by women and on women's side. Their accounts produced emotionality as suspect and post-natal depression as behaviour adopted by women to get their own way. Because of women's role as gatekeepers to children, considerable anxiety was expressed about how safe the men's investments in children were. While a minority sought to construct partnerships with the mothers of their children and the mothers' families in order to ensure they would stay involved with the children, most felt their only hope of continued involvement was through developing a sufficiently strong relationship *with the child*. Their status as 'birth' father was invoked and seemed to provide reassurance that this status would ensure they mattered to the child in a way no other man could. Rights talk by these young men seemed to be located in a context of precarious relationships with the mothers of their children and was code for marginalisation. The law and health and social care services were seen as failing and feminised.

In a very different context, Gatrell (2007: 353) suggests, from her research with married or cohabiting professional couples parenting pre-school children, that fathers challenged mothers' sphere of influence by asserting their paternal 'rights'. She argues that some fathers in dual-career couples may be mobilising paternal rights to counteract the professional power wielded by female partners.

An important point, returned to in Chapter Nine, is that 'rights talk' by fathers may be heard by social work professionals as evidence of selfishness or a lack of concern for children's welfare. At legislative and policy levels, the mobilisation of rights talk either in relation to children or parents is very limited (see Henricson and Bainham, 2005; and Chapter Eight). Contact, when discussed in such terms, is seen as the right of the child, not of the parent. There is no statutory presumption of contact as such with the 1989 Children Act providing that the child's welfare is the overriding consideration. However, the Act encourages both parents to share in their children's upbringing after separation and case law suggests a strong presumption of contact as long as it is safe.

Henricson and Bainham (2005) argue that the above policy and legislative focus is going to become harder to justify with legislation such as the 1998 Human Rights Act and the increasing internationalisation of law (see Choudry et al, forthcoming). They also point to the dangers attached to a more slippery language of welfare for both children and parents and argue:

> Rights provide a framework and point of reference for handling interests. They flush individual and collective entitlements out into the open. They create expectations of a balance of interests that cannot disappear so readily as it might under a discretionary welfare model of government investment. (Henricson and Bainham, 2005: 110)

Debates about the relationship between a rights-based approach and welfare-based approach are ongoing in socio-legal scholarship. Are they diametrically opposed, containing different sets of ethics and, indeed, ethics that are gendered – an ethics of care and an ethics of justice? Can they be synchronised via a notion of 'relational autonomy' as has been suggested (see Herring, forthcoming)?

Feminism and fathers' groups

Feminists and pro-feminist men regard activist groups of fathers with considerable suspicion, as has been noted. In the UK, post-separation contact has been a key battleground. Reece's (2006) exploration of contributions to a government consultation on contact offers important insights into what appears to be considered as legitimate grounds by feminists and fathers' activists for the refusal of contact. In the process, as Reece notes, it underscores how authoritative the discourse around contact being beneficial for children has become and, moreover, the complete marginalisation of any discourses that refer to women's or men's need for 'clean breaks'.

She argues that women's groups, in their lobbying in relation to contact, devoted their attention to the connection between child contact and domestic violence rather than the connection between child contact and mothers' autonomy, or subsumed questions of autonomy within the very wide definition of violence used. What does Reece mean by autonomy? While she does not offer a definition here she refers to a range of literature that has pointed out that the gendered division of labour exists in most families and that this is continued post-separation with serious implications for women's ability to construct 'new' lives. Basically, divorce and separation do not allow women to leave inequitable settlements behind, but may indeed reinforce or intensify such settlements.

The main argument from feminists in their submissions was that, when courts decide contact orders, they give insufficient weight and attention to fathers' violence, resulting in unsafe contact orders. The evidence of unsafe contact orders most frequently presented to the Select Committees was the contrast between the very large numbers of contact cases in which domestic violence is estimated to be present and the very small number of contact applications that are refused. The most common estimates of the former are that domestic violence exists in 16,000 cases that go through the family court system every year and 60% of Children and Family Court Advisory and Support Service cases, while the number of contact orders refused was cited as 601 in 2003 (Reece, 2006:542-3). Additionally, the Select Committees were told that, when Women's Aid surveyed 178 refuge organisations in 2003, only 3% believed that appropriate measures were being taken to ensure the safety of the children and resident parent in most contact cases involving domestic violence.

An interesting point made by Reece is that women's groups concentrated far more on the harm that domestic violence causes children than the harm it causes their mothers, arguing that such harm to children took many forms. Most starkly, they claimed that men who are violent to their female partners tend to be violent to their children as well. Mobilising arguments in relation to the risk to children, while important and understandable, has had unintended consequences in public law contexts, with mothers who 'fail' to leave being deemed negligent for failing to protect children from violent men (see Featherstone and Peckover, 2007; and Chapter Nine).[9]

Women's groups have been successful to an extent, according to Reece, and there has been significant recent change in the way that the judiciary approaches domestic violence in child contact cases. A range of initiatives has been introduced in recent years. Section 120 of the 2002 Adoption and Children Act amends the definition of harm in Section 31(9) of the 1989 Children Act to include impairment suffered from seeing or hearing the ill-treatment of another, thus clarifying that, if a child witnesses violence towards his or her mother, then this may be counted as harm to the child and child protection services can be involved. However, as indicated previously, this now runs the risk of mothers who are experiencing violence being judged as failing to protect children if they do not take steps to stop the violence (see Davies and Krane, 2006, for an important discussion of this in the Canadian context where such legislation came in earlier).

Furthermore, campaigners lobbied successfully for the Children and Adoption Bill (now the 2006 Children and Adoption Act) to be amended to include perpetrator programmes in the range of contact activities that *may* be required (not mandatory as they asked for). However, Women's Aid expressed concern that the Act does not specify the activities to be included within such programmes, giving rise to the possibility that the activities may be unsuitable (such as anger management). The question of how violent men should be worked with is returned to in Chapter Nine, as there is dissent and debate.

However, a persistent demand that the 1989 Children Act be amended to introduce a legal presumption against contact in domestic violence cases has never received official endorsement. Furthermore, fathers' groups can also claim some successes. Under Part 1 of the 2006 Children and Adoption Act there is a responsibility on the Children and Family Court Advisory and Support Service (CAFCASS) to enforce contact orders, if necessary by imposing penalties such as community service on resident parents. This Act adopts a three-track approach (see Collier and Sheldon, 2008: 160). It is concerned with the facilitation and monitoring of contact, addresses the issue of enforcement and encapsulates a broader intention to educate parents in behaviour modification. However, for some fathers' groups, the absence of any legal presumption of contact and shared 'equal' parenting remains grounded in problematic discriminatory assumptions.

Reece argues that campaigners constructed mothers solely as domestic violence victims, thus abandoning others who are likely to be labelled unreasonable or implacably hostile. In their framework there were no unreasonable mothers, but only domestic violence victims. However, violence is far from the only reason that mothers oppose contact. Important concerns can include fathers' unreliability, lack of parenting skills and so on.

Autonomy–based feminist critiques of child contact do not assume that unreasonable mothers do not exist, but argue that the term obscures the complexity of what is often going on and the fluidity of contact arrangements in which negotiation is ongoing. A paradox of the current approach to contact is that, while it promotes an ongoing cooperative project between the parents, it imagines this in static terms.

An important point is that a mother who does not prevent, but also does not promote, contact may be seen as implacably hostile.

Reece recognises that women's groups probably assumed they could not oppose contact (other than in cases of domestic violence) as it has achieved the status of an uncontested truth – contact is necessary. However, some judges have shown sensitivity towards mothers' autonomy claims – for example, where women have wished to move geographically for job reasons.

It is important to note here that the degree of importance placed on maintaining contact between children and fathers is a relatively newly constituted construction of children's welfare with a shaky empirical base:

> It is very important to note that the empirical evidence does not support the idea that the mere fact that a child maintains contact with a parent who is not living in the house, or that the child spends equal time with both parents after they have separated is beneficial for the child. Too much depends on the circumstances. If they become occasions for conflict, they cease to benefit the children, for it is widely agreed that overt parental conflict is damaging to children. (Eekelaar, 2006: 125)

Reece's (2006: 538) overall point is that women's groups facilitated the bifurcation of mothers into the domestic violence victim and the unreasonable mother. Bifurcating mothers in this way was to the detriment of both types of mothers because it facilitated the introduction of Part 1 of the 2006 Children and Adoption Act, an Act that both introduces more insidious powers to enforce contact orders against unreasonable mothers and paves the way for more intrusive regulation of contact in domestic violence cases.

Fathers' groups did not present an effective challenge to the consensus about the interconnections between domestic violence and child contact. Indeed, their repeated response to questions that had nothing to do with violence was to assert the strong proposition, never advocated by women's groups during the hearings, that violent fathers should not be allowed contact. On occasions they disputed the extent of the problem, expressing concern about false allegations and there were certain muted 'and hopeless' (Reece, 2006) attempts to hint at the need to obtain a conviction for the violence before it could be taken into account. Some were concerned that mothers would pretend to be domestic violence victims, whereas women's groups were concerned women would not realise they were!

Fathers' groups also argued that contact denial carried safety risks. They argued it was the new partner who would be the risk according to their reading of the research evidence. Here there is an interesting bifurcation of the birth father and step-social father. Fathers' groups used women's definition of violence (including emotional abuse) to argue that denial of contact by women was a form of violence as it was emotional abuse. The definition of domestic violence used was broad and facilitated this kind of appropriation. It, thus, mirrors some of the weaknesses raised in Chapter Five about the imprecision of terms such as 'marital conflict' or 'hostility'. While the latter terms are not only imprecise and run the very real danger of underestimating the seriousness of the threats that may be posed, the definitions often used by domestic violence activists are so broad that they have other dangers. Because they defined violence as the systematic, patterned and purposeful exercise of power and control, which, therefore, encompassed both physical and non-physical phenomena: 'any woman whose ex-partner hampered her autonomy or self-development after separation could be regarded as a domestic violence victim' (Reece, 2006: 561). There was very little overt challenge to the women's groups' understanding of domestic violence and, indeed, a more common strategy was for other interest groups to use the definition to their own advantage. It does seem, however, that the definition is so broad that, in the current context, where the law attaches such importance to contact between fathers and children, it would be inconceivable for the law to prejudice a father 'merely on the grounds that he had systematically and purposefully exercised power and control over the child's mother' (Reece, 2006: 561). The argument that the current arrangements allow fathers to exercise too much power and control over mothers was not explicitly stated.

Discussion

Overall, as identified previously, there is a tendency for the key fathers' organisations to pursue their demands through a language of children's welfare. While the focus in this chapter has been on those organisations concerned with private law and contact with children, the next chapter considers an ostensibly different organisation, the Fatherhood Institute, which locates its demands primarily within a concern to promote good outcomes for children.

As indicated in Chapter One, men's talk about children's welfare should not simply be constructed as either cynical or opportunist, but can be part of a movement on the part of men towards taking more responsibility for children. However, it needs to be continually interrogated in the context of the constructions of women that are mobilised by such organisations. How seriously do these groups address gendered inequalities and the consequences for women? For example, how many campaign against the gendered pay inequalities outlined in Chapter Two? How many address and acknowledge the amount of work women often have to do to make contact work? If they do not then it is hardly surprising that the concern may be that men are using contact to continue controlling women in a context where they can no longer do so through marriage and to roll back the possibilities that have emerged in recent decades for women to live independently of men.

An important question must be that, in a context where women are perceived as unreliable, are men seeking to establish direct unmediated relationships with children (to cut out the middle woman as it were)? It has been argued that demands for equality in post-divorce parenting can be read as more of a symbolic demand than a description of how children should be parented (Rhoades, 2006):

> The failure to accord fathers equal contact time with their children might thus be perceived to be not so much a practical problem as a psychological injury relating to men's sense of their worth as fathers; a perception of being accorded secondary importance to their children's mother. (Collier and Sheldon, 2006: 17)

As we saw with rights talk, it is possible to discern a displacement by men and an inability to articulate feelings of vulnerability and dependency. While this remains the case it will be very difficult for men and women to cooperate to build the kinds of settlements that allow earning and caring to be possibilities for both.

However, it is also not in women's interests to use welfare of children arguments to pursue their own desires to free themselves of men. These arguments have rebounded in the child protection arena where the recognition that domestic violence also harmed children did effect some important improvements, but ultimately has meant that women can be held responsible for failing to protect their children from the violence they experience (see Chapter Nine). As we have seen previously in the contact field such arguments can risk constructing some women as illegitimate and others as victims.

It does seem that, as difficult as it may be, we need to continue dialogue on what unites and divides us as parents, as men and women, and stop using the welfare of children as a weapon or a shield. Moreover, change in this area requires parents, men and women, to engage with the feelings of pain and loss and the vulnerability thrown up by separation (Collier and Sheldon, 2008).

Conclusion

This chapter has explored the emergence and claims of fathers' organisations, identifying the dominance of a language around children's welfare. It also suggests the need to recognise diversity between fathers and this will be further underscored in the next chapter by discussion of the organisation, the Fatherhood Institute. It is recognised that some men in situations of great pain and loss are looking for help and support, and their angry calls need to be decoded in that context. However, there is a very partial understanding of gendered inequalities and no commitment, generally, to challenge wider manifestations of men's continuing power. The chapter also suggests that it is not the denial of domestic violence by fathers' rights activists that should be a key concern for feminists. Rather, it is the effacement of the needs and wishes of mothers, and the attempts to construct fathers as essential to children's welfare.

Notes

[1] There are women involved in many of the organisations that campaign around fathers.

[2] In January 2008 the author commissioned Claire Fraser, a freelance researcher, to carry out a survey of websites for this chapter. The material gathered has been used to inform the thinking for this chapter but it is important to note that some of these organisations seem to be quite fluid in composition and duration. Moreover the subsequent publication of Collier and Sheldon's book in 2008 has proved more significant for the analysis, as this was informed by empirical research.

[3] The party lost power in 2007.

[4] One website focused specifically on Scotland, which has its own and quite distinctive legal system.

[5] Thanks to Richard Collier for this point.

[6] The page for this charter has the year 2008 printed on it. However, the charter's pdf version becomes the Father's Day Manifesto 2004.

[7] www.fathercare.org/ is the website of one individual who was certainly involved in F4J and seems to be continuing his own campaigns and linking in with others.

[8] Although it is not specified, this probably refers to the demand that family court proceedings be held in public rather than private, which has been a long-standing demand.

[9] Such women may, of course, be too frightened or undermined. They are, in effect, being judged negligent in relation to their children because they are being beaten up. Moreover, separation can escalate violence and women who do not leave may actually be taking what they consider the least damaging option. Cases of men killing themselves and their children post-separation have achieved considerable publicity in recent years.

EIGHT

Contemporary social policies

Introduction

The last decade has seen a limited focus on men as fathers within a wide-ranging project emphasising the importance of investing in children. There has been an array of developments in relation to strengthening the responsibilities of birth fathers and some opening up of possibilities for social fathering through legislation. There have been moves towards supporting both mothers and fathers in sharing care, although these are limited and do not seem concerned to promote gender equity. This chapter identifies the key developments in policies, analysing their rationale and, where possible, identifying effects. A brief attempt is made to locate such developments within a wider international context, although an extended discussion of this is beyond the scope of the chapter.

Policy matters

Policy analysts have debated the factors influencing/determining outputs for many years (Borchorst, 2006). There is little support for previously held ideas that policy makers react rationally to objective conditions and many differing theoretical approaches are apparent. Social constructivists, for example, argue that policy making involves a constant discursive struggle over criteria and framing of issues, and the way they are framed attributes meaning to them (Borchorst, 2006: 104; see also Bacchi, 1999). Comparisons of different countries highlight considerable differences in how and when issues reach the political agenda. For example, when British fathers were given a legal right in 2003 to take paid leave for a period of time when their child was born, this was almost 30 years after Sweden had introduced such a right (O'Brien, 2005). Furthermore, although child support legislation has been introduced in many countries, its framing is often very different (see Lewis, 2002).

Froggett (2002) has used psychoanalytic concepts to understand both social policies and practices in the post-war welfare state in the UK. This is part of a growing interest in thinking about the psychic dimensions of entitlement, risk, responsibility, compassion and dependency, and developing policies based on such thinking.

It is acknowledged that the causal relationship between family policies and family change can be quite complex (Ellingsæter and Leira, 2006a: 5). Policy interventions may play different roles in different historic periods and the timing of policy reform is also of importance. Welfare state policies may react, adapt or be proactive in relation to family policies. Moreover, not all family change becomes the subject of policy change. Policies to close gaps that have developed between policy regulations and social practices in effect support ongoing transformations and can be expected to be more successful than reforms trying to reverse social trends. Policies can, of course, try to reward certain types of behaviour (tax breaks for married couples) as well as punish other types. Moreover, language is very important in politics and government, and has been an interesting feature of analysis of policy developments in the UK (Fairclough, 2000; Featherstone, 2006).

New Labour: from welfare to investment

Since 1997 New Labour has sought to construct a social investment state (see Featherstone, 2004; Lister, 2006). Compatible developments are apparent across a range of countries (see Jenson, 2008, for example, for an analysis of developments in the EU). The notion of the social investment state can be understood as both an ideal and an analytical tool (Lister, 2006). Basically, it is argued that the post-war welfare state sought to protect people from the vagaries and insecurities of the market, whereas a social investment state seeks to facilitate the integration of people into the market. Jenson (2004) compares the citizenship regime of the old post-war welfare state and its social rights with social investment regimes. Post-war social rights accrued to the model citizen who was the waged – usually the male – worker. The other social rights were to meet the needs of non-participants in the workforce who, apart from women and children, were expected to be few in number. Full employment policies responded to this primary interest, as did the politics of workplace representation. Over much of the 20th century, social policy was premised on the need to compensate for the risks of unemployment, sickness or the absence of the male breadwinner.

As economies became more open, with shifts to global markets, the state emphasis moved from seeking to maintain stable employment in a relatively closed national economy to the need to enhance competitiveness through increasing flexibility and permanent socioeconomic innovation in open economies by intervening mainly on the supply side. Developing a labour force skilled enough to engage with a changing global labour market becomes central. Jenson (2008: 133) identifies three features of the 'new' paradigm: constant learning; a future orientation; we all benefit from good social investments or successful individuals enrich our common future. Briefly, security depends on learning for employability. In modern industrial societies, income security depended on the earnings of a salaried or independent worker. But in recent decades that pattern has changed. Rising rates of female employment have impacted on the role of the male breadwinner and the restructuring of wages has decreased the capacity of the family to live on a single wage. These changes have generated new ways of thinking about income security. It is considered that individuals' security depends less on protection from threats to male breadwinning and more on the capacity to confront and adapt successfully to challenges over the life course or coming from unstable markets. The key challenges are defined as those at life transition points such as entry into school, the school–work transition, breakdown of a couple relationship, as well as labour market conditions such as unemployment or sickness.

Reliance on acquired human capital rather than specific skills or training is proposed as a response to the changes associated with deindustrialisation, the growth of the service sector and the emergence of a knowledge-based economy. Spending on early years increasingly becomes emphasised.

Moreover, it is argued that we all benefit from good investments and that investment now is less costly than solving problems later. In addition, certainly in the EU, attention to demographic considerations obliges efforts to respond to social risks such as decreased fertility rates: 'Never in history has there been economic growth without population growth ... if appropriate mechanisms existed to allow couples to have the number of children they want, the fertility rate could rise overall' (European Commission, quoted in Jenson, 2008: 137). The future of European society is linked to the capacity to address new social risks such as that there may be too few adults of working age to provide care and support for older people. Indeed, generally, 'new social risks' are perceived to have arisen from family and labour market change (Bonoli, 2005).

The risks necessitate methods to reconcile work and family responsibilities. Lewis and Campbell (2007: 4) examine the developments that have emerged in the UK and assess how far they promote gender equality, which they define 'in terms of the possibility of making a "real" or "genuine" choice for men and women to "work and care"'. They note that part of the construction of the UK as a liberal welfare regime was linked to the extent to which care of dependants was treated as a private family issue, and the UK long occupied a place towards the bottom of EU league tables on most aspects of family policy including care leave and care services for children. However, under New Labour, the position has changed with an explicit family policy being developed along a number of dimensions. New forms of leave have been introduced and existing ones extended. There has been an investment in childcare and a new statutory right to request a flexible working pattern. The next section considers these developments, locating them in the context of background concerns about fathers.

'Distant' fathers

In the 1990s, a coalition of differing and oppositional constituencies emerged to articulate concerns in relation to, or on behalf of, the 'distant' father. These concerns seemed to cohere around how to understand and tackle men's lack of involvement in the home in relation to women and children (Williams, 1998: 77). The reasons promoted ranged from the lack of structural and cultural support for fathers to men's unhelpful responses to the rupture in the power relations between men and women. In the process, it was very clear that different versions of feminism were at play here, in a context where feminism as any kind of organised or visible movement had collapsed. Given that many of the key feminist players here went on to be either New Labour government ministers (Patricia Hewitt) or leading members of the Fatherhood Institute (Adrienne Burgess), it is worth noting some of the problems Williams identified with the analyses developed at the time. In her analysis of the pamphlet by the Institute for Public Policy Research (IPPR) written by Burgess and Ruxton (1996) she offers prescient insights into the difficulties with some of today's analyses and policies.

Williams argues that the feminist demands and analyses of 'the distant father' developed in the 1990s differed markedly from those of the 1980s. In the 1980s the inequality of power relations between men and women was seen as key:

> The aim was to change those policies which underpinned gender inequality especially in relation to the unequal division of labour in the home and unequal access to paid work and income. In the 1996 IPPR pamphlet, the

> analytical context has changed. Here it is men's *loss of power* and/or rights (rather than men's ... privilege or women's lack of power and/or rights) which is the key issue. Fathers are not only losing opportunities to be the breadwinner, it is argued, but also losing out on opportunities for involvement with their children. They have, as fathers and as workers, become marginalized, deskilled and excluded. In these terms, policies are proposed which *compensate* men – in terms of practical support and legal and moral recognition – in terms of their role as fathers. (Williams, 1998: 82, emphasis in original)

Men need compensatory policies. Moreover, there is a shift in the analysis away from fathers and their behaviour (for example, their resistance to doing more domestic labour) to a focus on institutions to change. Although Williams understates the need to have a strategy for services in relation to men (see Chapters Nine and Ten of this book), her prescience is sobering because a key concern about the current policy context is the reliance on services (often staffed by poorly paid women) to engage fathers. This is returned to in Chapter Ten.

Williams noted also that the analyses of the 1990s considered women's power at home as the cause of men's resistance, thus women needed to change and allow men in. Women were to blame for not allowing men to care.

The IPPR revisited the issue of fathers in 2005 (see edited collection by Stanley, 2005). Here, Stanley and Gamble (2005) located their analysis and recommendations within the earlier work by Burgess and Ruxton (1996). Their recommendations, aimed at a New Labour government, adopt an explicit hierarchy of goals. The primary objective is to enhance fathers' involvement in order to improve children's experiences and outcomes. The secondary objective is to improve gender equity and the final objective is to enable men to fulfil their own aspirations for their fathering role (Stanley and Gamble, 2005: 12).

While they do at least mention gender equity, their hierarchy is profoundly misconceived, based on a misunderstanding of the interconnectedness of relationships between men, women and children. Good outcomes for children will not be promoted by forcing father involvement against the wishes of mothers (Featherstone et al, 2007).

Williams (1998) also noted the emergence of a discourse from influential feminists in the 1990s in which men were encouraged to take up responsibilities through the inducement of further rights rather than on the basis of a commitment to gender equality. For example, the IPPR pamphlet in 1996 (Burgess and Ruxton, 1996) devoted far more attention to the need for unmarried fathers to have parental responsibility (at that time, only married fathers automatically had parental responsibility on the birth of their children) than the lack of availability of childcare provision.

As indicated previously, under New Labour, a range of developments have ensued. New employment legislation came on-stream in April 2003. As O'Brien (2005) notes, principles of both gender convergence (attention to similarities between men and women) and gender differentiation (attention to differences between men and women) coexist in the new legislation. Statutory Paternity Pay (SPP) has been introduced and is paid at the same flat rate as maternity pay. If the father's average weekly earnings are £90 or more (before tax), SPP is paid for one or two consecutive weeks at £123.06 per week (from April 2009) or 90% of his average weekly earnings if this is less. All pregnant employees are entitled to 52 weeks' maternity leave in total, making it the longest in Europe. Mothers and fathers have access to statutory parental leave, which is unpaid, for 13 weeks and comparable rights were introduced for adoptive parents as far as possible. In 2006 the government consulted on an Additional Paternity Leave scheme to be available to fathers from 26 weeks following the birth of the child (at the earliest), and paid at the same rate and under the same conditions as SPP. If a mother wanted to return to work before her child's first birthday, the father would be able to take some, or all, of the second half of the child's first year as paid leave. It depends on the mother having the leave in the first place and is conditional on her not using her full entitlement to maternity leave. Another key change, introduced in 2003, was the introduction of the right to flexible working, which enabled a parent with a child under six or a disabled child under 18 to make a request for flexible working, and placed a duty on employers to consider such requests seriously and only reject them for 'good' business reasons. In April 2007, the right to request flexible working was extended to carers of adults and it was planned to be extended to parents of children under 16.[1]

According to Lewis and Campbell (2007), securing gender equality has not been an explicit priority in the policies that have been developed under the rubric of work–family balance (WFB).[2] WFB policies have been developed as a result of concern about both economic and social objectives. As already noted, there is a specific concern about fertility rates. The desire to tackle child poverty is also an important factor, with the employment of both men and women seen as crucial. Indeed, a key emphasis of New Labour has been the encouragement of all into paid work, particularly where the alternative is reliance on state benefits.

An incremental approach to policy development has been obvious in the expectation that it might provoke least resistance from employers and the policies reflect increased attention to the English-speaking literature on child development, which favours one-to-one care in the very early years of a child's life (Lewis and Campbell, 2007).

Two overlapping agendas have been evident – the promotion of flexibility and fairness was most prominent before 2000 and, since 2000, flexibility and choice have been stressed. Choices are treated in all the relevant policy documents as gender neutral, although there is evidence that the erosion of the male breadwinner model has been understood. Policies have addressed the issues of enabling women's choices to balance work and care – and, to a much lesser extent, men's – but they have ignored the extent to which expanding women's choices depends on changing men's behaviour in the home. However, as Lewis and Campbell (2007) acknowledge, this neglect is relatively commonplace outside a small number of Nordic countries.

Furthermore, it would appear long working hours on the part of men are not considered a problem by the government. As we saw in Chapter Two, by contrast with other countries in the EU, the UK is distinguished by the extent to which men work 48 plus hours weekly. The opt-out from the limitation placed on working hours by the EU's 1993 directive has remained in place.[3] Indeed, it is clear that exhortation has been preferred rather than legislative change in this area. This tendency to favour exhortation, rather than entrench legislative rights, extends across a range of policy initiatives directed at men as fathers, as was argued in Chapter One of this book and will be returned to in a subsequent section and in Chapter Ten.

Overall, it would appear that, in the case of men, paid work is assumed to take precedence over unpaid for New Labour. Lewis and Campbell (2007: 21) note that the distinctive British pattern of long working hours for men and short working hours for women has been addressed through exhortation, rather than via legislation on hours or wage replacement for fathers' leave. The individual opt-out has been maintained and instead flexible working patterns have been promoted. This is a not dissimilar policy strategy to most of the UK's northern and many of its western European neighbours in seeking to underpin a pattern of family care during the child's very early years, followed by institutional childcare provision that enables women to enter the labour market. As an explicit policy aim, gender equality has taken a back seat and it is unlikely that government policy will effect a major change in men's behaviour. Research on the benefits of one-to-one care in the first year has been significant. It is recognised that policies that promote the future welfare of mothers and their children are not easy to design. Galtry and Callister (2005) have concluded that the best compromise may be a six-month leave for the mother followed by a six-month leave for the father. To some extent that is what UK policy is but, as indicated previously, the type of leave policies for fathers renders comprehensive take-up unlikely. However, there appear to be divisions between feminists about the desirability of seeking to effect such behaviour.

As highlighted in Chapters One, Two and Six, there are disagreements among feminists in relation to how government policies should be read, or indeed sometimes what should be argued for. Lewis and Campbell (2007) argue, for example, that there is considerable evidence from cross-national research on what parental leave should look like if fathers are to take it. It must be an individual entitlement, paid at a high rate of compensation, and be flexible, making possible shorter and longer blocks of leave either full or part time. New Labour, by contrast, has instituted a low flat rate of compensation for its two weeks' paternity leave. Additional paternity leave is not an individual right (it is a transfer from the mother's leave), and is not well compensated and flexible. Indeed, the government's own regulatory impact assessment makes it clear that it does not expect many fathers to take up this leave. As other academics have suggested, such proposals entrench the belief that mothers are the primary caregivers and fathers can take on such roles at mothers' discretion (O'Brien, 2005).

Moreover, in terms of supporting women to fulfil their responsibilities in relation to paid work, the government has opted for arrangements that do little to improve gender equality in terms of the division of unpaid care. The UK now has the longest maternity leave entitlement of any EU member state, whereas the research suggests that short leaves are better for gender equality. In the summer of 2008, Nicola Brewer's speech[4] at the launch of a consultation on 'Working Better', a programme of work seeking to explore work/care provision, got considerable publicity in the media and opened up the above debates to a broader audience.[5] She asked whether the level of maternity leave entitlements made too many assumptions about the choices families make and entrenched the stereotype that it is women who do the caring. Her comments were supported both by the Fawcett Society, a feminist organisation seeking gender equality, and the Fatherhood Institute, a think-tank on fatherhood issues explored on page 141 (Kennedy, 2008).

However, it is not clear that all feminists would want shorter leaves for women. For example, although she does not identify policy implications, Hollway (2006, 2008) emphasises very strongly the importance of mothers and fathers not being considered as interchangeable, especially for infants.

Moreover, as Lewis and Campbell (2007) note, there is considerable evidence that working mothers themselves welcomed longer maternity leaves. This links with the other evidence we have considered from Dermott (2008) on fathers' preferences. As explored in Chapters Two and Six, Dermott's research would suggest that the model of fatherhood that is favoured by fathers is based on establishing a strong emotional relationship between father and child, and not a gender-equality model of parenthood. There is, therefore, little appetite from fathers themselves for an extension of policies to advance gender equality. Dermott seems to be suggesting, therefore, that present policies accord with men's preferences.

However, feminists such as Lewis and Campbell see current policies as part of the problem and wish to challenge men's 'preferences' in the interests of fostering gender equity. Moreover, they emphasise the role played by constraint – low levels of pay for example.

Fraser (1994) identified two approaches by feminists towards reforming the welfare state in gender egalitarian directions – the 'universal breadwinner' and 'caregiver parity' approaches (See Orloff, 2007). The universal breadwinner approach would allow and encourage women to act as men do in the economy, as breadwinners, earning a family supporting wage and leaving care work to others – not the unpaid housewife of the 'traditional' household, but the paid service workers of the state, thus commodifying everyone while also commodifying care. By contrast, the 'caregiver parity' model does not neglect care, or women's work as caregivers, but instead tries to compensate them for the disadvantages this work creates. Thus women and men continue to be different, but women are protected from the consequences. Fraser outlined the problems with both approaches and advanced an influential synthesis of them – the 'universal caregiver' model in which men are made the focus of efforts to change rather than women. Therefore, the problem is considered to be that most men are unlike most women (caregivers who are also women). As Orloff (2007) notes, this is an important analytic innovation, decentring the masculine and valorising care while not leaving it solely to women. Fraser does note that a precondition for this kind of gender equity would be to end gender, as we know it, which, as Orloff notes, is a revolutionary demand indeed. But a more reformist version is to attempt to make men more like women by finding ways to encourage their participation in care with policies such as individual leave entitlements.

However, Orloff argues that such a position does not adequately engage with the deep investments people have in gender and the ways in which subjectivity and knowledge are grounded in gender categories. She argues that taking account of these investments matters insofar as it points to men's investments in preserving the power that current social arrangements give them, but also women's concerns to preserve their power in the domain of the private caregiving realm. Identities are formed in relation to whether men and women see themselves as caregivers or not.

For feminists, the question remains, though, about whether such identities can or should remain unchallenged and, moreover, there is evidence to suggest that some fathers and mothers do want to challenge matters.

Lewis and Campbell's (2007) approach to defining gender equality is derived from Sen's (1999) capabilities approach, which focuses not on equality of outcomes but rather on the importance of agency and the possibility of making a real choice. Lewis and Campbell argue that such an approach eschews prescription and instrumentalism, and allows the reframing of the current policy debates over choice that have become increasingly dominant in a number of European welfare states. The idea of 'real' or 'genuine' choice goes beyond seeing choice as a simple expression of preferences and acknowledges the important role of policy in addressing the constraints on choice. If care is a universal human need then, arguably, it should be possible for anyone to choose to do it. Lewis and Campbell argue that truly genuine choice can only exist in a universe of fair and adequate wages, generous family policies, and secure work and family situations.

These debates are returned to in Chapters Ten and Eleven. The next section explores some of the other developments under New Labour's family policy and the implications for fathers.

Rights, responsibilities and fathers

As Dean (2008: 1) notes, the crowning achievement of the 20th century, brought to fruition at the end of World War Two, was the consolidation of more or less systematic forms of social policy across the capitalist world, providing certain rights to social security, health care, education, housing, social protection and, for example, legal aid for the poor. He notes that the form and substance of welfare rights has always been contested with different welfare regimes exhibiting different notions of rights. For example, some such as the more liberal English-speaking countries have operated with a notion of welfare rights as a form of safety net, whereas corporatist continental European welfare states have tended to see such rights as compensatory rights for their workers. Social democratic welfare states, by contrast, have been inclined to regard welfare more in terms of universal rights for all citizens.

The consensus outlined by Dean has now broken down and the last decades have seen many countries redesigning their social policies. While conditionality was always a feature of welfare provision in most countries, it has become more clearly entrenched and tied to notions of responsibility. The relationship between rights and responsibilities is deeply contested and the last decades have seen a range of differing debates and developments. Neo-conservatives have questioned the rights of social citizenship because they were considered to undermine the responsibilities of citizens to provide for themselves through paid work and neo-liberals have questioned them because they were considered to undermine the ethical freedoms and civic duties of the individual property-owning subject (Dean, 2008: 6).

The Third Way, a political development promoted in the US by Clinton and by New Labour in the UK had, as central, the notion 'no rights without responsibilities' (Giddens, 1998: 65). This intensified an already existing concern with parents and their responsibilities. Fox Harding (1996) noted that, from 1979 onwards, the Conservative government had developed an interest in family responsibility and was particularly concerned about the relationship with state responsibility and the financial implications of who took responsibility for what. She noted the emergence of key pieces of legislation using the term 'parental responsibility': the 1989 Children Act, the 1991 Criminal Justice Act, and the 1991 Child Support Act. Although the different types of parental responsibility were not always consistent, the then Conservative government was using the concept in a unified way and that concept meshed with a wider strategy for broader family responsibility, more private dependency and fewer state-dependent families.

Collier and Sheldon (2008) suggest that the 1989 Children Act was a pivotal moment in an increasingly dominant political and policy consensus that fathers have a significant positive contribution to make to families, transcending the role of provider and encapsulating a historic shift from rights to responsibilities. Section 2(1) of the Act provides that, in cases where a child's mother and father are married to each other at the time of birth, they shall each have parental responsibility for the child. This encompasses all the rights, duties, powers, responsibilities and authority that by law a parent of the child has in relation to the child and his property (see Collier and Sheldon, 2008: 115). Collier and Sheldon suggest it reflects an acceptance of the view that fathers' relationships with their children should, wherever possible, be encouraged by law, although they do accept the importance of economic concerns in the formulation of parental responsibility at that time. This is explored further in the later section on child support. However, Collier and Sheldon suggest it was an important moment in promoting the idea of the 'involved father' in family life in ways that transcended the primary economic focus (see also Smart and Neale, 1999).

As has been well documented (see, for example, Williams, 1998; Featherstone, 2004), a set of diverse constituencies in the 1990s turned their attention to men's behaviour as fathers:

> It turns out the clichés about role models are true ... Little boys don't naturally grow up to be responsible fathers and husbands. They don't naturally grow up knowing how to get up every morning at the same time and go to work ... And most emphatically of all, little boys do not reach adolescence naturally wanting to refrain from sex, just as little girls don't become adolescents naturally wanting to refrain from having babies ... boys and girls grow into responsible parents and neighbours and workers because they are imitating the adults around them. (Charles Murray, quoted in Williams, 1998: 10-11)

Murray, an American New Right academic and cultural commentator, became popular particularly with some influential newspaper editors in the UK. However, concerns were also raised by quite different constituencies. Dennis and Erdos (1992) were ethical socialist sociologists who identified a link between the growth of fatherless families and the growth of crime (manifest in a series of disturbances in areas in the UK in the early 1990s). They argued that working-class communities and the families within them, with their virtues of hard work, respectability and cooperation, had been undermined through economic restructuring and women's independent lifestyles. Beatrix Campbell (1993: 303), in a feminist analysis, by contrast, argued: 'neither manners nor mothers are to blame, but ... there is an economic emergency in many neighbourhoods where the difference between what women and men do with their troubles and with their anger shapes their strategies of survival'. While women seek solutions rooted in notions of solidarity, men choose destructive approaches. She argued that the criminal behaviour of young men was an attempt to reassert the power and privileges attached to men and masculinity. It is interesting to contrast this feminist analysis, which locates a range of difficulties in men's resistance to change, with that advanced by other feminists at that time, who sought to compensate men for the changes that had occurred (see Williams, 1998).

Parton (2006: 85-6) offers a helpful analysis of the impact of the death of a little boy, James Bulger, at the hands of two other children in 1993. He argues that it was pivotal in bringing together a set of concerns about crime and family structure, and profoundly influenced the Labour Party, which had just lost its fourth election in a row. He traces the origins of the New Labour project for reforming the welfare state and remodelling society to the notion of being 'tough on crime and tough on the causes of crime', and links this explicitly with this particular death. The relationship between the state, the child and the parents was seen as in need of urgent realignment.

Thus, the year after New Labour came to power saw the publication of *Supporting Families: A Consultation Document* (Home Office, 1998) containing a raft of initiatives in relation to supporting and controlling parents. It also contained the following statements:

> 6.5 The Ministerial Group on the Family will carry on its work and during the course of next year reports will be published, and further measures will be taken to improve public policy. In particular, the Ministerial Group will be focusing on *the needs of young men and the support available to fathers.*
>
> 6.6 Increasingly, boys and young men seem to have difficulty maturing into responsible citizens and fathers. Declining educational performance, loss of traditional 'male jobs', the growth of a 'laddish' anti-social culture, greater use of drugs, irresponsible teenage fatherhood, and the rising suicide rate may all show rising insecurity and uncertainty among young men. This has worrying implications for the stability of family life and wider society. For example, recent research suggests that young men may not grow out of crime in their late teens, as they were once assumed to do.
>
> 6.7 Fathers have a crucial role to play in their children's upbringing, and their involvement can be particularly important to their sons. Most voluntary and professional organisations currently working with parents acknowledge that it is much more difficult to encourage fathers to participate in parenting support than mothers. Some

> organisations have already developed programmes which specifically target fathers. The Ministerial Group for the Family will be looking at ways of encouraging the development of more widespread support for fathers. (Home Office, 1998: 42, emphasis in original)

A range of projects directed at fathers were funded (see Featherstone, 2003, 2004; and Chapter Ten). These were time limited and were located in a variety of agency settings. Interestingly, despite the above emphasis on fathers providing role models for sons, and dealing with troublesome behaviour, very few initiatives have been funded directed at fathers and sons. Moreover, the Respect agenda (discussed on page 142) has not made this a focus either, even though, as outlined, it does appear that it is women who are on the receiving end of controlling and supportive measures to manage troublesome men and boys.

In more recent years, there is evidence of a move away from funding projects for limited periods towards 'mainstreaming', where services in a variety of settings from health to social care appear to be expected to 'engage fathers'. A host of issues, including the practice implications of these initiatives, are dealt with in the next chapters, but a point to note is that it has not, hitherto, been practice to name men as fathers in documents aimed at services. There has been a preference for the gender-neutral term parents.

New Labour has also part-funded organisations such as Families Need Fathers and an organisation originally known as Fathers Direct, which is now known as the Fatherhood Institute. This organisation differs from those outlined in the previous chapter and has been included in this chapter because of its explicit distancing from fathers' organisations and their usual focus on private law and contact campaigns. While Collier and Sheldon (2006) were able to establish parallels between organisations such as F4J in other countries, it is less clear where the Fatherhood Institute can be situated comparatively. Flood (2004) locates it with Dads and Daughters in the US as one of the organisations that promote positive and collaborative visions of men's relations with women and children.

The Fatherhood Institute (formerly Fathers Direct)

Fathers Direct emerged from discussions emanating from research entitled *Men and their Children: Proposals for Public Policy*, which was carried out by a think-tank, the Institute for Public Policy Research (IPPR), in the 1990s (Burgess and Ruxton, 1996).

In 2008, it changed its name to the Fatherhood Institute to signpost that it is an organisation concerned with fatherhood and how it impacts on the well-being of children, mothers and fathers, and not with supporting individual fathers or fathers' rights. A major review of international research conducted by Adrienne Burgess (2007) had been key also. The review had led the Institute to a number of key conclusions. The difference between poor fathering and good fathering has a greater impact – positive or negative – on children brought up in disadvantaged circumstances than other children. Only services designed for the purpose of engaging fathers make a noticeable difference to their behaviour and hence change outcomes for the child.

The Fatherhood Institute (2008b) summarises its key activities as follows:

- collate and publish international research on fathers, fatherhood and different approaches to engaging with fathers by public services and employers;
- help shape national and local policies to ensure a father-inclusive approach to family policy;
- inject research evidence on fathers and fatherhood into national debates about parenting and parental roles;
- lobby for changes in law, policy and practice to dismantle barriers to fathers' care of infants and children;
- remain the UK's leading provider of training, consultancy and publications on father-inclusive practice, for public and third-sector agencies and employees.

It has three ongoing concerns (Fatherhood Institute, 2008c):

- To change *work* so that fathers can be more available to care for their children. The aim is to see more fathers, including fathers on low incomes, working flexibly and part time and taking time off for caring.
- To change *education* so that boys are prepared for future caring roles and girls and boys are prepared for the future sharing of these roles.

> We want to see children and young people discussing gender inequalities and understanding that mothers and fathers experience pressure to specialise in caring and earning roles, and that mothers and fathers should have a similar range of choices over their caring roles, not limited by gender. We

want to see more encouragement of boys into childcare careers. (Fatherhood Institute, 2008c)

• To get *services* such as health, education and children and family support services to be *father-inclusive*. Fathers should be supported in their caring roles as seriously as those services currently support mothers.

The website and attendant materials establish explicit distance from fathers' rights organisations, and the concern to be evidence-based may, in part, signal a concern not to be identified with the individual, highly charged stories told by other fathers (for example, web searches routinely throw up examples of individual stories of pain and anger about the family courts). The Institute positions itself explicitly within a 'child outcomes' project, rather than a gender-equality project, echoing, though not explicitly signalling, alignment with New Labour discourses. Fathers are construed as central to such a project.

A key theme that emerges is the Institute's focus on the role of services. The service focus on mothers is assumed to be supportive of mothers (although, as we will see in the next chapters, this is not how it is experienced always by mothers and indeed there is a long tradition of research suggesting that, in certain sectors, mothers have been very poorly served by services). Therefore, fathers are assumed to be 'missing out' or being prevented by services from taking on 'caring roles' and employment practices are insufficiently flexible. This represents a very specific version of fatherhood that leaves out complexity and diversity, and crucially, as outlined in Chapter Six, the links between men's practices as fathers and male power at a range of levels. The dominant construction is of heterosexual families comprised of men and women seeking to balance work and care.

Antisocial behaviour and the Respect agenda

Parents' responsibilities in relation to their children's delinquency and criminality have been expanded under New Labour. As Parton (2006: 78-9) notes, throughout the 1990s, as New Labour was developing its political identity, the case was made by a number of diverse constituencies for developing new policies on crime and delinquency reduction, and this was to become an important area of policy.

Eschewing a conservative view that the collapse of a particular model of family was responsible for a range of social ills, and the left view that parents and children were victims of economic and social changes, a growing consensus emerged:

> It was recognised that turning the clock back to the 1950s was neither a serious nor a desirable option and that policies to 'strengthen families' and 'help parents' needed development. Family change should be managed not anathematised, with a firm policy emphasis on supporting parents, not stigmatising them. (Parton, 2006: 78-9)

In a changing world, parents and parenting behaviours were seen as important mediators between the stresses of adult life and children's development. Parton documents the family-based factors that were increasingly considered by influential researchers to be linked to a greater risk of offending:

- Neglect: where parents spend little time interacting with and supervising children.
- Conflict: where parents exert inconsistent or inappropriate discipline and where one party rejects the other.
- Deviancy: where parents are themselves involved in offending and/or condone law breaking.
- Disruption: where neglect and conflict arise from marital discord and the break up of the marriage with the subsequent absence of one parent, usually the father.

Anti-Social Behaviour Orders for Children aged 10 or older were introduced in the 1998 Crime and Disorder Act. This Act also introduced parenting orders. These court orders could require parents to attend counselling or guidance sessions, and to exercise control over the child's behaviour, ensuring, for example, that their child went to school every day. Local authorities gained the powers to apply local curfew schemes where police could return children home if they broke the curfew notices.

Within the Respect agenda (see Squires, 2006, for an outline) a range of developments that also expand the responsibilities of parents in unprecedented ways have ensued. It is interesting to note Eekelaar's (2006) comments on responsibility from a socio-legal perspective. By the 1980s, both public child protection law and private family law placed the interests of children (at least as perceived by courts and welfare agencies) above those of adult family members (see Eekelaar, 2006: 122). The 1989 Children Act, at the behest of the Law Commission, felt it necessary to attempt to banish the concept of a parent's 'rights' with respect to children, saying that parents had only responsibilities towards them. Eekelaar argues that responsibility for children was beginning to be seen as more of a matter for parents than for the state than it had been in the 30 or so years after World War Two (although there were limits to this – for example, there was no responsibility for their early care pre-school).

Eekelaar (2006: 128) explores the fault lines that have emerged in relation to the rights–responsibility axis in the last decade. For example, the responsibility of parents now includes an expectation that the agent should demonstrate an appreciation of the effects of their actions, or inactions, on other people by modifying their behaviour accordingly, even if this means modifying claims to one's entitlements. So, while we can say that a responsible person follows their legal obligations, responsibility does not stop there. Responsible people will exercise restraint within their legal rights, but they will also act beyond their legal duties. For example, a child who keeps in regular contact with his or her parents when he or she leaves home has no legal duty to do this but will usually be seen as acting more responsibly than one who does not. Responsible parents will try and ensure that their children behave considerately to others. None of these, hitherto, has legal obligations. However, it is now interesting that the government is trying to embrace a wider approach through the provisions in relation to antisocial behaviour within the law. As Eekelaar notes, the legislation in relation to antisocial behaviour clearly covers behaviour that, hitherto, escaped any form of legal action (but would probably have been thought to be irresponsible). The apparent failure of parents to prevent such behaviour might previously have been considered irresponsible, but it would have fallen outside the scope of official intervention. Eekelaar argues that there is no difficulty in principle with a policy that seeks to bring about such changes in behaviour. But the difference between encouraging and enforcing is pivotal as one loses the fuller sense of responsibility referred to above. The behaviour is now a legal duty.

Henricson and Bainham (2005) have questioned whether attributing blame to parents for children's behaviour can be considered compatible with human rights considerations. They also point out such an attribution underestimates children's independence and overestimates the ability of parents to control their children's behaviour as they grow older. Indeed, in an evaluation of a parenting programme with fathers who were compelled by the courts to attend because of their sons' offending, fathers made this very point to the author (Featherstone, 2001b, discussed further in Chapter Ten).

A number of writers have highlighted the gendered implications of policies that emphasise parents' responsibilities towards their children. Lister (2006) has noted that it is women-headed households that fail to control the behaviour of male children or boyfriends who are most likely to be the subject of complaints under antisocial order legislation and subject to sanctions such as eviction from their homes.

The research evidence suggests that it has been mothers, not 'parents', who have been made the subject of parenting orders because of their sons' behaviour (Ghate and Ramalla, 2002). The imposition of the order is determined, not by legal concerns about who has parental responsibility, but by who accompanies the child to court and this is usually related to residency (Holt, 2007). Holt notes that the mothers in her research were more likely to attend court because they were either unemployed or working part-time or flexible hours. She also notes the evidence from the research on parenting orders that economic difficulties were a key concern for mothers. This links with themes from the research identified in Chapter Two and suggests the importance of attending to the feminisation of poverty in many families.

Child support

In Britain, as in many other western countries, fathers emerged on the policy agenda at the end of the 1980s (Lewis, 2002).[6] While, superficially, the debates in many northern European countries and the US looked similar, revolving mainly around the responsibilities of fathers to maintain their children on separation/divorce, there were real differences in the drivers and nature of debates and policies. Lewis notes that this is linked to the differing balances drawn between fathers as providers of care and cash in differing welfare regimes. In Scandinavia,[7] where the dual-earner model is firmly established and where adult citizenship is tied to participation in the labour market, the focus has been more on the care provided by fathers and has been part of the debate about achieving greater equality in the division of unpaid as well as paid work. Britain has historically adhered to a strong male breadwinner model and placed more emphasis, therefore, on the ability of fathers to maintain their children financially.

It is interesting to note that, in relation to what the balance of responsibility should be about supporting children financially (between fathers, mothers and the state), the end of the 1980s was a *specific moment*. Not that long before, a quite different approach had been taken and there have been complex shifts since. For example, during the 1970s, lone mothers and their children were the focus of attention, and a government committee was set up to look at the circumstances (the Finer Committee discussed in Lewis, 2002). But its focus was very much the lone mother and not the father – the emphasis was on the way in which all lone mothers, whether divorced or unmarried, had 'extra needs' and the extent to which these would have to be met by the state. The Finer Committee did not deny the responsibility of men to maintain their children:

> However, it shied away from the degree of effort necessary to determine paternity and trace fathers, believing that the greater confidentiality of personal information in Britain, than in the Scandinavian countries, for example, would make this impossible ... It was also inclined to respond pragmatically to male behaviour, believing that it was impossible to dictate who a man should live with and support in a democratic society. (Lewis, 2002: 129)

Thus there was a pragmatic stance taken towards providing financial support for lone mothers and their children.

That pragmatism did not survive. Fathers, and their responsibilities in relation to economic maintenance, became a serious focus of attention in the late 1980s. The growth in divorce and cohabitation rates had resulted in a separation of marriage and parenthood. A key concern regarding men was how to tie them to families and reduce the social security budget. Thus, child support legislation was introduced (see Lewis, 2002). The child support system faced a host of problems after its inception in 1993 (Wikeley, 2007). Although the British Social Attitudes Survey in 1990 found that 90% of men and 95% of women thought that a father should pay for his children after divorce, the new agency, the Child Support Agency (CSA), was the subject of considerable controversy and protest. While there were many who could not pay (the Finer Committee had recognised the impossibility of making a low family wage stretch between two households), there was also tremendous hostility from those who could (Lewis, 2002: 143). Many researchers considered the complexities of the issues involved here. The formula was highly complex with little recognition of second families. There was a high threshold (104 nights a year) before overnight contact reduced the non-resident parent's child support liability.

A key issue was that all the money received in child support was deducted from the benefit entitlement of the parent with care. While child support systems were meant to cover the entire eligible population, in practice they focused on those receiving state benefits.

Where the parent with care was not on income support or income-based jobseeker's allowance, he or she had a choice about whether to pursue child support through the statutory system. According to Wikeley (2007), there are currently about 2.5 million parents with care in the UK who are entitled to receive child support, but the best data available suggests that just over half of parents with care have some sort of arrangement in place.

New Labour's revised scheme in 2003 clarified the formula but still took no notice of the non-resident parent's housing costs or other special expenditure. Second families were recognised more. It was planned to move all separated parents to the new scheme but this did not happen because of well documented problems with IT systems. This outraged those on the old system as they worked out how much better off they would be under the new scheme.

By 2006 it was clear that the government was presiding over two failing schemes: the old, which covered most applications for maintenance made from April 1993, and a new scheme that was only partially implemented. Sir David Henshaw was asked to undertake a fundamental redesign of child support policy and its operations.

Henshaw argued in his subsequent report that the system was failing to deliver as a result of policy and operational failures. He recommended that private maintenance arrangements should be supported, parents with care on benefit should keep more of the child support and there should be a new organisation with stronger enforcement powers as a back-up provided by the government (Henshaw, 2006). The recommendations were broadly accepted and have become law. All parents are now given the choice of invoking the statutory mechanism or not, which removes compulsion from those on benefits. There is a weekly (and enhanced) disregard for claimants.

'The policy shift towards encouraging private maintenance agreements is a further example of the emphasis on private ordering as a means of resolving disputes' (Wikeley, 2007: 446). Will there be a risk therefore (in the absence of adequate support and advice services) that any existing power imbalances between parents are reinforced to the detriment of children, as Wikeley suggests? Certainly, campaigners from the Child Poverty Action Group, One Parent Families/Gingerbread and Resolution have expressed concern about the implications for lone mothers (Robins, 2008).

Contact and child support are complexly linked (see Bradshaw et al, 1999; Dermott, 2008). Shared care (not defined) under the new child support system should be organised between the parties, with no third party involvement. Under the original system, overnight contact was at

104 nights before it affected child support liabilities. Then it became 52 and this differential treatment continues to be a source of resentment. This is an issue mainly affecting fathers. The issue is not properly tackled in the new proposals and, therefore, the potential remains for conflict over contact and child support arrangements to continue.

Some fathers' groups are broadly supportive of the emphasis on voluntary arrangements. Fathers Need Families argued that the proposals contain the grain of a positive approach to shared parenting (Robins, 2008). However, it expressed concern about the proposed clampdown on fathers who default on payments, which calls for the use of deduction from earnings orders to collect maintenance directly from wages, as well as powers to confiscate passports and driving licences, and introduce curfews, which it describes as punitive, draconian and internally contradictory (Robins, 2008). However, some observers argue they are necessary because previous measures were toothless (Robins, 2008).

During the review, a coalition of organisations worked together to try and influence it. This coalition, involving as it did academics, women's groups, Families Need Fathers, the Fatherhood Institute and lone parent groups, is an interesting example of a range of very diverse and often opposed constituencies getting together to seek change (Fatherhood Institute, 2006). For many, the subsequent proposals were disappointing, with an overemphasis on sanctions at the expense of support. The Australian model has received a degree of support from many within this coalition. Here a range of family relationship centres and a funded national service help non-resident fathers stay connected to their children and the formula for payments is based on a rational calculation of children's needs. This model expects, and gets, a good success rate in relation to the payment of child support, but also supports relationships continuing. It is important to note that within Australia some feminists are unhappy about this latter emphasis, as they argue it pressurises women to stay involved with men whom they are experiencing difficulties with, including violence. Certainly, it is important to note Reece's (2006) comments in the last chapter on the dangers of ignoring women's autonomy in some of these developments.

To summarise, there have been important shifts in relation to child support on the part of successive governments. The 1970s signalled a pragmatic acceptance of the role of the state and a corresponding lack of desire to pursue men. But, by the end of the 1980s, the responsibilities of birth fathers for all their children were emphasised and the subject of legislation. Currently, it is possible to see the revised child support developments outlined previously, in conjunction with the increased emphasis on lone parents taking up paid work, as representing another shift. Although many feminists are critical of the emphasis on lone mothers taking up paid employment that has run through New Labour policies, others argue that, for those with children of school age, it can be an important means out of poverty and is in line with long-standing feminist demands to ensure women's economic independence from men (see Featherstone, 2004, for a summary of the debates).

New Labour, fathers and the 'democratic' family

In the last decade, the responsibilities and rights of birth fathers have been strengthened in a range of domains as outlined above and in the last chapter in relation to child support and contact. Unmarried fathers whose name is on the birth certificate are now awarded parental responsibility under the law. Hitherto, this was dependent on marital status or a special application by the father. In June 2008, the government signalled its intention to make joint birth registration a legal requirement unless this was decided by the registrar to be 'impossible, impracticable or unreasonable' (DCSF and DWP, 2008: 30). This confers new rights although they are, as is usually the case, coupled with responsibilities, in particular that of child support. This development is particularly concerning given that only 7% of births are not registered by both parents. Those who register alone are overwhelmingly likely to be poor young women and the important points raised in the consultation about the pressure this could place women under at what might already be a difficult time appear to have been ignored (Williams, 2008). Suffice to say here that this is an example of the tendency noted in Chapter Two to impose a father on every arrangement (in this case it is clearly a birth father). At the same time, legislation has opened up possibilities for gay couples to adopt (2002 Adoption and Children Act)[8] and, as already indicated in Chapter Two, changes in the law in relation to reproductive technology have removed the need for clinics to consider 'the need for a father' when assessing women who seek treatment. Thus New Labour, while tending quite clearly to support and control birth fathers, have not carved out a clear path in relation to advocating one kind of father or indeed family (see Featherstone, 2004).

Collier and Sheldon (2008: 117) argue that, from a position in which marriage had been the primary mechanism for grounding fathers' rights, fathers are now seen to have a more direct unmediated relationship with their children. They also suggest that New Labour has promoted a particular model of the family:

> The new democratic family is marked by a commitment not simply to formal equality between men and women, to mutual rights and responsibilities, but also to a negotiated authority over children, a joint commitment to co-parenting and a political acceptance that law has a role to play in promoting 'responsible' parenting and lifelong obligation to children on the part of both women and men. (Collier and Sheldon, 2008: 118)

Collier and Sheldon are correct to signal that there has been much more engagement by New Labour with families than hitherto. Indeed, as outlined in Featherstone (2004), explicit family policy has been developed where previously there was none or implicit measures. They are also correct that New Labour's promotion of family life, based on shifting labour market participation of men and women, changing ideas of child welfare and social changes around marriage and parenting, have promoted shifts in notions of good mothering and fathering. The promotion of active parenting on the part of men is tension-ridden though. As we outlined in the last chapter, there is a consensus that fathers must retain contact with children post-divorce and must financially support them (these measures precede New Labour) but, in relation to work–family balance policies, the measures are weak, as discussed earlier. Moreover, other social care type measures discussed in the next chapters are important but contain important limitations.

Some comparative insights

Academics and think-tanks, as well as governments, have shown increasing interest in thinking about fathers in the context of exploring how differing welfare regimes have developed in relation to parenthood policy and in exploring the internationalisation of law and guidance in the area of gender equality.

O'Brien et al (2007) explore fathers' use of paternity leave, parental leave and flexible work practices across a number of industrialised countries. They note that, although the evidence base is still low, their new evidence makes a significant contribution to an emerging picture of fathers' work–family behaviour as distinct from their aspirations.

There are differing definitions of paternity and parental leave in different countries and the two are sometimes conflated.[9] Globally, gender differentiation of birth leave is the norm with mothers given more time away from employment. By contrast, leave for fathers is relatively recent (1974 in Sweden, for example). The emergence of father-targeted parental leave in a number of mainly Nordic countries has occasioned great interest in other countries and, certainly in the UK, is championed by some feminists (see, for example, Lister, 2006).

> Father-targeted parental leave includes periods of times that only fathers can take (sometimes referred to as a father's quota) ... policy analysis of Nordic governmental documents shows that the goal of these designated 'daddy periods' was to strengthen fathers' caring role with their infants, and also to encourage fathers to take a greater share of leave to support gender equity. (O'Brien et al, 2007: 377)

An analysis of 173 countries indicates that fathers have a paid entitlement to paternity leave or paid parental leave in 66 countries. One-hundred-and-sixty-nine countries offer maternity leave (only four do not – Liberia, Papua New Guinea, Swaziland and the US).

Overall, O'Brien et al (2007: 379) argue that the evidence:

> ... highlights the importance of a country's policy framework, particularly financial incentives, in shaping fathers' propensity to take family leave. In the absence of paid job-protected leave, poorer and less economically secure fathers may be less able to spend time with their infants and partners during the transition to parenthood.

An important development in the context of the concerns of this book is the work done by the group Critical Research on Men in Europe (CROME) – see Hearn and Pringle with members of CROME (Hearn and Pringle, 2006). Some of this work has expanded, not only comparative analyses (covering countries, especially with the break-up of the Soviet Union not hitherto explored), but also, very explicitly, what is studied. Hearn and Pringle (2006) argue that, in both academic and policy discussions, men's relations to children are often reduced to the issues of fatherhood, paternity and paternal leave and, increasingly, fathers' rights post-separation and divorce. Partly as a result of their concern to question whether the limited increases in paternal activity by some men in the home represent real 'progress' or new creations of patriarchal dominance in relatively novel forms (Hearn and Pringle,

2006: 376), they interrogate particularly lauded countries in terms of age, ethnicity, power and violence in considering men's relations to children. They argue that, while Nordic countries have made provision for child welfare a high priority, levels of violence against women and sexual violence 'do not seem so very different from those in much of Western Europe, even though both countries have high reputations for gender equality policies and practices' (Hearn and Pringle, 2006: 378). Moreover, when employing other and little used criteria to evaluate the relative performance of countries (such as levels of research, legal frameworks, training of welfare professionals) on violence to women and children, then the UK seems to perform better than many Nordic countries. However, such criteria do not seem to have reduced levels of violence. Moreover, there are very serious concerns about how child protection policies and practices in countries such as England deal with men's violence to women. Overall, Hearn and Pringle suggest that more needs to be done to make the welfare responses of the Nordic countries as comprehensive in relation to personal and bodily integrity as they already are in relation to other aspects of welfare.

As indicated at the beginning of this chapter, comparative analyses deserve a book of their own (see Hobson, 2002). A flavour is given here in line with the concern, in this book, to bring voices that do not always speak to each other together (as in those who study violence and those who study paternity leave).

Conclusion

At the time of writing, the legacy that New Labour might leave for a Conservative government to either build on or dismantle is under scrutiny as it hits electoral problems and extremely serious economic difficulties. What legacy will it leave? Has it promoted the kinds of cultural change that would ensure that fathers' rights to care and mothers' rights to work were inextricably located in understandings about the importance of gender inequality? Or has it promoted a particular role for fathers that asserts their 'importance' to children without asking them to do much of their everyday care.

Moreover, Conservative policies have started to be scrutinised as the possibility that it might be the next government looks more likely. David Cameron, the current leader of the Conservatives, has voiced support for significant improvements to parental leave and for this to be available for step-parents and lesbian partners, but at the time of writing policy still seems to be that couples will be privileged in the tax and benefit system, and marriage in particular supported. The influential Centre for Social Justice Report (2007) argued that 'dadlessness' exacerbated children's underachievement and that supporting marriage is essential. In this context, it is important to note comments on developments in Scandinavia in the last decades where it is suggested that partisan politics, as distinct from economic constraints, are the most important factor in shaping welfare states (see Ellingsæter and Leira, 2006b). The Danish experience, where the daddy quota was abolished in 2002 after a right-wing government attained power, is, therefore, instructive (Borchorst, 2006).

Notes

[1] As a result of the economic problems widely publicised in the autumn of 2008, planned leave changes are being threatened (Grice, 2008).

[2] Lewis and Campbell discuss the different terminology that has been used on occasion by the government. They suggest that the kinds of policies that have been adopted mean they should be called work–family balance policies rather than, for example, work–life balance, which implies the balancing of a wider set of considerations.

[3] In December 2008 the European Parliament voted that the opt-out must end and decreed that there should be no exceptions to the 48-hours maximum working time. It is unclear as yet what the response of the UK government will be to this vote.

[4] Nicola Brewer is chief executive of the Equality and Human Rights Commission, a commission established in 2007 that merged a range of separate bodies dealing with gender, 'race' and disability.

[5] The speech was (mis)reported in parts of the media as indicating support for employers who are reluctant to employ women because they were likely to take maternity leave – for a taste of the debates see the editorial in the *New Statesman*, 17 July 2008, and the subsequent letter from Professor Ruth Lister on 24 July 2008.

[6] As Lewis notes, there had been periods of concern before, most notably at the end of the 19th and beginning of the 20th century, about the behaviour of fathers at both ends of the social spectrum and their perceived distance from families.

[7] Scandinavia, strictly speaking, refers to Denmark, Norway and Sweden, and the Nordic countries often include Finland and Iceland, although the terms are used interchangeably in the literature (see Ellingsæter and Leira, 2006).

[8] Hitherto, gay individuals could adopt but not as a couple. As Collier and Sheldon point out, gay male couples can now adopt, though they are classified in law as parents, not as fathers.

[9] At a very basic level, paternity leave can be considered as a statutory entitlement to enable a father to be absent from work for a period of time when a child is born. Parental leave is a statutory entitlement to be absent from work after early maternity and paternity leave (O'Brien et al, 2007: 377).

NINE

Working with fathers

Introduction

This chapter and Chapter Ten focus on practice issues, drawing from a range of research and evaluation projects that the author has been involved in over the last decade. This chapter concentrates on a piece of research in a neglected and difficult area, that where families come to the attention of services because of concerns about violence and neglect. While the findings confirm some well-known issues, some, hitherto unidentified, tensions and dilemmas are explored.

Setting the scene

Service development and underpinning philosophies differ from country to country, reflecting views about the appropriate roles and responsibilities of parents, employers and the state in relation to children and childcare. A very brief outline of the policy context for the research focused on here is offered particularly for readers not familiar with the English context (see Parton, 1985, 1990, 2006).

For much of the 20th century, based on developments in the last quarter of the 19th century, the role of the state was essentially to support the family in the upbringing of children. When the state did intervene, it did so because families were perceived to be failing. As outlined in previous chapters, the post-war welfare state was based on a particular model of the family – the male breadwinner model (see Featherstone, 2004):

> Social work played a vital role in mediating the sometimes ambiguous relationship between the privacy of the family and the public responsibilities of the state to ensure that children did not suffer. While the family was seen as an essentially uncontested social good, acting in the interests of children, social work had a low profile. (Parton, 2006: 3)

Childcare officers, as they were known post-World War Two, were informed by the then influential theories of material deprivation, based on the work of Bowlby, as outlined in Chapter Five. There was a belief that the major social ills of poverty could be solved by the project of social democracy. Thus, if families continued to experience difficulties, this was due to factors such as the early childhood experiences of the parents. Women were the major recipients of services, with an acceptance of the gendered division of labour in the home. While workers were often pragmatic in their approach, the underlying theoretical premises were based on a form of psychodynamic thinking or attachment theory.

As Lewis (2002) notes, there was greater sympathy for the father than there had been in previous decades (see Chapter Three). After two world wars, the cooperation of fathers tended to be assumed and the work habits of working-class men who had proved themselves in battle were no longer regarded with suspicion, as they had been in previous decades. The father's role was considered of marginal importance when it came to the care of his children but his role as economic provider was vital. Unmarried mothers and fathers were considered 'abnormal' and victims.

Neglect and delinquency were the central issues to be tackled. However, in the 1960s, researchers drew attention to the 'battered baby syndrome' whose aetiology was considered to lie in the lack of 'empathic mothering' in parents' childhoods (see Featherstone, 1996). This research was to be pivotal in establishing awareness of 'child abuse' and placed medical professionals at the centre of definitional and diagnostic endeavours (see Parton, 1985). While attempts were made to engage fathers in the treatment required, these were not often successful and the focus remained on mothers.

The 1960s also saw the 'discovery' of poverty, in a context of gendered and generational challenges to post-war social democracy and prevailing power relations. Social work became subject to critique as part of this process. Radical social work challenged prevailing forms of practice. These were considered to be based on assumptions of personal and familial pathology, which failed to acknowledge the wider structural components of people's difficulties. While there were writers who seemed to see little possibility of change within social work, as it was an integral part of the capitalist state, others counselled the need to fight 'in and against' the state (Featherstone, 2005). In this literature, there was an explicit rejection of the psychodynamic underpinnings of earlier approaches (Pearson et al, 1988).

Feminist social work emerged in the 1970s, drawing inspiration from the wider movement. It emphasised the importance of women social workers working with women clients[1] in order to challenge how they were defined (as wives and mothers). The similarities between workers and clients, as women oppressed by patriarchal forces, were highlighted. Such similarities were considered resources to effect change. There is a considerable literature about how this early understanding ran aground in the face of organisational cultures and demands, as well as the changing political climate of the 1970s and 1980s. What is important to note is that, from the onset, feminist social work struggled with whether engaging with men was part of its project (see Cavanagh and Cree, 1996). From the mid-1980s, literature did begin to emerge, often from male practitioners, on the interrelationship between masculinity and problematic male behaviour such as offending.

The 1970s opened with a major reorganisation of services and with the emergence of social services departments funded by local rather than national government. These were designed to have an ambitious remit and move beyond the residualism of previous services. A shadow was cast over these departments very quickly. The death of Maria Colwell, a little girl killed by her stepfather while under social work supervision, meant for one commentator that the 'party had ended' for the new departments almost before they had begun to operate (Bamford, 1990: 3). The economic crisis, calling a halt to the expansion of local government in 1975, was, of course, also highly significant. As has been extensively documented, the death of Maria and the subsequent inquiry led to the development of many of the systems and procedures that characterise contemporary practices (see Parton, 1985). Throughout the 1980s, further high-profile inquiries into the deaths of children reinforced the development of systems for the identification and management of abuse. In comparison to other countries, therapeutic skills and approaches were not used widely, though they were used in the voluntary sector in some areas (see, for example, Dale et al, 1986).

Interestingly, while most of the deaths that received publicity were caused by fathers or father figures, there was little discussion about how to work with such men. The links between violence to women and violence to children became recognised (see Mullender and Morley, 1994) and, as discussed later, a substantial body of procedures and research began to emerge. The behaviour of men, including fathers, towards children was highlighted at the end of the 1980s with a high-profile inquiry into events in Cleveland in the North of England where over a hundred children were removed from their homes because of suspected sexual abuse. Feminists were very keen to focus attention on the importance of recognising that sexual abuse does happen in families and is perpetrated by 'normal' fathers rather than deviant strangers, and the need to explore why this is so. Others focused on the personal distress caused by the interventions of the doctors and social workers involved. It was difficult to get a hearing for perspectives that acknowledged the need to discuss both sets of issues, without being accused of seeking to deny either that sexual abuse occurred or that all men were sexual abusers.

As Parton (2006) notes, the post-war consensus about the role of social work was seriously dented by such high-profile deaths and inquiries. Social workers were deemed to be negligent or ineffectual in the cases involving deaths and over-intrusive in cases concerning sexual abuse. Moreover, a series of revelations concerning the abuse of children, removed from their families and placed in children's homes, contributed further to the denting of the consensus. Thus, social work became feared as too powerful and despised as too weak – perceptions variously shared by parents, children, other professionals and politicians.

In this context, it is probably not that surprising that an anxiety-ridden, defensive, procedurally based form of practice emerged despite periodic attempts, for example, to get social workers to develop more supportive approaches and to work in partnership with parents – for example, *Child Protection: Messages from Research* (DH, 1995). There was little emphasis on developing therapeutic skills (except, to some extent, in terms of working with children) and the contexts in which workers operated were often characterised by a sense of bombardment and overload. Such contexts often did not provide the kinds of environments where workers could think about the work they did.

In 2003, Scourfield published his book on gender and child protection, based on fieldwork carried out in social work offices in the late 1990s. He outlined the following social work discourses about men: as a threat, as no use, as absent, as no different from women and as better than women. The first two were dominant. Women were commonly constructed as oppressed, but responsible for the welfare of their children. By failing to engage men, women were also left to manage the consequences of their problematic behaviour. These points are returned to later.

When New Labour came to power in 1997, it introduced a range of policies for children. These were designed to facilitate early intervention in order to prevent undesirable outcomes such as a lack of employability, involvement in criminality and so on, in line with the desire to construct a social investment state. The practice sites for such policies often involved the creation of new organisations and new professional groupings. But concerns with protecting children from abuse have needed to be integrated into these policies as, yet again, another report from another inquiry into the death of a little girl (Laming, 2003) focused attention on the inadequacies of the systems set up to protect children. *Every Child Matters: The Next Step* (DfES, 2004) set out a broad agenda outlining the key outcomes for children to be achieved by a range of agencies working together.

This new agenda offered the possibility of social workers working with other workers to offer early interventions, to prevent early difficulties escalating and to move away from a focus on risk to considering the needs of children and their parents more holistically. However, it would appear that, while some elements of children's services such as those working in specific projects can do such work, the evidence to date suggests that statutory social work remains defensive and procedurally driven, with the emphasis on e-technology further reinforcing a focus away from relationship-based work. Rather the focus is on assessing, identifying and categorising. This is reinforced by the audit culture that has emerged as a consequence of the emphasis on meeting targets in relation to outcomes (see Peckover et al, forthcoming). The latter means that workers routinely assess within rigid timescales and in accordance with set protocols. Indeed, the tragic death of Baby P in 2007, which received considerable publicity at the end of 2008 after the jailing of the adults responsible, has further highlighted concerns that technological and performance management imperatives have completely eclipsed 'practising' in child protection. The case, moreover, highlights the vital importance of engaging fathers and father figures as addressed in subsequent sections in this chapter.

In the last decade a number of developments have emerged to challenge the above. *The Journal of Social Work Practice* has provided a focus for academics and practitioners who emphasise the importance of taking relationships seriously – relationships with service users and relationships within organisations. Some, such as Froggett (2002), have used Kleinian approaches to explore the importance of working with anger and hate, and represent a very clear rejection of what has become known as anti-oppressive social work. The latter, which to some extent emerged from earlier radical, feminist and anti-racist perspectives, operates with a highly rational view of people's difficulties and what should be done. Binaries such as victimised/good client and victimiser/bad system predominate here (Hoggett, 2000). Moreover, the approach to identity that is generally taken conceives of it in static terms and there is a tendency to think in terms of categories or in additive ways about oppression.

Furthermore, an interesting development has been the exploration of what kinds of social policies can support interconnectedness, which has emerged from those espousing an ethic of care (Williams, 2004). A further development has been a resurgence of interest in attachment theory, although its potential to offer a critique of contemporary directions in practice has been questioned (Taylor, 2004).

Fathers Matter: round 1

The next section explores the first research project in England[2] to focus exclusively on the issues experienced by fathers and paternal relatives whose children are involved with social care services.[3] Most of the research was concerned with social work practice but not all, which is why the term social care was used.

There were two rounds of funding and two phases of the project. The research covered the period when the abolition of social services departments was occurring and the terminology reflects this with many departments in round 1 being called social services, but, by round 2, most were children's services. In terms of the organisation of services, changes were announced in 2004 in *Every Child Matters: The Next Step* (DfES, 2004) with the abolition of the generic social services departments (SSDs) established in the 1970s. Services are now organised into those working with children and those working with adults.

The first round of funding emerged from a successful bid in 2004 by the Family Rights Group, in conjunction with Children Law UK, Fathers Direct (now the Fatherhood Institute), Grandparents Association and a local inner-city London youth organisation SKY Partnership, to develop a project that aimed to identify barriers to the inclusion of fathers and paternal relatives of children within the child welfare system, and to start examining what works and why. The impetus behind the funding bid emerged from increasing numbers of calls from non-resident fathers and paternal relatives to the advice line run by the Family Rights Group. The Grandparents Association had also found that 70% of its calls were from paternal relatives with concerns about their treatment by social services.

The aims of the project were to:

- explore the barriers encountered by fathers and paternal relatives whose children are involved with social services;

- identify effective ways of working with fathers and paternal relatives;
- recommend steps that could be taken by the judiciary, the courts, national government, statutory and voluntary agencies.

Eighteen young fathers were involved in a focus group and 13 older fathers were interviewed individually. Eleven grandparents (five maternal and six paternal) were either involved in a focus group or interviewed individually. Furthermore, eight young mothers were involved in a focus group. The analysis outlined here focuses mainly on the fathers. Mothers' views of social services were more fully considered in round 2 and are dealt with in a subsequent section.

Of the 18 young fathers, their experiences were more often of professionals such as health professionals rather than of social services. Their children were mostly under five, with a number having children under a year old. The majority of the young fathers were from minority ethnic groups and were aged between 15 and 29. Nearly half classified themselves as students and, although one described himself as long-term disabled, no one described himself as unemployed (three indicated they were looking after home/family). While most were still in relationships with the mothers of their children, their living situations were fluid.

The older men ranged in age from 30 to 59. Nearly half were in full-time employment and one in part time. Eleven described themselves as White British. The ages of their children ranged from one to 15 years, with seven children being less than five years of age. Three had children living with them. Two had children who were accommodated,[4] and the rest of the children were living with their mothers. Only one of the men was living with the mother of his children.

The next section draws from the analysis conducted by Featherstone and White (2006) of the transcripts of the focus group with the young fathers and the individual interviews with 11 of the older men.

Dads talk about services

As already discussed in Chapter Seven, the fathers repeatedly spoke of not having any rights. The UK was constructed as 'behind the times', both because fathers had no rights and laws and because services were considered to reflect outmoded notions of fatherhood that constructed fathers as either absent or disinterested.[5]

The state and state agencies were constructed as problematic for men in a number of ways. The state offered women an alternative to economic reliance on men ('now most of them just live off the government'). In general, state services were perceived to be on the side of women, positively offering them money or judging them either more favourably or less harshly than men.

For the men in the focus group, the controlling aspects of the state such as the police and child support agencies were highlighted (their minority ethnic status is of clear relevance here). There was also a sense that, if the police got involved with them and their partner, there would be an automatic assumption that domestic violence by them was an issue. There was also some ignorance about changes in the law that might be construed as positive for such men (such as the law on parental responsibility).

The minority of men who had sought to and succeeded in getting full-time care of their children in the context of a mother's inability, for whatever reason, told stories of struggling against the odds to be involved, listened to and taken seriously. It appeared to require considerable persistence on their part to succeed.

For those with varying degrees of involvement/contact with their children, at least one spoke of being inconsistently mobilised as a resource for the child by social workers. One social worker enlisted him in monitoring the mother's mental health. However, a change of worker meant that his accounts of the mother's deteriorating health were accorded little credibility. More commonly, non-resident fathers' accounts were treated with the utmost suspicion if court proceedings were ongoing.

For those where there were allegations made in relation to men's abuse (mainly sexual abuse), the accounts given denied the abuse and constructed the allegations as part of the woman's campaign to deny contact. This was also alleged to be the case with some allegations of domestic violence.

Across the board, there were very few positive constructions of social workers. Overall, their constructions coalesced around the following themes.

Predictably unpredictable

In general, social workers were constructed as unreliable and unfair (for example, it was OK if they were late for contact visits, but parents were considered to be lacking in commitment if they were). Examples were given of situations where a change in worker had suddenly changed the direction of a case in a bewildering way, or where a change in pace or urgency had not been adequately explained. Furthermore, there were examples of fathers drawing attention to a difficulty/injury and having a child protection investigation that involved them as suspects launched.

The fathers' depiction of the service and workers as predictably unpredictable mirrored how they often constructed the mothers of their children, as discussed later.

Going by the book

Workers were perceived often as doing things because it said so in a book (this did not always refer to procedures but also text or theory books). They did not see people as individuals but as members of categories. These categories, such as 'unemployed' for example, could be profoundly unfair and misleading (they could have just lost their job rather than be long-term unemployed).

On the woman's side

This construction has already been alluded to. It was, however, much more likely to be mobilised by men who had allegations made against them and was also directed at judges and members of the legal profession. However, one father was very anxious about the treatment his ex-partner had received also. There was a recognition that social workers did not treat parents well, although there were felt to be specific issues for fathers, particularly those who were non-resident and without parental responsibility.

Constructions of fathers, mothers and children

The 'father as economic provider' discourse was absent from the men's accounts. This cannot be attributed solely to the economic marginality of these men. A number were at or had been to university, a number were in white-collar jobs. A number had given up work to look after children. Moreover, there was little evidence of investment in a discourse that 'children need fathers'.

Overall, the accounts were of distrust and conflict between women and men. Generally, there was a sense that adult relationships were precarious and, in this context, children were imbued with considerable significance. Children were generally endowed with positive characteristics in stark contrast to their mothers. Indeed, much of the men's accounts constructed children as the source of deep emotional connections, a language that was strikingly absent from their accounts of the relationships with the mothers of their children.

There were indications that most of the men had difficulties with articulating vulnerability in a way that moved them away from an adversarial relationship with their partners. There was evidence of a gendered split around emotionality noted by Hollway (1989) in her analysis of men's and women's accounts of their relationships. Basically, men identified emotionality with women, but they also considered that women used emotionality to get their own way.

As indicated, the state was seen to be on the women's side in terms of welfare benefits and services were often seen, particularly by those involved in private law battles, as on the women's side. While this was also the case in relation to social services, accounts emphasised a more general concern with an unpredictable and inconsistent service.

As already explored in Chapter Seven, rights-based language was the currency traded in to articulate the men's concerns about their treatment by the state and by women. Interestingly, it was also apparent that many in the focus group were unaware of the rights they did have as unmarried fathers (they were unaware, for example, that the law had changed in 2003). They were also unaware of some of the rights they did not have. Some of the older men who had substantial involvement with social services articulated a concern that social workers were also poorly informed about the law.

But what did mothers say?

It is of great interest in light of the above that the majority of the ten young mothers who took part in discussions in round 1 wanted midwives, doctors and nurses to involve the father before, during and after the birth and thought there were many opportunities missed by professionals to help fathers become involved and confident. The mothers also recognised that the months after the birth were a difficult time for the father and that at this time the mothers might be mainly focused on the baby. They acknowledged that as mothers they found it difficult to trust others with the care of the child, but that it might be helpful for the fathers' confidence to have times when they looked after the baby on their own. The mothers recognised the barriers that could be placed in young fathers' way by grandparents and housing for young families.

Fathers Matter: round 2

Further funding was received in 2006 to take the findings of round 1 forward (for a full account of this project and its findings, see Roskill et al, 2008). Just two of the strands of this research will be explored here: work with a number of children's services authorities to develop best practice models and a survey of higher education institutions.

In relation to the work with children's services authorities, there were many elements to this including an audit of case files, meeting with relevant officers, an analysis of relevant policies and focus groups, and interviews with senior managers, senior practitioners and social workers, voluntary organisations working with fathers, and fathers and mothers involved with services. The following areas are focused on here: mothers' views of services for fathers, fathers' views and their presence/absence.

Mothers' views of services for fathers

In all, 17 mothers took part in focus groups. The mothers' living and relationship situations were often complex. This is not surprising given that the audit of cases, discussed further later, highlighted that only a minority of cases involved birth mothers and birth fathers living together with their children:

> There were varying experiences influenced by a kaleidoscope of changing family relationships ... it was sometimes difficult for the mothers to explain exactly what was happening in these complex relationships. (Roskill, 2008: 40)

The mothers were asked specifically about their views on services for birth fathers.

Many of them recognised the need for more groups, parenting courses and services for fathers in their own right. Karen, who lived with the children's father, said:

> You see dads out there over the weekends taking the kids somewhere and I can't help thinking I wish my kids' dad was like that ... He just needs to be pointed in the right direction and guided and supported. (Roskill, 2008: 39)

Furthermore, the absence of parenting courses designed for fathers was perceived as problematic. In particular it meant that parents lacked the opportunity to resolve divergent views on discipline (see also Featherstone, 2004). Mothers often favoured fathers attending a project designed exclusively for them. However, there was recognition of the need to develop a range of provision, as some fathers would never attend a fathers' group.

The mothers also articulated a sense that fathers were missing out on positive sources of support. For example, some mothers valued the specific help they had received and felt strongly that fathers should have something similar of their own.

Anger management courses were mentioned as a resource that children's services should provide, especially in situations of domestic violence. It is important to note, in this context, that it was apparent that domestic violence, alongside substance misuse issues was a feature of many of the cases on workers' caseloads (see Roskill, 2008).

While women recognised and, indeed, some had experience of situations where fathers needed to be removed, many did want social work practice to change in terms of involving fathers. A quote from one mother captures much of what was said:

> They [the social workers] don't ask the fathers anything or try and involve them. Because they don't know what to do they are nervous ... should be encouraging them and showing them that it's OK to be involved. They should remember and not just ignore them. (Roskill, 2008: 42)

A key issue that emerges from the audit of cases is that there were many gaps in the recording of the legal status of both mother and father – the child's birth father was not named on file in 13 out of 67 cases. There were 17 children where there was no information on parental responsibility of the father. Of the sample of 67, 13 birth fathers lived in the household.

Only eight fathers were involved in data gathering, as they proved difficult to recruit. Their views are mentioned briefly, as there are similarities with the analysis presented above. Workers were considered to be unreliable and uninterested in listening to fathers. The fathers also argued that power needed to be more evenly shared between workers and parents.

Survey of education

In round 1 accounts, fathers suggested that not all workers appeared to have an accurate knowledge of the law. Moreover, their accounts suggested a lack of consultation and involvement in assessment and intervention processes. It was also felt their potential to offer a positive contribution to their children was not mobilised adequately.

It was, therefore, decided to seek funding in round 2 to survey higher education institutions offering qualifying social work training in order to identify the following: teaching inputs on fathers; the placement opportunities for working specifically with fathers; the involvement of fathers as service users on courses; and their self-assessment of strengths, obstacles and the help required.

A full account of this study is available (Featherstone, 2008) but the following offers a summary of some of the key themes that emerged from a survey of institutions (27 out of 110), a seminar with nine educators and telephone interviews. The author is unaware of a previous audit of teaching about fathers on qualifying courses in social work in the UK, although one survey has been carried out and is in the process of being written up in Canada (Walmsley, 2008, personal communication). So, while what follows is from a small study, it is of interest.

The main teaching about fathers took place on human growth and development courses although it was unclear what exactly was taught there. This is an important issue as it is unclear whether developmental psychological inputs are being used without any critical interrogation, as Taylor (2004) suggests is happening.

Just under half indicated they did *not* teach about fathers in their law teaching. Of those who did, two indicated it was brief or cursory and related to 'rights', a further one said it was concerned solely with domestic violence.

Just over half indicated they provided some input on working with men and women on their relationships, but three said this was solely or primarily in the context of domestic violence. One also indicated it was 'in passing'. One institution ran a module on Sexuality in Social Work Practice, which encompassed exploring sex and intimacy in heterosexual and gay relationships (and looked at the role of gay fathers).

Eight indicated their courses did examine working with men around domestic violence and fathering issues, although one indicated this was 'in passing'. One course had specific expertise in this area as it was involved in evaluating a project in this field of work. One respondent indicated that his/her emphasis was to promote a positive view of fathers and therefore this input would be too negative. One respondent noted they did not do this work, even though there was a 'prison within minutes of the campus'.

Fifteen indicated some input in their course about Family Group Conferences (FGCs), but, of those, six said it was brief or very limited. One did indicate that this particular teaching had highlighted the importance of fathers being involved with a video and case study, addressing this as an 'example of good practice'.

The response rate to the survey was low and most of those who responded indicated that they were not teaching much about fathers. Moreover, at the seminar held to discuss the findings of the survey, the respondents felt that the culture on social work courses was geared towards equipping students with rather limited and short-term approaches to practising as social workers. Students were equipped with knowledge of the latest procedures and policies rather than being educated to be critical and reflective practitioners. Respondents felt that the curriculum increasingly reflected a construction of practice that had moved away from relationship-based work and that was based on social workers meeting quite rigid targets for the completion of assessments and so on. Moreover, it was considered that gender was not emphasised in the curriculum, or in practice, in comparison with previous decades.

Discussion

There is a small but growing literature from a range of countries on the challenges in involving fathers in services where there are concerns about abuse or neglect.[6] For example, Ferguson and Hogan (2004) researched fathers, mothers and workers in the Republic of Ireland; Sabla (2007) is conducting research in Germany; Fleming (2007) in Australia; Dominelli (2007) in Canada; Scourfield (2003) has researched occupational culture in the UK; and Daniel and Taylor (2001) and Featherstone (2001a, 2003) have reviewed the research literature.

A host of issues have been rehearsed in the literature above: the woman-dominated nature of the workforce, societal assumptions that child welfare is women's business and workers' fears of violent men. The Fathers Matter research above highlights some less well-rehearsed issues. These are explored in turn and echo some of the issues already highlighted in previous chapters. They include the following. Who is the father? What do mothers want? The issues involved in working with men and domestic violence are explored. The power of language is also considered briefly. Finally, some reflections are offered on the context in which services to children and their mothers and fathers are delivered currently.

Who is the father?

First, who should be engaged with? Should a birth father be engaged with even though a stepfather has been involved for many years? What about a mother's boyfriend? What criteria can and should be used to make a case for 'engaging' him? What if that causes conflict with the birth father? What if the children in the family have differing fathers?

The Fathers Matter research underscores the complexity of the task and the emotionally laden territory that we may be asking workers to enter. While the women, many of whom were living apart from the birth father, wanted services involved, there is a need to do more research on this. Furthermore, it seems social work courses may not be equipping social workers with the kinds of training they need to enter such territory. Family Group Conferences have emerged as an important method for engaging with the complexities of family relationships and also seem to have some success in engaging men, but, as the findings above outline, there is often little input on them on training courses and they are not available routinely (see Featherstone, 2004, for an exploration of the concept of FGCs; and Featherstone et al, 2007, for a discussion of the research on engaging men).

What do mothers want?

This research begins an important conversation about mothers' views about father involvement and the role of services. It is very limited, however, and much more research is needed (see Ferguson and Hogan, 2004, for research with mothers in the Republic of Ireland). An important finding from the Fathers Matter research is that women wanted services for fathers, including birth fathers. While the study was not a study of maternal identities, and did not enquire into what kinds of involvement the women wanted the men to have with their children, some of the comments suggested that it was either to 'back up' the women around discipline issues, or to engage in leisure activities with the children at weekends.

As has already been explored in Chapters Five and Six, mothers can play important roles in facilitating as well as obstructing father involvement. Doucet's (2006a) research suggests that mothers lead in taking down gender borders, or opening gates, so that men can participate more fully in parenting. However, there is a need to do more research in this area and it is likely that there will be diverse conceptions of what father involvement might consist of. Furthermore, one mother's perception of involvement as supportive may not be matched by that of another, who may perceive it as supplanting or usurping her role.

There may also be a need for caution about assumptions that fathers who are, or wish to be, actively involved in childcare, are doing so for positive reasons. For example, a small-scale study, by Harne (2005) with fathers who were violent towards their partners (what she called 'domestically violent' fathers), found that for some men a key way of further undermining the mother and reducing her self-esteem was to take over childcare.

Women wanted services for men in situations where men were being violent and, indeed, anger management courses were mentioned specifically. (It was noted in Chapter Seven that feminists offering services in this area do not consider such courses are appropriate.) The issues in relation to what should be offered are returned to in a later section. Here, it is important to reflect on some of the tensions in the current policy and practice climate in relation to men, fathering and domestic violence.

There have been important legislative, policy and practice developments in relation to domestic violence and child protection in the last decade, particularly under New Labour (see Featherstone and Peckover, 2007). Recognition that violence to women may also be accompanied by violence to children, and, moreover, that children are adversely affected by witnessing violence towards their mothers, means the issue has been placed firmly on the child protection agenda.

The research evidence suggests, however, that women's and children's needs are still being inadequately addressed in practice. Indeed, not only may they not receive appropriate services, women may be considered as 'failing to protect' their children if domestic violence is ongoing and the man remains in the household whether against their will or not. (The concept of 'failure to protect' does not seem to be used against violent men, however.)

Scourfield (2003) has called for practices to engage directly with such men. Featherstone and Peckover (2007) have argued for a joining up of government agendas in relation to fostering father involvement in families and tackling domestic violence, thus challenging the split constructions of 'father' and perpetrator underpinning policies.

Furthermore, programmes for violent men are often offered only to those mandated to attend by the courts. However, according to the research into police call-outs, there is a range of 'fateful moments' at which resources might be offered. According to Webb (2006), drawing from the work of Giddens discussed in Chapter Six, fateful moments are 'critical moments at which consequential decisions have to be taken or courses of action initiated by people that may leave them feeling helpless, resulting in the need for support' (Webb, 2006: 15). The response to such 'fateful moments' currently seems to suggest that women who call out the police to incidents are often left feeling helpless. Furthermore, they are likely to receive a response from social services that suggests that, by getting beaten up, they are failing to protect their children.

Rather than simply attempting to rectify this by offering appropriate support directed at women, a crucial part of the intervention must be to find ways of engaging men about their behaviour. A way in is to appeal to men as fathers. Naming such men as fathers opens up a number of possibilities. In a situation of resource constraints, resources may be more easily available if it is argued that it will have some spin-off for children. Appealing to men as fathers may help key into fathers' own desires in relation to a more nurturing fatherhood model.

However, as noted previously, research suggests that some fathers' involvement with their children can be linked to their desire to retain control and further undermine women. Moreover, there are dangers in appealing to and developing policies for violent men as fathers as it may reinforce the belief that domestic violence matters only when it impacts on children. It is thus important that the resources offered are located within understandings of gendered inequalities and men's responsibilities. As outlined in Featherstone et al (2007), a model of treatment has become hegemonic in work with the perpetrators of domestic violence in England and Wales. This work stresses the importance of engaging with power and control issues, and favours cognitive behavioural approaches to the treatment offered. However, it is important to avoid orthodoxy and dogma in this very difficult and anxiety-provoking area and adopting one model, while offering the comfort of certainty, runs many dangers. There is a need to engage with individual biographical experiences of power and powerlessness and work with men's stories of why they do what they do, rather than assuming the answers can be contained in a manual. This does not preclude the need for very clear ground rules as well as paying the utmost attention to safety planning for women and children.

What 'should' happen when women do not want men involved and there is no violence? What 'should' happen when men want to be involved more than women want them to be? Smart and Neale (1999) have explored this issue in relation to divorce and separation in ways that are of interest for practitioners. They identified two modes of exercising power and correspondingly two types of experiences of powerlessness in the post-divorce situation:

> … there might be a deployment of *debilitative* power, which
> is experienced as an effacement of the self, and on the other
> hand there is a *situational* power (deriving from the fact that
> women are mostly the primary carers of children while
> men are usually responsible for financial support) which is
> experienced as an inability to control others and a denial of
> rights. (Smart and Neale, 1999: 146, emphasis in original)

Debilitative power was seen as an attempt to stop the other from
becoming a new self or from discovering their old selves. Situational
power referred to tangible resources such as court orders in relation
to residence, time available with children and so on. Fathers in divorce
situations commonly experience women as having too much situational
power. Mothers, by contrast, in Smart and Neale's study suggested
that they suffered most from the exercise of debilitative power where
the partner took more than they gave and put obstacles in the way of
personal autonomy. We saw in Chapter Seven that this latter form of
powerlessness is raised rarely as an issue even by women's groups. Indeed,
Smart and Neale suggest that it is only situational power imbalances
that are recognised as legitimate. They argue that 'any mediation or
conciliation process that does ignore the interaction between these
differential forms of power continues to place mothers' needs below
those of fathers and fails to acknowledge the importance of the mother's
self-esteem to the future welfare of the children' (Smart and Neale,
1999: 147). The tensions and dilemmas raised here are returned to in
the next chapter when discussing the case of Paul.

The power of language

The Fathers Matter research suggests the need for more careful
explorations of 'talk'. There was evidence of a misfit between social
workers' and other professionals' repertoires for ascribing moral worth
to parents and many fathers' accounts of fatherhood. In particular, rights-
based arguments are likely to fall on fallow ground with professionals
who invoke notions of parents' responsibilities and are likely to consider
fathers who invoke rights as selfish or not appropriately concerned
with their children's welfare. Fathers too, because of their perceptions
of agencies and often their ambivalence about help-
seeking, may resist engaging in the kinds of talk that are required to
ensure more positive outcomes.

Professionals need to be able to engage with fathers' talk and versions
of events in an open and exploratory way – that is, to adopt a position

of 'respectful uncertainty' and 'not knowing', avoiding premature foreclosure and precipitous categorisations. This is compatible with Ferguson and Hogan's (2004) call for 'conversations of curiosity'.

Reflections on complexity in a context of denial

As already indicated, social work with children and families in statutory settings has been dominated by defensive and procedurally driven approaches for a number of decades. Offering workers time and space to reflect on the pain, anger and deprivation they encounter daily does not appear to be a feature of everyday practices. To some extent, practices with men around fathering expose writ-large endemic features of the contemporary context. As Ferguson and Hogan (2004) note, and as discussed further in the next chapter, men's bodies become encoded with danger in a context where workers feel highly anxious about danger and the consequences for them of not spotting dangers to children. As the research from the Fathers Matter project indicates, fathers may struggle to accept that they have responsibilities towards others, particularly in contexts where they are behaving oppressively.

While there are a host of recommendations that can be made to ensure that services engage fathers in more positive ways than they do currently, and these are outlined further in the next chapter, it is hard not to feel pessimistic about an overall context that denies workers the time and space they need to engage with the complexities they encounter daily.

Conclusion

This chapter outlines findings from a small piece of research into a neglected area – fathers and social care services, particularly where there are concerns about the abuse of children. An interesting finding is that women want services to engage fathers, although family situations were often complex in relation to who or where the father was and much more research is required in this area. It would appear that practitioners might not be equipped to deal with the complexities of the relationships they encounter. Many of the men who responded to this research reported considerable anxiety about how much power the mothers of their children had and little belief that services were interested in their needs. Those who had involvement with social workers reported an unreliable and inconsistent service.

Notes

[1] This was the terminology of the time. It has, over the decades, been replaced by service user.

[2] The Family Rights Group (FRG) campaigns in England and Wales but funding was from the Parenting Fund, which is concentrated on England, so the data was collected in England. There is a small amount of evidence available in round 2 on social work courses in England, Scotland, Wales and Northern Ireland.

[3] While not a member of the original funding bid for round 1, the author was approached at the end of 2004 to become a member of the steering group and became involved in a range of activities with the project including the work outlined in Featherstone and White (2006). In round 2, she took the lead in the research with social work courses.

[4] This means they were living in some form of state care, either with a foster family or in residential care.

[5] Services were 'behind the times' was a point emphasised by the young Black father at the Fathers Matter conference in May 2008.

[6] There are considerable difficulties with terminology here, especially when discussing different countries.

TEN

Reflections on a decade of working with fathers

This chapter reflects on a range of research and evaluation projects engaged with by the author in a variety of contexts in the last decade. As Chapter Eight noted, a boost to work in this area in England was the funding of a range of initiatives under the family support grant at the Home Office[1] in 1999. Since then a range of specialist and mainstream initiatives have been funded. The chapter explores some of the research and evaluation initiatives the author has been involved in. It identifies some of the key issues when considering who will engage fathers, the differing contexts in which the work will be carried out, and the implications of engaging with diversity, complexity and vulnerability in relation to men who father.

Meeting fathers: a learning process

In 1999 the author was involved in the evaluation of a project seeking to engage young fathers in a centre offering a variety of activities to men, women and children (see Featherstone, 2003, 2004). The men who eventually did engage with the specially recruited woman worker were mainly White, young and unemployed.

The centre hosting the project was involved in government developments to foster employability and the men were initially attending in that context. Thus workers who asked about their fatherhood status and invited them to take part in activities were treated with suspicion. Why were the men being called upon as fathers? Was it for child support purposes? And, indeed, the fathers' suspicions keyed into an important aspect of this agenda. This was an early lesson in the need to engage with the variety of differing agendas motivating this work and the delicate tensions in relation to government sponsored initiatives in this area.

The importance of working with mothers was highlighted in this evaluation. Many of the men were not living with the mothers of their children and had contact difficulties. The worker often had little choice but to get involved with such difficulties. Her work often seemed to reassure mothers anxious about contact and fathers' parenting skills. As has already been noted in Chapter Seven, the fear of violence is not the only reason women may resist contact by men.

This project did highlight that workers can work with men and women around very difficult issues in a way that was able to acknowledge pain and disappointment, and move matters forward in helpful and respectful rather than damaging ways. One young father's story (Paul)[2] is of interest here. Having spent his childhood in local authority care, he was thrilled to become a father, but the relationship with the mother broke down. She had a new partner and was now denying him contact. Paul did not have parental responsibility and it was prior to the change in the law. The resources offered by the project, including the support offered by other fathers, were very important. It is pertinent in this context to reflect on the research in Chapter Seven suggesting that men often turn to fathers' groups because they seek support in such circumstances. In this case the worker was obliged to work with conflicting needs and there were no happy endings in any straightforward sense. While law and policy increasingly incline towards birth fathers, it is important to continue to affirm the mother's concerns as legitimate also. This does not mean that she, or indeed he, will get what they want, but it does mean that they are both recognised as needing to be heard. Merely intoning, as is often the case, that all that matters is the welfare of the child is just a means to short-circuit painful discussions. It is also useful to reflect on Smart and Neale's (1999) observations about different types of power, as outlined in the previous chapter.

A parenting group for fathers was also evaluated (Featherstone, 2001b). As outlined in Chapter Eight, New Labour extended and developed initiatives compelling parents to take responsibility for their children's behaviour. These included attending parenting programmes. The majority of those who have participated in such programmes have been mothers (see Ghate and Ramalla, 2002). This evaluation of a small parenting programme directed at fathers opened up interesting and important issues, particularly in relation to the danger of 'one size fits all' approaches. All of the men but one had been compelled by court order (under the 1998 Crime and Disorder Act) to attend the programme because their sons were offending. These were men who were separated from the mother of the child (or in one case the mother had died) and had only recently taken on full-time care. All characterised themselves as unemployed and as White British. The one man attending voluntarily was a lone father of many years duration. He was desperately seeking help to manage a son who had been diagnosed with a form of attention deficit disorder. He did not identify with the other men on the programme and considered them as 'deadbeat' fathers. Indeed, it appeared that he had been inappropriately placed in a provision because of categorical thinking and that his resentment of this was justified. As far as he was concerned he had more in common with mothers who were caring for children than the other fathers who had been made subject of court orders in order to access help.

Analysis of group discussions and individual interviews suggested that the other fathers were, indeed, ambivalent about their identities as fathers and the process of receiving help. It is also important to note that this was not straightforward and reinforces the significance of interrogating the context in which help is being offered. A number of the men recognised they needed help, although they rejected the need for compulsion. They considered the imposition of a court order on them because of their sons' behaviour unfair (see Chapter Eight). All had considerable personal needs of their own in terms of mental health, addiction and relationship issues. A prescribed programme, focused on improving parenting skills, was rejected by the men, who considered they needed to get to 'know' their children and wanted sessions with them and their children together. In the author's opinion, attention to their own needs might also have increased their appreciation of the help being offered. Although it is unwise to draw parallels too closely, it is interesting, in this context, to note that workers on parenting groups directed at mothers were often able to overcome women's resistance because they attended to their concerns about violence, debt and so on (see Ghate and Ramalla, 2002).

Clearly, this evaluation raised the importance of attending to diversity within the category 'father', as well as complexity. Furthermore, fathers at different stages of their lives may be negotiating a range of complex relationships including former and current partners and children from different relationships, and have been intermittently absent from and present in children's lives. This is returned to later.

The author was also involved in a consultancy for a local Sure Start programme seeking a review of the literature on engaging with fathers in relation to post-natal depression and domestic violence (Featherstone and Manby, 2003). When advising the project on whether, and how, it should work with fathers around violence issues, it became apparent that resources would also need to be devoted to safety planning for women and children (see Featherstone and Peckover, 2007). This area of work exposed writ large the dangers of working only with men. However, when considering how best to work on post-natal depression, the limitations of working only with women were apparent. The roles that men could play as buffers for children in the context of a mother's depression as well as support the mother are important. Acknowledgement of the contribution that men's violence or unsupportive behaviour can make to women's depression is also important.

Engaging fathers: policy and practice

As outlined in Chapter Eight, there appears to have been a change in language in some of the government documents directed at practitioners, reflecting an increased emphasis on naming parents as mothers and fathers. A number of these are as follows: *Every Parent Matters* (DfES, 2007); *Aiming High for Children: Supporting Families* (HM Treasury and DfES, 2007); *The Children's Plan: Building Brighter Futures* (DCSF, 2007).

Many of the documents repeat each other, so this section takes *Every Parent Matters* as typical in exemplifying some of the difficulties with contemporary policy injunctions for services:

> Fathers matter to children's development. Father–child relationships – be they positive, negative or lacking – have profound and wide ranging impacts on children that last a lifetime, particularly for children from the most disadvantaged backgrounds. Research shows that where fathers have early involvement in a child's life: there is a positive relationship to early educational achievement; there is an association with good parent–child relationships in adolescence; and children in separated families are protected from mental health problems. (DfES, 2007: 6)

While the above statements capture important elements of the research, they are also misleading. It is worth reminding ourselves of the points made in Chapter Five. A systematic review of studies where maternal involvement had been controlled for, and where data had been gathered from different independent sources, found a beneficial impact of 'positive' father involvement in children's lives (Pleck and Masciardrelli, 2004). As noted in Chapter Five, what counts as positive depends to some extent on the theoretical models of the psychologists and sociologists and the age of the child, but there are certain commonalities: activities likely to promote an emotionally secure environment and well-being in its broadest sense, such as warm, responsive and sensitive interaction, monitoring and guiding behaviour to set limits, spending time to listen and talk about the child's concerns, encouraging age-appropriate independent action, caring for the child's physical welfare. A key point made by many researchers is that:

> Father involvement cannot be separated from the network of family relationships within which it is embedded. The couple relationship is a key one, setting the scene against which parents negotiate and balance their family and employment roles and responsibilities. Research suggests that high paternal involvement is 'grounded' in harmonious couple relationships. (O'Brien, 2005: 9)

This is important, alerting us to the dangers of abstracting father involvement or activities from the overall relationship context in which they operate. Government documents repeatedly point out the educational benefits for children if fathers are 'involved' with them. The evidence highlights the importance of locating father involvement contextually. For example, Goldman (2005) points out that fathers are more likely to be involved if the child's mother is involved in the child's learning and education, they have good relations with the mother, they or the child's mother have relatively high educational qualifications, they get involved early on, their child is in primary school rather than secondary school and the school welcomes parents. The strongest association is with the level of mother's involvement.

However, in the documents outlined above, the father–child relationship is constructed as a dyad, with mothers disappearing as key players. For example, the Children's Plan argues for engagement with both mothers and fathers except where there is a clear risk to the child to do so. While this may be intended to encompass a range of potential possibilities in relation to risk, it avoids any discussion of gendered inequalities in relation to violent behaviour and produces children as the only legitimate objects of concern.

The promotion of gender equality is not mentioned as a policy objective. Moreover, there is an absence of discussion on what would be considered success in engagement or any real attention to the detail of what involvement might look like. Would it be sharing equally in housework, for example?

Where mothers do appear in the documentation their construction is problematic. For example, *Every Parent Matters* (DfES, 2007) outlines the barriers to father involvement with services as follows: insensitive services; the overtly female focus and culture of services, which is manifest in a lack of confidence about explaining to female service users why it is important to engage fathers; finally, services are considered to underestimate the significance of a father's involvement if he is not visible or living with the child. All of these factors are located in a service deficit approach that locates the 'failures' to engage fathers solely at the hands of services. Thus there is no engagement with the complexities of gender and help-seeking and, indeed, some men's resistance to engaging with their children. These points are returned to later. Here, what is of interest is that mothers or 'female service users' are portrayed so simplistically. They do not understand the importance of father involvement. Moreover, women workers have not got the confidence to explain it to them. However, as discussed in a range of places in this book, maternal gatekeeping is quite a complex phenomenon. Women can range from actively obstructing men's involvement to positively embracing it for a variety of very complex reasons linked to their investment in gendered identities and their understandings of children's needs. These are interrogated in the context of their own particular experiences of real men and children. Their lack of knowledge about the importance of father involvement may be a factor, but research on divorce discussed in Chapter Seven suggests it is unlikely to be a key factor.

While most of the documents aimed at workers are guidance only and may have limited impact, the Gender Equality Duty, which came into force in April 2007, obliges a range of public bodies to proactively promote equality between men and women and take into account their differing needs when making policies and providing services, and not just react to complaints when things go wrong.

In the next sections the author explores some of the issues that she considers of importance in thinking about taking work with fathers forward. First she considers issues in relation to who and where, before looking at how in the context of diversity and complexity. Finally, a key question must be why?

Who will do this work?

Certain areas of employment tend to be seen in gendered terms as primarily masculine or feminine (Christie, 2006). However, gender and professional identities are reproduced in work environments that are changing. One aspect of late modernity is the way that many forms of paid work are becoming feminised, with knowledge and skills associated with femininity gaining new status.

The extent of the change that is under way should not be exaggerated. For example, Rolfe et al (2003) highlighted that men comprise only 2% of the childcare and early years sector. The sector is dependent on young, predominantly White, women and difficulties with recruitment have emerged as such women have been able to get other, better-paid, opportunities in the last decade. More generally, the demand for care workers has been increasing at the same time as demographic and economic trends have been reducing the pool from which they would usually come.

Brannen et al (2007) studied the work and family lives of four groups of workers caring for vulnerable children: residential social workers; family support workers; foster carers; and childminders. Using a time perspective, they examined what motivated care workers to care, why and when they entered the childcare workforce and what developing a career in childcare work might mean in practice. Although they found a similar demographic picture as outlined above, their sample of foster carers comprised a third from minority ethnic groups and, as they indicate, may partly reflect the geographical base of their study.[3] They suggest that gender is likely to remain a crucial issue affecting the different routes that men and women take in care work, including the rewards they seek and the competencies they bring. Interestingly, rather than advocating men being brought into working with children, they advocate more possibilities for women to become managers and increase their qualifications.

There are a number of studies that have explored the issues for men entering 'women's' occupations such as social work (see, for example, Christie, 2006). Not surprisingly, a key theme here is the ways in which men negotiate their identities within dominant understandings of masculinity. Cameron et al (1999) have explored 'men in the nursery', identifying a range of important issues in relation to confusion over why men were being introduced and what models of masculinity they were being expected to promote.

As Hearn (2002) notes, men are present in welfare organisations as service users, workers, managers and policy makers. The views of managers and workers were sought in the Fathers Matter project outlined in the last chapter in relation to the issues involved in engaging fathers. Scourfield (2003) also explored some compatible issues in relation to gender and occupational culture. It does not seem possible, in the view of the author, to discern gendered differences between men and women managers or workers in relation to this area. It would seem that there is a need for research that explores whether occupational culture overrides gender identity.

An interesting area concerns men as foster carers. As part of the research for this book a male foster carer who had worked in this area for many years (John),[4] and who had also organised a number of men in foster care groups, was interviewed. A number of issues that would benefit from further research emerged from this interview. Some men attending the groups did so to voice their anger at their treatment by social workers. They felt marginalised in relation to their role (for example, when social workers rang up, they asked to speak to their female partners). This could lead to them deciding to absent themselves from what might have been embarked on as a joint enterprise and, in worst-case scenarios, redefine it as 'the woman's job' and not offer support.

A very important issue was that the emphasis on 'safe care' (this is the training that foster carers receive on how to care for children safely and is very anxiety provoking for them in a high-risk climate) often seemed overly focused on men. There was very little emphasis on what men could offer that was positive. Single male foster carers are rare and have to develop strategies to ensure their practices as carers are not misconstrued (see Gabb, 2008, for a discussion of sexuality, intimacy and risk issues).

It seems unlikely in the near future that many men will enter, or if they do will stay long term, many of the social care sectors at the level of offering a direct service. In this context it is important to note that, for those men who have engaged in projects exploring their needs as fathers, the gender of the worker is often not as important as their attitude. However, we do need to reflect on whether many of the government initiatives outlined above are going to continue to rely on low-paid women workers to carry out the project of 'engaging fathers'.

Where will this work be done?

The question of 'place and social care' has been interrogated from a variety of perspectives. Workers of both genders often deal with men, women and children and their 'private' troubles in 'private' places and translate them into public concerns needing public remedies. Social work has been called an invisible trade (Pithouse, 1987) where workers talk to people in homes and then bring back accounts to their managers or other agencies. Home visits can offer particular challenges when dealing with vulnerability, pain, anger and violence in contexts offering few opportunities for containment.

Centre-based work brings differing issues. Many practice guides talk of the importance of making spaces such as centres more male-friendly, putting up posters of men and babies and so on. This is not unimportant but does need to be integrated into more thoughtful discussions about the meanings of space in the context of gendered identities. The men in Doucet's (2006a) study spoke of their own and women's discomfort on entering 'women's' spaces.

Cameron et al (1999) emphasised the importance of managers and workers taking time to discuss and reflect on such discomfort and the anxieties that might arise.

If the Gender Equality Duty is interpreted simplistically as about men having the 'right' to attend services, as some fathers' groups seem to want to argue, this is likely to be unhelpful (see Ghate et al, 2000, on research on fathers and family centres). Workers, in order to do the kinds of work explored further later, need to be able to engage with their fears and anxieties about men entering what have often been 'women-only' spaces.

How will work be done?

A literature of the 'how to' variety has emerged. Lloyd (2001) and Bartlett and Burgess (2005) offer practice guidelines on the following: the recruitment of fathers to projects, their retention, staffing issues and the organisational barriers and supports. Both these texts are based on some limited research as well as 'practice wisdom'. The latter would seem to be important given that practice developments are still at a relatively early stage. More conventional academic research projects include Ghate et al's (2000) study of how family centres do or do not engage men and the barriers and obstacles. Daniel and Taylor (2001) have brought together literature including research findings on practice developments from a range of disciplines and countries in order to support health and social care practitioners seeking to engage fathers. The funding of Sure Start programmes since 1999 has provided impetus for work on engaging fathers in early years settings and has been subject to evaluation (Lloyd et al, 2003). This book does not offer a checklist of what works. In this section, it offers some thoughts on the issues involved in working with diversity and complexity.

In relation to diversity, it has been noted that much of the policy focus has been on the rights and responsibilities of birth fathers, but, as the research suggests, they are often absent from the families that some services engage with. Kiernan (2006) suggests that non-resident fathers may go through diverse paternal careers in terms of financial contributions, residence and contact. As the analysis of the parenting programme outlined previously indicates, fathers can 'come back' into children's and young people's lives and play an important role. However, as the Fathers Matter research shows, social workers often know little about these fathers and do not even record their details. Research suggests that workers need to be wary of making any assumptions about the 'absence' of the 'absent' birth father. It is unwise to assume that, because a father is not resident, he is not actively involved in caring for, and about, his children. Equally, a father may be present but absent through long hours at work, for example. Presence and absence are unreliable guides in terms of assessing caring about, and caring for usually implies caring about but not always.

Insights from the research on stepfathers are important to engage with. The category of stepfather is often problematic, as it can obscure relationships of considerable diversity in relation to duration and commitment. Some researchers suggest stepfathers face challenges materially and emotionally. Chapter Two, for example, indicates the families are usually larger. Brannen et al's (2002) research with children in differing family types[5] would indicate that, while love and care provided consistently on an everyday basis is more important to children than family structure, birth parents, no matter what family form they lived in, were very important and stepfathers often struggled with a range of emotional and practical issues.

There are also a host of issues to consider in relation to ethnicity. As indicated in Chapter One, South Asian fathers in one consultation undertaken by the author spoke of the need for flexibility in relation to service provision and, in particular, the need to develop differing opening hours. More difficult questions are raised when services engage with diverse cultures and beliefs in a context of considerable mobility of populations. While much remains to be done, a number of practice resources have emerged, as outlined by the Fatherhood Institute (2008d). For example, a conference, 'Searching for Dad, Exploring Muslim Fatherhood', which was a collaboration between An-Nisa Society (a Muslim women's group), Fathers Direct and *Q News* (a Muslim magazine) in 2006 highlighted a range of projects in differing contexts. Moreover, a guide, *Working with Muslim Fathers, A Guide for Practitioners*, was developed and at the time of writing is available (Fatherhood Institute, 2008d). An-Nisa, an organisation managed by women working for the welfare of Muslim families since 1985, has developed a range of projects from a faith-based perspective: Islamic counselling, supplementary religious education, sexual health, gender, marital issues, parenting and fathering.

The website of the Fatherhood Institute also has a section on African-Caribbean fathers. As has been explored in a number of chapters in this book, a great deal of attention has focused on such fathers in more recent years in the UK. There is a long tradition in the US of concern about 'absent' Black fathers (see Chapter Six). Indeed the remarks by President Barack Obama (Bosman, 2008) during his campaign about the need for Black fathers to shoulder their responsibilities sharply reignited debates that have been in evidence there since the publication of a report by Daniel Moynihan on Black disadvantage in the 1960s (see Daniels, 1998).

The deaths of young boys in gun and knife crime incidents in recent years in the UK have opened up such debates here. For example, when the Reach Report was published in 2007 calling for more Black role models, Black journalists such as Joseph Harker (2007a) suggested that this obscured very important issues about the roles and responsibilities of fathers. As we saw in the last chapter, organisations such as the SKY Partnership have been working with young Black fathers and mothers around what they perceive as their needs from a frame that seeks to build their capacity to care for their children (see also Fatherhood Institute, 2008e).

Recently, the issue of diversity in relation to fathers has been considered within a frame of 'vulnerability' (see, for example, Burgess, 2007). Here, issues such as age, substance misuse, mental health problems, disability, involvement in crime and imprisonment are considered. In terms of age, it is important to think about the needs of young fathers, but also recognise the role that grandfathers may play in some children's lives.

An important contribution has come from Ferguson and Hogan (2004) who have also used the term 'vulnerable' in relation to the kinds of men in the families encountered by social workers. Here, children are being neglected and abused, and both mothers and fathers are struggling with their own experiences of emotional pain and economic and social marginality to be the kinds of parents and partners they often want to be.

Ferguson and Hogan (2004) argue that changing fathers is not simply about finding ways of equipping them with techniques to manage destructive behaviours and acquiring better parenting 'skills' in some limited technical sense. Where significant change occurs, therapeutic and support work with the men, often in tandem with their partners and children, leads fathers to question the basis of their identity as men (Ferguson and Hogan, 2004: 73). They argue that it is important to use Connell's (1995) notion of hegemonic masculinity, not because it is how men are, but because it helps to understand cultural ideals and influences. As already highlighted, Ferguson and Hogan suggest that constructions of hegemonic masculinity in welfare practices are heavily infused with notions of risk and danger. It is the most marginal men who are seen to embody danger and risk and who are most likely to be judged in this way. This way of seeing men constitutes what Ferguson and Hogan call a 'hegemonic fixation' that has to be worked through by professionals.

In his book in 2004, Ferguson argues for the need to construct such fears and anxieties openly, rather than hide behind procedures. There, are, of course, serious difficulties with doing so in the current climate of defensive managerialism in many welfare organisations, such as social work, as outlined in the previous chapter.

Ferguson and Hogan (2004) also identified men's feeling of failure on becoming the subject of interventions and having to let go of something precious to see how they saw themselves as men. Featherstone et al (2007) in explorations of differing practice models in working with men have also talked of men's resistance to admitting they needed help, which can be compounded by being forced, for example, by the courts.

The particular issues for men at different stages of their lives or with differing needs have been studied to an extent using insights from the men and masculinities literature. For example, Kilkey's (2007) research with disabled fathers is of interest here:

> A striking theme emerging from the accounts of fathering practices is that of adapting what they do as fathers within the constraints imposed by physical and/or sensory impairments. The men who had become disabled when well into adulthood (whether before or after becoming fathers) reported, without exception, of having subscribed to the construction of the 'masculine' rough and tumble, physical father. (Kilkey, 2007: 26)

She suggests that the responses adopted by these fathers to their inability to conform to the expectations of physicality bound up with hegemonic masculinity may be understood as lying on the rejection/reformulation end of the continuum of strategies pursued by disabled men. Rejection involves replacement whereas reformulation is a middle ground where there is a renegotiation in a more achievable manner.

An important insight for Ferguson and Hogan (2004) is excluded young men's tendency towards a 'protest' masculinity:

> Men's practices of drinking, violence and criminality ... constitute a public acting out of a 'hard-man' image. Their status and definition of themselves as men is given meaning

through protest, an acting out of being against everything that is seen as socially valid. (Ferguson and Hogan, 2004: 136)

The growing boy puts together a tense, freaky façade, making a claim to power where there are no real resources for power (Connell, 1995: 111). However, a conventional stereotype of masculinity is not being adopted. As Ferguson and Hogan's (2004) data showed, some of these young men were perfectly at ease with non-traditional gender roles that involved attempts at egalitarian relationships with women and nurturing their children. Connell (1995) argues that with these men there is a lot of concern with façade, and Ferguson and Hogan (2004) consider how social workers should deal with this façade. A key challenge for professionals is to see beyond young men's enactment of a protest masculinity and to recognise that, in a context of overwhelming failure, vulnerable young men can see fatherhood as an opportunity to succeed in a meaningful way in their lives.

An important issue in relation to *how*, which links with *why* and *who*, concerns workers' own gendered identities and investments. It has already been acknowledged that many settings are characterised by a highly rational and procedural approach to working with children and families. There is little space to think about the complexities of what motivates painful and destructive behaviour, for example. Linked with this, there is often little space to reflect on the impact on workers who are often, but not exclusively, women. We have all been children, had mothers and fathers whether we lived with or knew them or not. We carry past stories, which we can seek to integrate into current narratives. There needs to be space within the project of engaging fathers to think about what fathering has meant and continues to mean to those designing and delivering services.

Why do it?

Practitioners in those sectors directly concerned with child neglect and abuse (often but not exclusively women) are often very concerned with exploring 'why' rather than concentrating on 'how' in relation to engaging fathers. This is partly because many of them are concerned with men who are posing difficulties for women and children in a variety of ways, either through what they do (actual abuse) or do not do (neglect and lack of support). 'Why' is a key question in the context of the concerns of this book.

As discussed in Chapter Eight, Stanley and Gamble (2005) have identified an explicit hierarchy of goals for their project around enhancing 'active fatherhood'. Their primary objective is to enhance fathers' involvement in order to improve children's experiences and outcomes. The secondary objective is to improve gender equity and the tertiary objective is to enable men to fulfil their own aspirations for their fathering role. While this may seem a sound pragmatic political strategy in a policy climate where outcomes for children are accorded central priority, it is unacceptable ethically and misconceived in that it is not located in concrete understandings of parental and partnering relationships and their dynamics. First, the concept of a hierarchy is problematic – one set of considerations should not be assumed to trump another. It is very important that those who support father involvement locate it explicitly in a project that is critical of current gendered inequities, because not doing so runs the risk of supporting men who do want to 'turn the clock back'. Moreover, Stanley and Gamble's hierarchy rests on mistaken and misleading assumptions about being able to disentangle the needs and interests of children, women and men when, in practice, they are entangled in messy as well as beneficial ways. Good outcomes for children generally rest on mothers and fathers being able to cooperate and the possibilities of such cooperation are surely jeopardised if attention is not paid to their concerns or, worse, their concerns are not recognised. Basically, father involvement cannot foster good outcomes for children if it rides roughshod over women's desires.

The author is often asked what should practitioners be aiming for? What would gender equality look like in practice? Is there a fixed notion? These are very legitimate questions that she continues to struggle with. Sometimes, she has used the work of Ferguson to talk of the importance of practitioners supporting 'democratic families'. For Ferguson (2001: 8) such families are those 'where children are heard as well as seen and feel safe, women as well as men are treated with respect, and men as well as women are enabled to have expressive emotional lives and relationships'.

This still seems useful, although it could support assumptions about all parents being heterosexual. However, we are still left with questions about means. How do you get there? What kinds of social policies as well as practices are required, for example? Should men be compelled to take time off (via a daddy quota) to participate in childcare or should they be encouraged?

In the first chapter, Doucet's (2006a) formulation was offered as a very useful guide to the author's position in writing this book:

Theoretically and politically, the feminist position that guides my work on fathers calls for the inclusion of men where it does not work to undermine women's own caregiving interests ... my feminist position on fathering is one that works towards challenging gendered asymmetries around care and employment, encouraging and embracing active fathering, while always remembering and valuing the long historical tradition of women's work, identities and power in caregiving. (Doucet, 2006a: 30)

But, as she acknowledges herself, context is crucial. Which men? Which women? In which contexts? Who decides who is being undermined? As practitioners know only too well, everyday lives in everyday families are full of differing and shifting stories about who deserves what, where does equality lie, is equality even the right word?

To explore this further, it is important to make a brief detour into debates within feminism. As Doucet (2006a: 23) notes, a key set of debates cohere around equality and difference feminism. Equality feminism is a strand of feminism underpinned by liberal feminism, which minimises or denies differences between women and men because they represent obstacles to socioeconomic equality. There is a strong emphasis on facilitating women's participation in paid work on an equal footing. Bryson (1999) outlines the many critiques there have been. At its heart is the notion of the independent autonomous human being. People are thus abstracted from physical and social connections, and the neglect of physical bodies and social relationships has serious implications for understanding and valuing women's work.

Difference feminism covers a broad and very contested spectrum of approaches but a key theme is the celebration of work associated with women, as well as challenging the value accorded it by society. In recent years, many feminists have aligned with the ethic of care that values women's work as caregivers and extends the implications to men and wider social policies and structures (see, for example, Williams, 2004).

There is a consensus among scholars that, in certain theoretical and historical contexts, the concepts of gender equality and gender differences are highly interdependent. Doucet (2006a) argues that, in order to move out of the equality–difference gridlock, the following is of use. She shifts her analytic lens from equality to differences and disadvantages, and the difference that difference makes. Difference does not always lead to disadvantage and difference does not always mean unequal: 'My belief is that gender difference ... can co-exist with equality, and indeed, what should be emphasised is gender symmetry rather than gender equality' (Doucet, 2006a: 233).

As indicated in Chapters One and Eight, the author considers that the notion of equality can be used at a political level, but it is far removed from some liberal notions that ignored the private and encouraged women to focus on the public. Lewis and Campbell's (2007) arguments in relation to fostering genuine equality at the level of policies are very important and support the resistance of policy developments that rest on dyadic constructions of fathers and children. Our increased understanding that 'fathers matter' must be located within an appreciation of how 'mothers matter' also.

While the author recognises that it leaves many questions unanswered, the aim of this book has been to support practitioners in engaging men to be more active caregivers. This does not mean that they should become mothers, adopt a prescriptive accounting mentality to who does what with childcare, or undermine mothers by taking over.

Each practice situation obliges the weighing up of the hopes, fears, constraints and resources of those involved. Individual practitioners, however, cannot bear the brunt of this project alone – social policies are crucial, as are well-resourced (this includes emotionally resourced) work environments. Workers not only need time and space to engage with the complexities of what they are doing but also, as indicated previously, their own gendered investments in mothering and fathering.

Conclusion

This chapter has reflected on the issues emerging from research on engaging with fathers in a variety of welfare settings in the last decade. It highlights some key issues in relation to who will do this work, where, how and why. While avoiding prescription, it does appear that attending to how men and women navigate their ways through material and emotional landscapes saturated with gendered meanings is vital if current policy developments are to be implemented.

Notes

[1] The Home Office was a government department with responsibility for criminal justice and security among other duties. Its role in taking on responsibility for family policy in the early years of New Labour has been a source of interest (see Featherstone, 2004).

[2] This is a pseudonym.

[3] Half of the foster carers in the study came from a London authority and this might account for the larger number of foster carers from minority ethnic groups than in the overall population of foster carers.

[4] This is a pseudonym – identifying details have been changed also.

[5] The research looked at four different types: two parent, lone mother, stepfamilies and foster care.

ELEVEN

Concluding remarks

This book would probably not have been considered relevant to practitioners 20 years ago. It would certainly not have been able to draw from the wealth of literature it has drawn on. It emerges from a period of profound change in relationships between men, women and children and attempts by governments to adapt to these changes. Alongside examples of cooperative gendered settlements, achieved against considerable odds, are to be found tendencies among men and women, in a range of differing sectors of society, to invest in children but treat the mothers or fathers of those children with hostility and suspicion. Indeed, a number of times in this book it has been suggested that children have become the site for gendered power battles.

A feature of the current political context, certainly in England, and one actively influenced by fathers' groups, is an emphasis on encouraging father 'involvement' in order to aid good outcomes for children. Birth fathers are prioritised and the wishes of women are not addressed or the benefits are assumed to be clear-cut. Ignoring women negates, not only the important work they do and have done in caring for children, but also the work they put into helping men to father. Gender equality does not appear to be an objective of this particular policy emphasis.

This book had an ambitious remit, as outlined in the first chapter, to:

- trace the emergence of ways of thinking about fathers in different disciplines;
- bring together in one book voices from disciplines that do not always speak to one another;
- identify important policy and practice developments and debates;
- identify some of the learning that has emerged for the author over the last decade of evaluating service developments;
- reflect throughout on the insights that feminist and pro-feminist perspectives can bring to understandings and practices.

In relation to the first aim, the author has tried to highlight some of the key themes within the differing disciplines that inform either wider cultural thinking or the professional training of practitioners.

Inevitably, this has led to offering overviews rather than engaging in-depth, although every effort has been made to offer comprehensive sources of reading. As someone whose first degree was in sociology and then trained as a social worker, the author has straddled disciplines, although she would never claim not to have disciplinary preferences. Social work draws from a number of disciplines, as its critics often disparagingly note, and, indeed, it is clear that there can be an uncritical appropriation of knowledge from other disciplines. The author has tried in this book to explore where ideas have come from in order to offer readers the possibility of interrogating these and making up their own minds.

Apart from the limitations imposed by disciplinary boundaries, there are very differing legal and policy developments that impact on fathering that workers in specific settings might be unaware of. For example, those who work in the child protection arena may be unaware of debates about contact in the private law arena or what is happening in relation to child support and, yet, these issues might be relevant to a specific family. While it is impossible to keep abreast of what are often complex and ever-changing developments, it seemed important in this book to capture key themes of this particular practice moment and think about parallels in other areas. In particular, the policy drive to get services to engage fathers needs to be located within understandings of some of the complex and difficult issues that have emerged for all concerned in the arena of post-divorce parenting.

In terms of the author's aim of reflecting on service developments in the last decades, a host of issues have emerged. A primary concern has been to insist on the need to interrogate the potential of such developments to undermine or support desirable caring practices. Assessing what is desirable is, of course, value-laden. The author outlined her own perspective in the first chapter but, as Chapter Ten indicates, she is left with as many questions as answers. While ongoing dialogue continues to be necessary, she would contend that a bottom line has to be the location of active fathering within a discussion of what the costs and benefits for women might be.

Finally, it seems appropriate to return to Doucet's (2006a) point in relation to 'the epistemology of reception' raised in Chapter One. As she notes, we are obliged to consider 'how and under what circumstances social scientific knowledge is received, evaluated, and acted on and under what circumstances' (May, 1998, quoted in Doucet, 2006a: 247). The author's own experience of presenting material on engaging fathers, and being 'accused' by one section of an audience of vilifying men and another section of the same audience of being too supportive to them, is not unique (see, for example, Dermott, 2008). How this book might be received is beyond the author's control, but it is hoped that it provides intellectual and emotional support to those who continue to dream of, and work towards, a world where opportunities to care for and about children are open to men and women in a variety of 'family' arrangements and are fundamental aspects of ongoing dialogue with policy makers and practitioners.

References

Allan, G. (1999) 'Introduction', in G. Allan (ed) *The Sociology of the Family: A Reader*, Oxford: Blackwell, pp 1-7.

Allen, S.M. and Hawkins, A.J. (1999) 'Maternal gatekeeping: mothers' beliefs and behaviours that inhibit greater father involvement in family work', *Journal of Marriage and the Family*, vol 60, pp 809-20.

Aries, P. (1962) *Centuries of Childhood*, London: Jonathan Cape.

Ashley, C., Featherstone, B., Roskill, C., Ryan, M. and White, S. (2006) *Fathers Matter: Research Findings on Fathers and their Involvement with Social Care Services*, London: Family Rights Group.

Bacchi, C. (1999) *Women, Policy and Politics: The Construction of Policy Problems*, London: Sage.

Backett, K. (1982) *Mothers and Fathers: A Study of the Development and Negotiation of Parental Behaviour*, Basingstoke and London: Macmillan.

Bamford, T. (1990) *The Future of Social Work*, Basingstoke and London: Macmillan.

Barlow, A., Duncan, S. and James, G. (2002) 'New Labour, the rationality mistake and family policy in Britain,' in A. Carling, S. Duncan and R. Edwards (eds) *Analysing Families: Morality and Rationality in Policy and Practice*, London: Routledge, pp 110-29.

Bartlett, D. and Burgess, A. (2005) *Working with Fathers*, London: Fathers Direct.

Beck, U. (1992) *The Risk Society*, Cambridge: Polity.

Beck, U. and Beck-Gernsheim, E. (1995) *The Normal Chaos of Love*, Cambridge: Polity.

Beck, U. and Beck-Gernsheim, E. (2002) *Individualization*, London: Sage.

Benjamin, J. (1995) *Like Subjects, Love Objects: Essays on Recognition and Sexual Difference*, New Haven, CT: Yale University Press.

Bonoli, G. (2005) 'The politics of the new social policies: providing coverage against new social risks in mature welfare states', *Policy & Politics*, vol 33, no 3, pp 431-49.

Borchorst, A. (2006) 'The public–private split rearticulated: abolishment of the Danish daddy leave', in A.L. Ellingsaeter and A. Leira (eds) *Politicising Parenthood in Scandinavia: Gender Relations in Welfare States*, Bristol: The Policy Press, pp 101-21.

Bosman, J. (2008) 'Obama sharply assails absent black fathers', *New York Times*, 16 June, 2008.

Boyd, S.B. (2006) '"Robbed of their families?" Fathers' rights discourses in Canadian parenting law reform processes', in R. Collier and S. Sheldon (eds) *Fathers' Rights Activism and Law Reform in Comparative Perspective*, Oxford and Portland, OR: Hart Publishing, pp 27-53

Bradshaw, J., Stimson, C., Skinner, C. and Williams, J. (1999) *Absent Fathers?*, London: Routledge.

Brannen, J., Heptinstall, E. and Bhopal, K. (2000) *Connecting Children: Care and Family Life in Later Childhood*, London: Routledge Falmer.

Brannen, J. and Nilsen, A. (2006) 'From fatherhood to fathering: transmission and change among fathers in four generation families', *Sociology*, vol 40, no 2, pp 335-52.

Brannen, J., Statham, J., Mooney, A. and Brockmann, M. (2007) *Coming to Care: The Work and Family Lives of Workers Caring for Vulnerable Children*, Bristol: The Policy Press.

Brewer, N. (2008) Speech at the launch of Working Better consultation (www.equalityhumanrights.com/en/newsandcomment/speeches/Pages/SpeechbyNicolaBrewerlaunchof%27WorkingBetter%27.aspx).

Britton, R. (1989) 'The missing link: parental sexuality in the Oedipus complex', in R. Britton, M. Feldman and E. O'Shaughnessy (eds) *The Oedipus Complex Today: Clinical Implications*, London: Karnac Press, pp 83-101.

Bryson, V. (1999) *Feminist Debates*, Basingstoke: Palgrave Macmillan.

Burgess, A. (1997) *Fatherhood Reclaimed: The Making of the Modern Father*, London: Vermilion.

Burgess, A. (2005) 'Fathers and public services', in K. Stanley (ed) *Daddy Dearest: Active Fatherhood and Public Policy*, London: IPPR, pp 57-74.

Burgess, A. (2007) *The Costs and Benefits of Active Fatherhood* (www.fatherhoodinstitute.org.uk).

Burgess, A. and Ruxton, S. (1996) *Men and their Children: Proposals for Public Policy*, London: IPPR.

Burkitt, I. (2008) *Social Selves*, 2nd edn, London: Sage.

Burman, E. (1994) *Deconstructing Developmental Psychology*, London: Routledge.

Butler, J. (2000) *Antigone's Claim: Kinship between Life and Death*, New York: Columbia University Press.

Calasanti, T. (2003) 'Masculinities and care work in old age', in S. Arber, K. Davidson and J. Ginn (eds) *Gender and Ageing: Changing Roles and Relationships*, Maidenhead: Open University Press, pp 15-31.

Cameron, C., Moss, P. and Owen, C (1999) *Men in the Nursery*, London: Chapman.

Campbell, B (1993) *Goliath: Britain's Dangerous Places*, London: Virago.

Carrigan, T., Connell, R. W. and Lee, J. (1985) 'Towards a new sociology of masculinity', *Theory and Society*, vol 14, no 5, pp 551-604.

Cassell, P. (ed) (1993) *The Giddens Reader*, London: Macmillan.

Castells, M. (1997) *The Power of Identity*, The Information Age, vol 11, Oxford: Blackwell.

Cavanagh, K. and Cree, V. (eds) (1996) *Working with Men*, London: Routledge.

Cawson, P., Wattam, C., Brooker, S. and Kelly, G. (2000) *Child Maltreatment in the United Kingdom: A Study of the Prevalence of Child Abuse and Neglect*, London: NSPCC.

Centre for Social Justice (2007) 'Breakthrough Britain: ending the costs of social breakdown' (www.centreforsocialjustice.org.uk/default. asp?pageRef=226).

Chodorow, N. (1978) *The Reproduction of Mothering*, Berkley, CA: University of California Press.

Chodorow, N. (1995) 'Individuality and difference in how women and men love', in A. Elliott and S. Frosh (eds) *Psychoanalysis in Contexts: Paths between Theory and Modern Culture*, London: Routledge, pp 89-105.

Choudry, S., Herring, J. and Wallbank, J. (eds) (forthcoming) *Rights, Gender and Family Law*, London: Routledge.

Christie, A. (2006) 'Negotiating the uncomfortable intersections between gender and professional identities in social work', *Critical Social Policy*, vol 26, no 2, pp 390-411.

Clapton, G. (2002) *Birth Fathers and their Adoption Experiences*, London: Jessica Kingsley.

Clatterbaugh, K. (1990) *Contemporary Perspectives on Masculinity*, Boulder, CO: Westview Press.

Collier, R. (1995) *Masculinity, Law and the Family*, London: Routledge.

Collier, R. (2006) '"The outlaw fathers fight back": fathers' rights groups, Fathers 4 Justice and the politics of family law reform – reflections on the UK experience', in R. Collier and S. Sheldon (eds) *Fathers' Rights Activism and Law Reform in Comparative Perspective*, Oxford and Portland, OR: Hart Publishing, pp 53-79.

Collier, R. and Sheldon, S. (2006) '"Fathers" rights, fatherhood and law reform – international perspectives', in R. Collier and S. Sheldon (eds) *Fathers' Rights Activism and Law Reform in Comparative Perspective*, Oxford and Portland, OR: Hart Publishing, pp 1-27.

Collier, R. and Sheldon, S. (2008) *Fragmenting Fatherhood: A Socio-legal Study*, Oxford and Portland, OR: Hart Publishing.

Coltrane, S. and Parke, R.D. (1998) *Reinventing Fatherhood: Toward an Historical Understanding of Continuity and Change in Men's Family Lives*, Philadelphia, PA: National Centre on Fathers and Families, University of Pennsylvania (www.ncoff.gse.upenn.edu).

Connell, R.W (1995) *Masculinities*, Cambridge: Polity.

Connell, R.W (1996) 'The politics of changing men', *Arena*, 5, pp 53-72.

Connell, R.W., Hearn, J. and Kimmel, M.S. (2005) 'Introduction', in M.S. Kimmel, J. Hearn and R.W. Connell (eds) *Handbook of Studies on Men and Masculinities*, London: Sage, pp 1-13.

Cooper, D. (1971) *The Death of the Family*, Harmondsworth: Penguin.

Cornell, D. (1998) 'Fatherhood and its discontents: men, patriarchy and freedom', in C.R. Daniels (ed) *Lost Fathers: The Politics of Fatherlessness in America*, Basingstoke and London: Macmillan, pp 183-203.

Crompton, R. (2006) *Employment and the Family: The Reconfiguration of Work and Family Life in Contemporary Societies*, Cambridge: Cambridge University Press.

Crowley, J.E. (2006) 'Organizational responses to the fatherhood crisis: the case of fathers' rights groups in the US', *Marriage and Family Review*, vol 39, nos 1/2, pp 99-120.

Dale, P., Davies, M., Morrison, T. and Waters, J. (1986) *Dangerous Families: Assessment and Treatment of Child Abuse*, London: Tavistock.

Daniel, B. and Taylor, J. (2001) *Engaging with Fathers: Practice Issues for Health and Social Care*, London: Jessica Kingsley.

Daniels, C.R. (1998) 'Introduction', in C.R. Daniels (ed) *Lost Fathers: The Politics of Fatherlessness in America*, Basingstoke and London: Macmillan, pp 1-11.

Davies, L. and Krane, J. (2006) 'Collaborate with caution: protecting children, helping mothers', *Critical Social Policy*, vol 26, no 2, pp 412-26.

Day Sclater, S. (1999) *Divorce: A Psychosocial Study*, Aldershot: Ashgate.

Day Sclater, S. and Yates, C. (1999) 'The psycho-politics of post-divorce parenting', in A. Bainham, S. Day Sclater and M. Richards (eds) *What is a Parent? A Socio-legal Analysis*, Oxford and Portland, OR: Hart Publishing, pp 271-95.

DCSF (Department for Children, Schools and Families) (2007) *The Children's Plan: Building Brighter Futures*, London: The Stationery Office.

DCSF and DWP (Department for Work and Pensions) (2008) *Joint Birth Registration: Recording Responsibility*, London: The Stationery Office.

Dean, H. (2008) 'Social policy and human rights: re-thinking the engagement', *Social Policy and Society*, vol 7, no 1, pp 1-12.

Dennis, N. and Erdos, G. (1992) *Families Without Fatherhood*, London: IEA Health and Welfare Unit.

Dermott, E. (2006) *The Effect of Fatherhood on Men's Pattern of Employment*, End of Award Report, Swindon: ESRC.

Dermott, E. (2008) *Intimate Fatherhood*, London: Routledge.

DfES (Department for Education and Skills) (2004) *Every Child Matters: The Next Steps*, London: The Stationery Office.

DfES (2007) *Every Parent Matters*, London: The Stationery Office.

DH (Department of Health) (1995) *Child Protection: Messages from Research*, London: The Stationery Office.

DH (2004) *National Service Framework for Children, Young People and Maternity Services*, London: The Stationery Office.

Diduck, A. (2007) '"If only we can find the appropriate terms to use the issue will be solved": law, identity and parenthood', *Child and Family Law Quarterly*, vol 19, no 4, pp 458-80.

Dixon, M. and Margo, J. (2006) *Population Politics*, London: Institute for Public Policy Research.

Dominelli, L. (2007) '"Here's my story": fathers of "looked-after" children recount their experiences of the child welfare system', *Gender and Child Welfare: An Interdisciplinary Conference*, University of York, 19 September.

Donovan, C. (2006) 'Genetics, fathers and families: exploring the implications of changing the law in favour of identifying sperm donors', *Social and Legal Studies*, vol 15, no 4, pp 494-510.

Doucet, A. (2006a) *Do Men Mother?*, Toronto: University of Toronto Press.

Doucet, A. (2006b) '"Estrogen-filled worlds": fathers as primary caregivers and embodiment', *The Sociological Review*, vol 54, no 4, pp 696-716.

Duncan, S., Edwards, R., Reynolds, T. and Alldred, P. (2003) 'Motherhood, paid work and partnering', *Work, Employment and Society*, vol 17, no 2, pp 309-30.

Duncombe, J. and Marsden, D. (1999) 'Love and intimacy: the gender division of emotion and "emotion work"', in G. Allan (ed) *The Sociology of the Family: A Reader*, Oxford: Blackwell, pp 91-111.

Dunn, J. and Deater-Deckard, K. (2001) *Children's Views of their Changing Families*, York: Joseph Rowntree Foundation.

Dunn, J., Davies, L., O'Connor, T. and Sturgess, W. (2000) 'Parents' and partners' life course and family experiences: links with parent–child relationships in different family settings', *Journal of Child Psychology and Psychiatric and Allied Disciplines,* vol 41, no 8, pp 955-68.

Dunne, G. (1999) *The Different Dimensions of Gay Fatherhood,* End of Award Report, Swindon: ESRC.

Eekelaar, J. (2006) *Family Law and Personal life,* Oxford: Oxford University Press.

Elder, G.H. Jnr (1978) 'Approaches to social change and the family', *American Journal of Sociology,* vol 84, pp 31-8.

Ellingsæter, A.L. (2007) '"Old" and "new" politics of time to care: three Norwegian reforms', *Journal of European Social Policy,* vol 17, no 1, pp 49-60.

Ellingsæter, A.L. and Leira, A. (2006a) 'Introduction: politicising parenthood in Scandinavia', in A.L. Ellingsæter and A. Leira (eds) *Politicising Parenthood in Scandinavia: Gender Relations in Welfare States,* Bristol: The Policy Press, pp 1-27.

Ellingsæter, A.L. and Leira, A. (2006b) 'Epilogue: Scandinavian politics of parenthood – a success story?', in A.L. Elingsæter and A. Leira (eds) *Politicising Parenthood in Scandinavia: Gender Relations in Welfare States,* Bristol: The Policy Press, pp 265-79.

Eriksson, M. and Hester, M. (2001) 'Violent men as good-enough fathers? A look at England and Sweden', *Violence against Women,* vol 7, no 7, pp 779-98.

Eriksson, M. and Pringle, K. (2006) 'Gender equality, child welfare and fathers' rights in Sweden', in R. Collier and S. Sheldon (eds) *Fathers' Rights Activism and Law Reform in Comparative Perspective,* Oxford and Portland, OR: Hart Publishing, pp 101-25.

Etchegoyen, A. (2002) 'Psychoanalytic ideas about fathers', in J. Trowell and A. Etchegoyen (eds) *The Importance of Fathers: A Psychoanalytic Re-evaluation,* Hove: Brunner-Routledge, pp 20-43.

Everingham, C. and Bowers, T. (2006) 'Reclaiming or re-shaping fatherhood', *Health Sociology Review,* vol 15, pp 96-103.

Fairclough, N. (2000) *New Labour, New Language,* London: Routledge.

Fatherhood Institute (2006) 'Family sector leaders meet govt to issue call for transformation of separated family policy' (www. fatherhoodinstitute.org/index.php?id=4&cID=467).

Fatherhood Institute (2008a) 'When father hurts mother' (www. fatherhoodinstitute.org/index.php?id=5&cID=166).

Fatherhood Institute (2008b) 'About us' (www.fatherhoodinstitute. org/index.php?Nid=1).

Fatherhood Institute (2008c) 'Our work' (www.fatherhoodinstitute. org/index.php?nID=73).

Fatherhood Institute (2008d) 'Bringing up Muslim children in the UK' (www.fatherhoodinstitute.org/index.php?id==8&cID=530).

Fatherhood Institute (2008e) 'Young black fathers tell the truth about their struggle' (www.fatherhoodinstitute.org/index.php?id=7&cID-294).

Fathers 4 Justice (2008) 'Fathers 4 Justice to end campaign' (www. fathers-4-justice.org/f4j/).

Fawcett, B., Featherstone, B. and Goddard, J. (2004) *Contemporary Child Care Policy and Practice*, Basingstoke: Palgrave.

Fawcett Society (2008) 'Keeping mum' (www.fawcettsociety.org. uk/index.asp?PageID=644).

Featherstone, B. (1996) 'Victims or villains? Women who physically abuse their children', in B. Fawcett, B. Featherstone, J. Hearn and C. Toft (eds) *Violence and Gender Relations: Theories and Interventions*, London: Sage, pp 178-89.

Featherstone, B. (2000) 'Researching into mothers' violence: some thoughts on the process', in B. Fawcett, B. Featherstone, J. Fook and A. Rossiter (eds) *Research and Practice in Social Work: Postmodern Feminist Perspectives*, London: Routledge, pp 120-36.

Featherstone, B. (2001a) 'Putting fathers on the child welfare agenda: a research review', *Child and Family Social Work*, vol 6, no 2, pp 179-86.

Featherstone, B. (2001b) *An Evaluation of a Parenting Group for Fathers*, Huddersfield: Nationwide Children's Research Centre.

Featherstone, B. (2003) 'Taking fathers seriously', *British Journal of Social Work*, vol 33, pp 239-54.

Featherstone, B. (2004) *Family Life and Family Support: A Feminist Analysis*, Basingstoke and London: Palgrave.

Featherstone, B. (2005) 'Feminist social work: past, present and future', in S. Hick, J. Fook and R. Pozzuto (eds) *Social Work: A Critical Turn*, Toronto: Thompson Educational Publishing, pp 203-19.

Featherstone, B. (2006) 'Why gender matters in child welfare and protection', *Critical Social Policy*, vol 26, no 2, pp 294-314.

Featherstone, B. (2008) 'Fathers and the social work curriculum', in C. Roskill, B. Featherstone, C. Ashley and S. Haresnape (eds) *Fathers Matter, Volume 2: Further Findings on Fathers and their Involvement with Social Care Services*, London: Family Rights Group, pp 55-62.

Featherstone, B. and Evans, H. (2004) *Children Experiencing Maltreatment: Who do they Turn to?*, London: NSPCC.

Featherstone, B. and Green, L. (2008) 'Judith Butler', in M. Gray and S. Webb (eds) *Theories and Methods in Social Work*, London: Sage, pp 53-62.

Featherstone, B. and Manby, M. (2003) *Sure Start: Local Evaluation Report*, Huddersfield: Nationwide Children's Research Centre.

Featherstone, B. and Peckover, S. (2007) '"Letting them get away with it": fathers, domestic violence and child protection', *Critical Social Policy*, vol 27, no 2, pp 181-203.

Featherstone, B. and White, S. (2006) 'Dads talk about their lives and services', in C. Ashley, B. Featherstone, C. Roskill, M. Ryan and S. White, *Fathers Matter: Research Findings on Fathers and their Involvement with Social Care Services*, London: Family Rights Group, pp 69-81.

Featherstone, B., Rivett, M. and Scourfield, J. (2007) *Working with Men in Health and Social Care*, London: Sage.

Ferguson, H. (2001) 'Promoting child protection, healing and welfare: the case for developing best practice', *Child and Family Social Work*, vol 6, no 1, pp 1-13.

Ferguson, H. (2004) *Protecting Children in Time*, Basingstoke: Palgrave Macmillan.

Ferguson, H. and Hogan, F. (2004) *Strengthening Families Through Fathers*, Dublin: Family Affairs Unit, Department of Social and Family Affairs.

Fisher, K., McCulloch, A. and Gershuny, J. (1999) *British Fathers and Children*, Colchester: University of Essex, Institute for Social and Economic Research Working Paper.

Flax, J. (1992) 'The end of innocence', in J. Butler and J.W. Scott (eds) *Feminists Theorise the Political*, London: Routledge, pp 445-64.

Fleming, J. (2007) '"If we get the mums in we are doing well": father absence in the context of child welfare', *Gender and Child Welfare – An Interdisciplinary Conference*, University of York, 19 September.

Flood, M. (2004) 'Backlash: angry men's movements', in S.E. Rossi (ed) *The Battle and Backlash Rage On: Why Feminism Cannot Be Obsolete*, Philadelphia, PA: Xlibris, pp 261-78.

Flouri, E. (2005) *Fathering and Child Outcomes*, Chichester: Wiley.

Flouri, E. and Buchanan, A. (2003) 'What predicts father's involvement with their children? A prospective study of intact families', *British Journal of Developmental Psychology*, vol 21, pp 81-98.

FNF (Families Need Fathers) (2008a) 'About us' (www.fnf.org.uk/about-us).

FNF (2008b) 'Families Need Fathers Charter' (www.fnf.org.uk/about-us/families-need-fathers-charter).

Foucault, M. (1979) *The History of Sexuality Vol 1: An Introduction*, London: Allen Lane/Penguin.

Fox Harding, L. (1991) *Perspectives in Child Care Policy*, London: Longman.

Fox Harding, L. (1996) 'Parental responsibility: the reassertion of private patriarchy?', in E.B. Silva (ed) *Good Enough Mothering? Feminist Perspectives on Lone Motherhood*, London: Routledge, pp 130-48.

Fraser, C. and Featherstone, B. (2007) *Parents' Views of Parent Support*, Bradford: Bradford Metropolitan District Council.

Fraser, N. (1989) *Unruly Practices: Power, Discourse and Gender in Contemporary Social Theory*, Cambridge and Oxford: Polity in association with Blackwell Publishers.

Fraser, N. (1994) 'After the family wage: gender equality and the welfare state', *Political Theory*, vol 22, no 4, pp 591-618.

Freud, S. (1939 [1985]) 'Moses and montheism', in S. Freud *The Origins of Religion*, Harmondsworth: Penguin.

Froggett, L. (2002) *Love, Hate and Welfare: Psychosocial Approaches to Policy and Practice*, Bristol: The Policy Press.

Frosh, S. (1987) *The Politics of Psychoanalysis: An Introduction to Freudian and Post-Freudian Theory*, New Haven, CT: Yale University Press.

Frosh, S. (1997) 'Fathers' ambivalence (too)', in W. Hollway and B. Featherstone (eds) *Mothering and Ambivalence*, London: Routledge, pp 37-54.

Frosh, S., Phoenix, A. and Pattman, R. (2001) *Young Masculinities*, Basingstoke and London: Palgrave Macmillan.

Gabb, J. (2008) *Researching Intimacy in Families*, Basingstoke and London: Palgrave Macmillan.

Gadd, D. and Jefferson, T. (2007) *Psycho-social Criminology*, London: Sage.

Galtry, J. and Callister, P. (2005) 'Assessing the optimal length of parental leave for child and parental well-being: how can research inform policy?', *Journal of Family Issues*, vol 6, no 2, pp 219-46.

Gatrell, C. (2007) 'Whose child is it anyway? The negotiation of paternal entitlements within marriage', *The Sociological Review*, vol 55, no 2, pp 352-72.

Gauthier, A., Smeeding, T.M. and Fustenberg, F. (2004) 'Are parents investing less time in children? Trends in selected industrialized countries', *Population and Development Review*, vol 30, no 4, pp 647-71.

Gavanas, A. (2002) ' The Fatherhood Responsibility Movement: the centrality of marriage, work and male sexuality in reconstructions of masculinity and fatherhood', in B. Hobson (ed) *Making Men into Fathers: Men, Masculinities and the Social Politics of Fatherhood*, Cambridge: Cambridge University Press, pp 213-45.

Gergen, K. (1994) *Realities and Relationships: Soundings in Social Construction*, Cambridge, MA: Harvard University Press.

Ghate, D. and Ramalla, M. (2002) *Positive Parenting: The National Evaluation of the Youth Justice Board's Parenting Programme*, London: Policy Research Bureau.

Ghate, D., Shaw, C. and Hazel, N. (2000) *Fathers and Family Centres: Engaging Fathers in Preventive Services*, London: Policy Research Bureau/Joseph Rowntree Foundation.

Giddens, A. (1992) *The Transformation of Intimacy: Sexuality, Love and Eroticism in Modern Societies*, Cambridge: Polity.

Giddens, A. (1998) *The Third Way: The Renewal of Social Democracy*, Cambridge: Polity.

Giddens, A. (1999) *Runaway World: How Globalisation is Reshaping our Lives*, Cambridge: Polity.

Gillis, J.R. (1997) *A World of Their Own Making: A History of Myth and Ritual in Family Life*, Oxford: Oxford University Press.

Goldman, R. (2005) *Fathers' Involvement in their Children's Education*, London: National Family and Parenting Institute.

Golombok, S. (2000) *Parenting: What Really Counts?* London: Routledge.

Gomez, L. (1997) *An Introduction to Object Relations*, London: Free Association Books.

Gordon, L. (1986) 'Feminism and social control: the case of child abuse and neglect', in J. Mitchell and A. Oakley (eds) *What is Feminism?*, Oxford: Blackwell, pp 63-85.

Gordon, L. (1989) *Heroes of their Own Lives*, London: Virago.

Grice, A. (2008) 'Mandelson halts flexitime reforms' (www.independent. co.uk/news/uk/politics/backlash-at-mandelsons-assault-on-flexitime-967675.html).

Grosz, E. (1990) *Jacques Lacan: A Feminist Introduction*, London: Routledge.

Grosz, E. (1994) 'The labors of love: analyzing perverse desire: an interrogation of Teresa de Lauretis's *The Practice of Love*', *Differences*, vol 6, nos 2/3, p 275.

Hakim, C. (1992) 'Explaining trends in occupation segregation: the measurement, causes, and consequences of the sexual division of labour', *European Sociological Review*, vol 8, no 2, pp 127-52.

Hakim, C. (2000) *Work–lifestyle Choices in the 21st Century*, Oxford: Oxford University Press.

Harker, J. (2007a) 'Role models should come from the home, not the TV' (http://guardian.co.uk/commentisfree/2007/aug/14/comment. society).

Harker, J. (2007b) 'Blears' band of bruthas' (http://guardian.co.uk/ commentisfree/2007/dec/07/blearsbandofbrothers).

Harne, L. (2005) 'Researching violent fathers', in T. Skinner, M. Hester and E. Malos (eds) *Researching Gender Violence: Feminist Methodology in Action*, Cullompton: Willan Publishing, pp 167–87.

Harrison, C. (2006) 'Damned if you do and damned if you don't? The contradictions between public and private law', in C. Humphreys and N. Stanley (eds) *Domestic Violence and Child Protection: Directions for Good Practice*, London: Jessica Kingsley, pp 137–55.

Hawkins, A.J. and Dollahite, D.C. (1996) *Generative Fathering: Beyond Deficit Perspectives*, Thousand Oaks, CA: Sage.

Hearn, J. (1992) *Men in the Public Eye*, London: Routledge.

Hearn, J. (2002) 'Men, fathers and the state: national and global relations', in B. Hobson (ed) *Making Men into Fathers: Men, Masculinities and the Social Politics of Fatherhood*, Cambridge: Cambridge University Press, pp 245–73.

Hearn, J. and Pringle, K. (2006) 'Men, masculinities and children: some European perspectives', *Critical Social Policy*, vol 26, no 2, pp 365–89.

Henricson, C. and Bainham, A. (2005) *The Child and Family Policy Divide: Tensions, Convergence and Rights*, York: Joseph Rowntree Foundation.

Henriques, J., Hollway, W., Urwin, C., Venn, C. and Walkerdine, V. (1998) *Changing the Subject: Psycholgy, Social Regulation and Subjectivity*, 2nd edn, London: Methuen.

Henshaw, D. (2006) *Recovering Child Support: Routes to Responsibility*, Norwich: The Stationery Office.

Henwood, K. and Procter, J. (2003) 'The "good father": reading men's accounts of paternal involvement during the transition to first-time fatherhood', *British Journal of Social Psychology*, vol 42, no 3, pp 337–55.

Herring, J. (forthcoming) 'Autonomy and family law', in S. Choudry, J. Herring and J. Wallbank (eds) *Rights, Gender and Family Law*, London: Routledge.

Hicks, S. (2008) 'Gender role models ... who needs 'em?!' *Qualitative Social Work*, vol 7, no 1, pp 43–59.

Hill, A. (2008) 'Fathers fight for lead role in childcare' (www.guardian. co.uk/money/2008/jan/20/childcare.fathers/print).

HM Treasury and DfES (2007) *Aiming High for Children: Supporting Families*, London: The Stationery Office.

Hochschild, A.R. (1989) *The Second Shift: Working Parents and the Revolution at Home*, New York: Basic Books.

Hoggett, P (2000) *Emotional Life and the Politics of Welfare*, Basingstoke: Palgrave Macmillan.

Hollway, W. (1989) *Subjectivity and Method in Psychology: Gender, Meaning and Science*, London: Sage.

Hollway, W. (2006) *The Capacity to Care: Gender and Ethical Subjectivity*, London: Routledge.

Hollway, W. and Jefferson, T. (2000) *Doing Qualitative Research Differently*, London: Sage.

Holt, A. (2007) 'Parenting orders, youth justice policy and the discursive shaping of subjectivity', Paper presented at 'Monitoring parents: childrearing in the age of intensive parenting', University of Kent, 21-22 May.

Home Office (1998) *Supporting Families: A Consultation Document* (www. homeoffice.gov.uk/vcu/suppfam.htm).

James, A. and James, A.L. (2004) *Constructing Childhood: Theory, Policy and Social Practice*, Basingstoke: Palgrave Macmillan.

Jamieson, L. (1998) *Intimacy: Personal Relationships in Modern Societies*, Cambridge: Polity.

Jenks, C. (1996) *Childhood*, London: Routledge.

Jensen, A.-M. (2001) 'Property, power and prestige – the feminization of childhood', in M. du Bois-Reymond, H. Sunker and H. Kruger (eds) *Childhood in Europe: Approaches – Trends – Findings*, New York: Peter Lang Publishing, pp 185-231.

Jenson, J. (2008) 'Writing women out, folding gender in: the European Union "modernises" social policy', *Social Politics*, vol 15, no 2, pp 131-54.

Jenson, J. (2004) 'Changing the paradigm: family responsibility or investing in children', *Canadian Journal of Sociology*, vol 29, no 2, pp 169-94.

Kennedy, S. (2008) 'Paid maternity leave does us no favours either, say fathers', *The Times*, 15 July (www.women.timesonline.co.uk/tol/life_and_style/women/families/article4333843.ece).

Kiernan, K. (2005) *Non-residential Fatherhood and Child Involvement: Evidence from the Millennium Cohort Study Case Paper No 65*, London: Centre for the Analysis of Social Exclusion, London School of Economics.

Kilkey, M. (ed) (2007) *Disabled Fathers: Identifying a Research Agenda*, Hull: Working Papers in Social Policy, University of Hull.

Laing, R.D. and Esterson, A. (1964) *Sanity, Madness and the Family*, London: Tavistock.

Lamb, M.E. (1997) 'Fathers and child development: an introductory overview and guide', in M.E. Lamb (ed) *The Role of the Father in Child Development* (3rd edn), Chichester: Wiley, pp 1-19.

Lamb, M.E. (ed) (2004) *The Role of the Father in Child Development* (4th edn), Chichester: Wiley.

Lamb, M.E. and Lewis, C. (2004) 'The development and significance of father–child relationships in two-parent families', in M.E. Lamb (ed) *The Role of the Father in Child Development* (4th edn), Chichester: Wiley, pp 272-307.

Laming, H. (2003) *The Victoria Climbiè Inquiry*, London: The Stationery Office.

Lewis, C. and Lamb, M.E. (2007) *Understanding Fatherhood: A Review of Recent Research*, York: Joseph Rowntree Foundation.

Lewis, J. (1992) 'Gender and the development of welfare regimes', *Journal of European Social Policy*, vol 12, no 3, pp 159-73.

Lewis, J. (2001) *The End of Marriage?*, Cheltenham: Edward Elgar.

Lewis, J. (2002) 'The problem of fathers: policy and behaviour in Britain', in B. Hobson (ed) *Making Men into Fathers: Men, Masculinities and the Social Politics of Fatherhood*, Cambridge: Cambridge University Press, pp 125-50.

Lewis, J. and Campbell, M. (2007) 'UK work–family balance policies and gender equality', *Social Politics*, vol 14, no 1, pp 4-30.

Lee, K. (2008) *Fragmenting Fatherhoods? Fathers, Fathering and Family Diversity*, unpublished PhD thesis, London: City University.

Lister, R. (2006) 'Children (but not women) first: New Labour, child welfare and gender', *Critical Social Policy*, vol 26, no 2, pp 315-36.

Lister, R. (2008) 'Maternity rights and wrongs', letter to *New Statesman* (www.newstatesman.com.letters).

Lloyd, N., O'Brien, M. and Lewis, C. (2003) 'Fathers in Sure Start local programmes' (www.ness.bbk.ac.uk).

Lloyd, T. (2001) *What Works With Fathers?*, London: Working with Men.

Lupton, D. and Barclay, L. (1997) *Constructing Fatherhood: Discourses and Experiences*, London: Sage.

Mallon, G.P. (2004) *Gay Men Choosing Parenthood*, New York: Columbia University Press.

Marsh, I., Keating. M., Eyre, A., McKenzie, J., Campbell, R. and Finnegan, T. (1996) *Making Sense of Society: An Introduction to Sociology*, London: Longman.

McKee, L. and O'Brien, M. (1987) 'The father figure: some current orientations and historical perspectives', in L. McKee and M. O'Brien (eds) *The Father Figure*, London: Tavistock Publications, pp 1-26.

McMahon, A. (1999) *Taking Care of Men: Sexual Politics in the Public Mind*, Cambridge: Cambridge University Press.

Messner, M. (1997) *The Politics of Masculinity*, Newbury Park, CA: Sage.

Mitchell, J. (ed) (1986) *The Selected Melanie Klein*, London: Penguin.

Morgan, D. (1996) *Family Connections*, Cambridge: Polity.

Morgan, D. (2002) 'Epilogue', in B. Hobson (ed) *Making Men into Fathers: Men, Masculinities and the Social Politics of Fatherhood*, Cambridge: Cambridge University Press, pp 273-87.

Mullender, A. and Morley, R. (eds) (1994) *Putting the Abuse of Women on the Child Care Agenda*, London: Whiting and Birch.

New Statesman (2008) 'You're hired, Mum's fired', editorial (www. newstatesman.com/politics/2008/07/women-leave-bnp-salary-hired).

Nussbaum, M. (2000) *Women and Human Development*, Cambridge: Cambridge University Press.

O'Brien, M. (2004) 'Social science and public policy perspectives on fatherhood in the European Union', in M.E. Lamb (ed) *The Role of the Father in Child Development* (4th edn), Chichester: Wiley, pp 121-46.

O'Brien, M. (2005) *Shared Caring: Bringing Fathers into the Frame*, Norwich: University of East Anglia.

O'Brien, M. (2008) 'Fathers' working hours and work–family policies: the UK experience', International Sociological Association Family Research Conference, *Family Diversity and Gender*, Lisbon, Portugal, 9-13 September.

O'Brien, M., Brandth, B. and Kvande, E. (2007) 'Fathers, work and family life: global perspectives and new insights', *Community, Work and Family*, vol 10, no 4, pp 375-87.

O'Brien, M. and Shemilt, I. (2003) *Working Fathers: Earning and Caring*, Manchester: Equal Opportunities Commission.

ONS (Office for National Statistics) (2005) *Focus on Families*, London: ONS.

Orloff, A. (2007) 'Should feminists aim for gender symmetry? Why a dual-earner/dual-carer society is not every feminist's utopia' (www. ssc.wisc.edu/~mscaglio/2006documents/Orloff_2007_Gender_Symmetry.pdf).

Parton, N. (1985) *The Politics of Child Abuse*, London: Macmillan.

Parton, N. (1991) *Governing the Family: Child Care, Child Protection and the State*, London: Macmillan.

Parton, N. (2006) *Safeguarding Childhood: Early Intervention and Surveillance in a Late Modern Society*, Basingstoke: Palgrave Macmillan.

Pearson, G., Treseder, J. and Yelloly, M. (eds) (1988) *Social Work and the Legacy of Freud,* London: Macmillan.

Pease, B. and Pringle, K. (eds) (2002) *A Man's World: Changing Practices in a Globalized World*, London: Zed Books.

Peckover, S., White, S. and Hall, C. (forthcoming) 'Making and managing electronic children: e-assessment in child welfare', *Information, Communication and Society*.

Phoenix, A. and Husain, F. (2007) *Parenting and Ethnicity*, York: Joseph Rowntree Foundation.

Pithouse, A. (1987) *Social Work: The Social Organisation of an Invisible Trade*, Aldershot: Avebury.

Pleck, J.H. and Masciadrelli, B. (2004) 'Paternal involvement by US residential fathers: levels, sources and consequences', in M.E. Lamb (ed) *The Role of the Father in Child Development* (4th edn), Chichester: Wiley, pp 222-72.

Pleck, E.H. and Pleck, J.H. (1997) 'Fatherhood ideals in the United States: historical dimensions', in M.E. Lamb (ed) *The Role of the Father in Child Development* (3rd edn), Chichester: Wiley, pp 33-49.

Pollock, L. (1987) *A Lasting Relationship: Parents and Children over Three Centuries*, London: Fourth Estate.

Popenoe, D. (1998) 'Life without father', in C.R. Daniels (ed) *Lost Fathers: The Politics of Fatherlessness in America*, Basingstoke and London: Macmillan, pp 33-51.

Poster, M. (1978) *Critical Theory of the Family*, London: Pluto.

Reach (2007) *An Independent Report to Government on Raising the Aspirations and Attainment of Black Boys and Young Black Men*, commissioned by Department for Communities and Local Government, London: The Stationery Office.

(The) Real Fathers For Justice (2008) 'Home page' (www. reaffathersforjustice.org/).

Reece, H. (2006) 'UK women's groups' child contact campaign: "so long as it is safe"', *Child and Family Law Quarterly*, vol 18, no 4, pp 538-61.

Rhoades, H. (2006) 'Yearning for law: fathers' groups and family law reform in Australia', in R. Collier and S. Sheldon (eds) *Fathers' Rights Activism and Law Reform in Comparative Perspective*, Oxford and Portland, OR: Hart Publishing, pp 125-47.

Riddell, M. (2007) 'Happiness is more than a good dad', *The Observer*, 25 November.

Riley, D. (1983) *War in the Nursery: Theories of the Child and Mother*, London: Virago.

Robins, J. (2008) 'DIY child support deals will hurt lone parents, warn campaigners', *The Observer*, 2 March.

Rogers, W.S. and Rogers, R.S. (2001) *The Psychology of Gender and Sexuality*, Buckingham: Open University Press.

Rolfe, H., Metcalf, H., Anderson, T. and Meadows, P. (2003) *Recruitment and Retention of Child Care, Early Years and Play Workers*, London: National Institute of Economic and Social Research.

Rose, N. (1991) *Governing the Soul: The Shaping of the Private Self*, London: Routledge.

Roseneil, S. (2006) 'The ambivalences of angel's "arrangement": a psychosocial lens on the contemporary condition of personal life', *The Sociological Review*, vol 54, no 4, pp 846-68.

Roskill, C. (2008) 'Report on research on fathers in two children's services authorities' in C. Roskill, B. Featherstone, C. Ashley and S. Haresnape, *Fathers Matter Volume 2: Further Findings on Fathers and their Involvement with Social Care Services*, London: Family Rights Group, pp 19-54.

Roskill, C., Featherstone, B., Ashley, C. and Haresnape, S. (2008) *Fathers Matter Volume 2: Further Findings on Fathers and their Involvement with Social Care Services*, London: Family Rights Group.

Rustin, M. (1996) 'Attachment in context', in S. Kraemer and J. Roberts (eds) *The Politics of Attachment*, London: Free Association Books, pp 212-29.

Ruxton, S. (2002) *Men, Masculinities and Poverty in the UK*, Oxford: Oxfam.

Ryan, M. (2006) 'The experiences of fathers involved with social services departments: a literature review', in C. Ashley, B. Featherstone, C. Roskill, M. Ryan and S. White, *Fathers Matter: Research Findings on Fathers and their Involvement with Social Care Services*, London: Family Rights Group, pp 13-22.

Sabla, K.-P. (2007) 'Fathers and child welfare services in Germany', *Gender and Child Welfare – An Interdisciplinary Conference*, University of York, 19 September.

Scott, J. W. (1992) 'Experience', in J. Butler and J. W. Scott (eds) *Feminists Theorize the Political*, London: Routledge, pp 22-41.

Scourfield, J. (2003) *Gender and Child Protection*, Basingstoke and London: Palgrave Macmillan.

Scourfield, J. (2006) 'The challenge of engaging fathers in the child protection process', *Critical Social Policy*, vol 26, no 2, pp 440-50.

Scourfield, J. and Drakeford, M. (2002) 'New Labour and the "problem of men"', *Critical Social Policy*, vol 22, no 4, pp 619-40.

Segal, L. (1987) *Is the Future Female? Troubled Thoughts on Contemporary Feminism*, London: Virago.

Segal, L. (1990) *Slow Motion: Changing Men, Changing Masculinities*, London: Virago.

Segal, L. (1999) *Why Feminism?*, Cambridge: Polity.

Sen, A. (1999) *Development as Freedom*, London: Knopf.

Sheldon, S. (2005) 'Reproductive technologies and the legal determination of fatherhood', *Feminist Legal Studies*, vol 13, no 3, pp 349-62.

Smart, C. (2007) *Personal Life*, Cambridge: Polity.

Smart, C. and Neale, B. (1999) *Family Fragments?*, Cambridge: Polity.

Smart, C., Neale, B. and Wade, A. (2001) *The Changing Experience of Childhood: Families and Divorce*, Cambridge: Polity.

Solomon, Y., Warin, J., Lewis, C. and Langford, W (2002) 'Intimate talk between parents and their children: democratic openness or covert control?', *Sociology*, vol 36, no 4, pp 965-83.

Somerville, J. (2000) *Feminism and the Family: Politics and Society in the UK and USA*, Basingstoke and London: Palgrave Macmillan.

Squires, P. (2006) 'New Labour and the politics of antisocial behaviour', *Critical Social Policy*, vol 26, no 1, pp 144-68.

Stacey, J. (1998) 'Dada-ism in the 1990s: getting past baby talk about fatherlessness', in C.R. Daniels (ed) *Lost Fathers: The Politics of Fatherlessness in America*, Basingstoke and London: Macmillan, pp 51-85.

Stacey, J. (1999) 'Virtual social science and the politics of family values in the US', in G. Jagger and C. Wright (eds) *Changing Family Values*, London: Routledge, pp 185-205.

Stanley, K. (2005) *Daddy Dearest? Active Fatherhood and Public Policy*, London: Institute for Public Policy Research.

Stanley, K. and Gamble, C. (2005) 'Introduction: fathers and policy', in *Daddy Dearest? Active Fatherhood and Public Policy*, London: Institute for Public Policy Research, pp 1-16.

Steiner, J. (1996) 'Revenge and resentment in the "Oedipus situation"', *International Journal of Psychoanalysis*, vol 77, pp 433-43.

Stone, L. (1977) *The Family, Sex and Marriage in England 1500-1800*, London: Weidenfeld.

Strega, S., Fleet, C., Brown, L., Dominelli, L. Callahan, M. and Walmsley, C. (2007) 'Connecting father absence and mother blame', *Children and Youth Services Review* (doi.10.1016/j.childyouth 2007.10.012).

Target, M. and Fonagy, P. (2002) 'Fathers in modern psychoanalysis and in society: the role of the father in child development', in J. Trowell and A. Etchegoyen (eds) *The Importance of Fathers: A Psychoanalytic Re-evaluation*, Hove: Brunner-Routledge, pp 45-67.

Taylor, C. (2004) 'Underpinning knowledge for child care practice: reconsidering child development theory', *Child and Family Social Work*, vol 9, no 3, pp 225-35.

Taylor, C. and White, S. (2000) *Practising Reflexivity in Health and Welfare: Making Knowledge*, Buckingham: Open University Press.

Tosh, J. (2007) *A Man's Place: Masculinity and the Middle-class Home in Victorian England*, New Haven, CT and London: Yale University Press.

Trowell, J. and Etchegoyen, A. (eds) (2002) *The Importance of Fathers: A Psychoanalytic Re-evaluation*, Hove: Brunner-Routledge.

TUC (Trade Union Congress) (2008) *Hard Work, Hidden Lives: The Full Report of the Commission on Vulnerable Employment*, London: TUC.

Urwin, C. (1998) 'Power relations and the emergence of language', in J. Henriques, W. Hollway, C. Urwin, C. Venn and V. Walkerdine *Changing the Subject: Psychology, Social Regulation and Subjectivity*, 2nd edn, London: Methuen and Routledge, pp 264-323.

Walkerdine, V. (1998) 'Developmental psychology and the child-centred pedagogy: the insertion of Piaget into early education', in J. Henriques, W. Hollway, C. Urwin, C. Venn and V. Walkerdine *Changing the Subject: Psychology, Social Regulation and Subjectivity*, 2nd edn, London: Methuen and Routledge, pp 153-203.

Walkerdine, V. and Lucey, H. (1989) *Democracy in the Kitchen: Regulating Mothers and Socialising Daughters*, London: Virago.

Wallbank, J. (2007) 'Getting tough on mothers: regulating contact and residence', *Feminist Legal Studies*, vol 15, no 2, pp 189-222.

Webb, S. (2006) *Social Work in a Risk Society*, Basingstoke: Palgrave Macmillan.

White, S. (2006) 'Unsettling reflections: the reflexive practitioner as "trickster" in interprofessional work', in S. White, J. Fook and F. Gardner (eds) *Critical Reflection in Health and Social Care*, Maidenhead: Open University Press, pp 21-40.

Whitehead, S. (2002) *Men and Masculinities*, Cambridge: Polity.

Wikeley, N. (2007) 'Child support reform – throwing the baby out with the bathwater', *Child and Family Law Quarterly*, vol 19, no 4, pp 434-57.

Williams, F. (1998) 'Troubled masculinities in social policy discourses: fatherhood', in J. Popay, J. Hearn and J. Edwards (eds) *Men, Gender Divisions and Welfare*, London: Routledge, pp 63-101.

Williams, F. (2004) *Rethinking Families*, London: Calouste Gulbenkian Foundation.

Williams, Z. (2008) 'The names of the fathers', *The Guardian*, 11 June.

Zarestsky, E. (1973) *Capitalism, the Family and Personal Life*, New York: Harper Row.

Index